MW01030870

Praise for

Wages for Housework

"Wages for Housework is arguably the most misunderstood, maligned, and mythologized movement in the annals of radical feminist history. Its impact was, and still is, bigger than its numbers, and its liberatory possibilities greater than we've realized. Emily Callaci sweeps away decades of misrepresentation and wrestles with the archives, memories, and perspectives of its brilliant founders, producing a groundbreaking account of a movement that brought the war on gendered racial capitalism home. Illuminating, honest, nuanced, *Wages for Housework* is a must-read for anyone seeking to make a just and sustainable world for all."

—Robin D. G. Kelley, author of *Freedom Dreams*

"What a wonderful book! Callaci beautifully captures the excitement and energy of the Wages for Housework campaign. A global history of the movement told through some of its principal figures, *Wages for Housework* takes us from the villages of Italy to the squats of Camden and New York City to UN conferences in Nairobi and Beijing. This book thrums with the voices of women: organizers, activists, housewives, students, mothers, writers, and caregivers of all kinds. If you are a woman who has ever been conscripted into unpaid work in the name of love, you will see yourself in this book."

—Maggie Doherty, author of *The Equivalents*

"Callaci's rich, perceptive account of the immensely influential, intensely charismatic, frequently invoked, yet often misunderstood Wages for Housework movement is the one I've been waiting for—one that does justice to the complexity of its most famous figures, demands, and campaigns while also bringing attention to overlooked thinkers and ideas, like Wilmette Brown's vision of environmental repair. As Callaci shows, while Wages for Housework's feminist critique of capitalism zeroed in on the seemingly mundane space of the home, its creative theorizing drew on struggles from around the world—and its powerful perspective on the kinds of work that capitalism neglects has implications for the future of life on our planet. Callaci's meticulous history, honest assessment, and sharp analysis are beautifully and aptly paired with eloquent reflections on her own experiences of balancing care with other forms of work. I learned so much from this book and loved reading every page."

—Alyssa Battistoni, coauthor of *A Planet to Win*

"Callaci has given us a beautifully clear history of the light that feminist Marxists shone on home sweet home, exposing it as a site of radical exploitation. Through a deft analysis of key figures and ideas, the book shows the extraordinary reach of Wages for Housework as a devastating critique of global, racial capitalism, and containing within itself a way of reclaiming the earth."   —Hannah Dawson, King's College London

"A subtle portrait of the Wages for Housework movement and its central figures. From Britain and the United States to Italy, Barbados, and Zambia, Callaci traces the development of this complex political struggle that began from the important truth that housework is work. This is a timely history that should be read by anyone interested in how we might transform our everyday lives—both by those who live and breathe these feminist battles and by those who have yet to join them."

—Katrina Forrester, author of *In the Shadow of Justice*

"This powerful book reminds us of the radical campaign to end capitalism by demanding recognition of the extraordinary extent it relies on unpaid work—of rearing children, caring for the sick, disabled, and for elders; of maintaining communities and tending the earth. Callaci's account of this everyday socialism extends from Black Power to Italian feminism, from opposing structural adjustment programs to inspiring those demanding a Green New Deal. I can't wait to teach this book and give a copy to everyone I know."   —Laura Briggs, author of *Taking Children*

"Callaci shows why Wages for Housework matters through the women who provoked a movement and her own attempt to juggle care work with academic labor. This stunning intellectual portraiture of Selma James, Mariarosa Dalla Costa, Silvia Federici, Wilmette Brown, and Margaret Prescod connects the personal with the political, illuminating the ways that racial capitalism has depended on reproductive labor—and how tending to people and the earth offers a perspective in which to fight back. Theory has never been more readable."

—Eileen Boris, University of California, Santa Barbara

WAGES

FOR

HOUSEWORK

THE FEMINIST FIGHT
AGAINST UNPAID LABOR

EMILY CALLACI

SEAL PRESS

New York

Copyright © 2025 by Emily Callaci
Cover design by Chin-Yee Lai
Cover images © Bettye Lane Photo; © Itsmesimon / Shutterstock.com
Cover copyright © 2025 by Hachette Book Group, Inc.

Hachette Book Group supports the right to free expression and the value of copyright.
The purpose of copyright is to encourage writers and artists to produce the creative works that
enrich our culture.

The scanning, uploading, and distribution of this book without permission is a theft of the author's
intellectual property. If you would like permission to use material from the book (other than for
review purposes), please contact permissions@hbgusa.com. Thank you for your support of the
author's rights.

Seal Press
Hachette Book Group
1290 Avenue of the Americas, New York, NY 10104
www.sealpress.com
@sealpress

Printed in the United States of America

Originally published in 2025 by Penguin Random House UK
First US Edition: March 2025

Published by Seal Press, an imprint of Hachette Book Group, Inc. The Seal Press name and logo is a
registered trademark of the Hachette Book Group.

The Hachette Speakers Bureau provides a wide range of authors for speaking events. To find out
more, go to hachettespeakersbureau.com or email HachetteSpeakers@hbgusa.com.

Seal books may be purchased in bulk for business, educational, or promotional use. For more
information, please contact your local bookseller or the Hachette Book Group Special Markets
Department at special.markets@hbgusa.com.

The publisher is not responsible for websites (or their content) that are not owned by the publisher.

Typeset by Jouve (UK), Milton Keynes

Library of Congress Control Number: 2024948703

ISBNs: 9781541603516 (hardcover), 9781541603523 (ebook)

LSC-C

Printing 1, 2025

Contents

List of Illustrations

Introduction

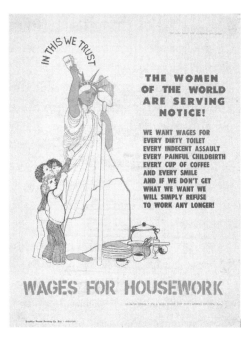

New York Wages for Housework Committee Poster (Library of Congress)

A poster created by the New York Wages for Housework Committee in 1974, inked in red-and-blue stencil, proclaims: "The women of
the world are serving notice! We want wages for every dirty toilet
every indecent assault every painful childbirth every cup of coffee
and every smile. And if we don't get what we want, we will simply
refuse to work any longer!" In the center of the poster stands the
Statue of Liberty, her face weary, a broom in one hand and a fistful
of cash in the other. Children grab at her robes, and dirty dishes lay
stacked up at her feet.[1]

Some years back, I ordered a print from the Library of Congress, framed it, and hung it in my living room. I acquired it as a kind of curiosity; an attractive vintage artifact of 1970s feminism, and a provocative conversation piece. It is directly in my line of vision from my place at the kitchen counter where I mix smashed banana into oatmeal for my sons' breakfast, or portion extracted breastmilk into 4oz bottles to be sent with the baby to daycare. It hovers in my peripheral vision as I, toddler plopped in my lap, read *I Am a Bunny* aloud for the tenth time in a row, and when I am bleary-eyed at the kitchen table with my laptop late at night after my kids are in bed, preparing a lesson plan for class the next day. I've thought about the concept often: Wages for Housework. In the duller moments of my life, it awakens something in my imagination, connecting my daily efforts to lives and labors beyond the four walls of my house.

For most of my life, I did not think very much about housework. A middle-class teenager in the "Girl Power" 1990s, I learned that my liberation would come through education, creative expression, and professional success. Thanks to the efforts of feminists who came before me, I never felt I had to rebel all that hard against the expectation of feminized domesticity. I intended to spend my time on earth on more meaningful things: love, politics, music, beauty. What did housework have to do with me? It seemed like a quaint preoccupation – the relic of an older generation's outdated and irrational beliefs about gender. That women were associated with housework seemed a category mistake: correct that mistake, and you fix the problem.

But then, when I became a mother, housework became inescapable. I experienced the housework of motherhood differently than my mother, who quit her job as a social worker to raise me and my brothers until my youngest brother was old enough for school. I remember her at the dinner table in the evenings with the three of us while my father was out, doing what I imagined as very romantic work as a union organizer. In stories about my father's childhood, I picture his mother, my brilliant grandmother, who left a job as a journalist when her first child was born, tending lovingly and skillfully to five children, often while my grandfather wrote poetry in his attic study. (She returned to journalism when she was in her sixties, after her children were grown.) When their children were school-aged, both my mother and grandmother became public-school teachers, choosing careers that adapted to the rhythms of their children's lives. These images of my mother and grandmother invoke in me feelings of warmth, safety, and love. Still, I never expected to play a role similar to them. It seemed unproblematic to me to identify with the men and their work: I'd emulate the union organizer, the poet.

I have not had to fight all that hard against an expectation that, as a woman, I should do a disproportionate amount of house-work, yet housework is nevertheless a struggle that I share with my partner. In at least one way, our household is typical for our generation of Americans: both adults in our house work full-time outside the home for money, and the work of maintaining our family gets squeezed into the time that is left after we've satisfied the demands of our employers.[2] We live in a country that, over the past few decades, has collectively experienced declining real wages, shrinking social services, and rising costs of education and health-care. We negotiate housework between us (as I write these words, he is at home with our two boys while I sit alone in my friend's empty house to write free from distraction), but we also distribute it beyond us. To be able to work, we rely on paid childcare; to pay for childcare, we need to work; and this entire cycle relies on the fact that the extremely skilled women who care for our children are paid less money for their work than we are for ours. There is no way around it: I am a beneficiary of an exploitative social arrangement. By participating, I also feel that I am undermining myself: I consent to a world in which the work of caring for children – the work that, for the past few years, I have spent most of my time on – is valued less than the work of being a professor.

Housework weighed most heavily on me when I returned to my full-time job as a history professor, four months after my first son was born. If housework is work– and it certainly was work in the physical meaning of the word – then together with my paid job, I was working eighteen-hour days. These were clearly poor working conditions. I know from growing up in a union family that one of the most effective ways to contest poor working conditions is by going on strike. But the feminism I grew up with had put me in a bind: if feminism was the right to pursue success and equality in the workplace, then to refuse my salaried job was to refuse the very thing that I had learned was the source of my liberation, autonomy, and sense of accomplishment. To refuse the work of caring for my child would be to harm the most vulnerable of beings, and the person I loved most in the world. Parenting young children during the pandemic only deepened my growing sense of a loss of power: that motherhood, the work that I knew I could never refuse, made me vulnerable to exploitation.

I was drawn to Wages for Housework because I wanted to understand what had changed in my life, and to make sense of my mixed feelings about it. Put another way, I wanted to understand how motherhood had changed my relationship to capitalism. And I wanted alternatives. I turned to feminist writings from the 1970s, wondering how the diverse, ambitious, imaginative, revolutionary ideas of that generation had gotten narrowed into the version of feminism that had been offered to me as a young woman. One of the places I looked for insight was in Silvia Federici's 1975 manifesto "Wages Against Housework," a rousing and elegant call to confront housework head-on as a site of women's systemic oppression, rather than imagining that, as individuals, we can find a way out of it.

Around that time, I learned that Silvia Federici was assembling her archive at Brown University, located in the town where I grew up and where my parents still live. So, on a long visit during my maternity leave, I left my son and several bottles of extracted breast-milk with my mother while I went (breastmilk pump in tow) to explore Federici's collection of writings, manifestos, and gorgeous black-and-white photographs of women marching in the streets of New York and London and Rome. One flyer from the New York

Committee seemed to address me directly. In it, they demanded support for the work of mothering in the form of collectivized day-care, subsidized by the government, not in order to free mothers up to work harder at our jobs, but to free us up for . . . *whatever the hell we want.* A nap. Art. A swim in the ocean. Slow, luxurious sex. Time to nurture our friendships. Time to participate meaningfully in politics. Having grown up with a feminism that equated liberation with the right to pursue success at work, this was a revelation: a feminism that was unabashedly anti-work.

Silvia Federici's archives led me to other feminist thinkers in the Wages for Housework campaign: Mariarosa Dalla Costa, the student militant who started the Italian Salario al Lavoro Domestico campaign in the wake of Italy's wave of wildcat strikes and student uprisings; Selma James, wife and comrade of the Trinidadian Marxist C. L. R. James, who launched a Wages for Housework campaign out of their apartment in London; Wilmette Brown, a poet and former Black Panther who, together with the Barbadian community organizer Margaret Prescod, launched Black Women for Wages for Housework in Brooklyn and Queens.

I started from questions about my own life, but Wages for Housework took me far beyond it. Housework is everywhere, once you start looking for it.

Feminists launched the Wages for Housework campaign in 1972. But the word "campaign" doesn't quite capture it. Wages for Housework is perhaps best understood as a political perspective, which starts from the premise that capitalism extracts wealth not only from workers, but also from the unpaid work of creating and sustaining workers. An employer who hires an employee gets more than what they pay for: they get the labor of the person who shows up to work, and they get the labor of a second person who is at home sustaining him (for in the early writings of the campaign, the waged worker was presumed to be a "him"). That second person feeds the worker, makes his home livable, does his laundry, does the shopping, nurtures his body and soul, raises his children. It is all this hidden labor that makes it possible for him to come to work all day producing profit for his boss. Housework is, therefore, not unproductive or external to the economy. It is the most essential part of the capitalist system because it produces and maintains the most important source of value: the worker. Yet those who perform this work are not entitled to a share of the wealth they create. To the contrary, they are often among the most impoverished and dependent members of society.

The systemic exploitation of women's unpaid work is hidden by a powerful myth: that women are naturally suited to housework. For a woman, keeping house and caring for family fulfills her natural desires, and should be reward enough. Compensation would sully the virtuous nature of this work, for the home is imagined as a refuge from the impure, punishing world of work and market relations. Capitalism relies on this myth to keep women in these roles, allowing others to profit from their work. Wages for Housework was so jarring to people because it demanded compensation for something that was supposed to be free from market forces, and which women were supposed to provide out of love. Campaign members saw this as a form of emotional blackmail. As one of my favorite Wages for Housework slogans sums it up: *They say it is love. We say it is unwaged work.*

By demanding payment for work that women had historically done for free, members of the Wages for Housework campaign made visible their role in capitalism. They aimed to destroy what they saw as a false distinction between work done in the marketplace for wages and unpaid housework done in the home and community. In so doing, they aimed to call into being a truer, more expansive, inclusive working class to dismantle capitalism and all its forms of oppression.

Wages for Housework is a critique not only of women's oppression, but of global capitalism in its entirety. It argues that, because women do housework for free, work that resembles housework is undervalued: the more similar a job is to housework, the lower its status and the less it is paid. Moreover, when governments cut social services, such as childcare, education, healthcare, elder care, and disability services, they exploit the fact that women will step in and provide these services without pay. The analysis can be applied at a global scale. The scholar-activist Andaiye, who launched a Wages for Housework campaign in her home country of Guyana in the early 2000s, applied the perspective to structural adjustment policies: the austerity measures imposed by the IMF and World Bank on countries in the global south as a condition for foreign aid and bank loans. With stunning clarity, she writes: "Structural adjustment . . . assumes correctly that what women will do in the face of the deterioration that it brings is to increase the unpaid work that we do without even thinking about it in an attempt to ensure that our families survive."[3] Wages for Housework puts austerity politics in a new light: what politicians call fiscal conservatism or "belt-tightening," Wages for Housework reframes as freeloading on the unpaid work of women.

Wages for housework is a strategy not just for unwaged workers, but for all workers, for we are all affected by housework's unwaged status. In the 1970s, the Wages for Housework campaign argued that men were made vulnerable in the workplace by their wives' financial dependence on them. If a worker wants to demand better working conditions, or go on strike, having a wife with no income makes it harder for him to assert himself: to do so would put his entire family at risk. Moreover, a woman working outside the home has more power in her workplace if she is already paid for the work she does at home: she has negotiating power to decide the terms on which she will take on additional work, and she can refuse shitty, demeaning jobs without the threat of complete destitution that is so often used as a stick to discipline poor and working-class mothers. Wages for Housework is not wages for housewives: it is bargaining power to the working class as a whole. It begins by re-defining "working class" with unpaid women's work at the center.

Wages for Housework was controversial when it was proposed in the 1970s. Few feminists disagreed with the insight that housework was essential, and hidden, and that it would be politically powerful to recognize it. But many were uncomfortable about the money part. Some argued that it would invite capitalism into their homes, bringing even more areas of life into the wage relation and commodification. Others chafed at the suggestion that, having struggled so hard to escape housework as their destiny, women should then identify with housework by demanding payment for it. The most common critique was that wages for housework would institutionalize women as housewives, doubling down on the link between women and housework, rather than destroying it. Many struggled to understand: how does getting paid for housework allow you to refuse that work? If you are demanding to get paid, aren't you then agreeing to do that work?

In the history of the campaign, I have encountered ambiguity on this point. Some have stated that the money was never the goal, but rather a provocation that aimed to change consciousness and catalyze social transformation. By contrast, others in the campaign have insisted that the money is the most important thing: Wages for Housework is not an intellectual exercise, they insist, but a fight to get money into women's hands. What members of the campaign all agree on is that the wage was never the end goal but rather the first step in a much larger struggle for power. This is why the word "wage" was so important. When Margaret Prescod, founder of Black Women for Wages for Housework, used her platform at the historic 1977 US National Women's Conference to insist that welfare be called a wage rather than a benefit, more than semantics was at stake. To recognize that welfare is payment for the work of mothering, rather than poverty alleviation, changes the entire political relationship. Wages for Housework reframes women's poverty as systemic impoverishment: women are not unfortunate victims in need of charity, rather, they are exploited workers in need of justice.

By my count, there were Wages for Housework branches in the United States, United Kingdom, Italy, Germany, France, Switzerland, Canada, Trinidad and Tobago, and Guyana, and their influence reaches far beyond. As the idea spreads, it inspires new forms of action. Recently, a women's collective in Andhra Pradesh with connections to the campaign demanded support for their work replenishing the land, protecting it from extractive industries that pollute the environment and contribute to global warming. Some advocates for a Green New Deal, in both Europe and the United States, cite Wages for Housework in their vision of an economic model that centers care for human beings and the environment, as an alternative to the relentless planet-destroying production of commodities. In a project called Wages for Facebook, artist Laurel Ptak provokes users of social media to demand a share of the wealth created through the mining of their personal data. Some prison abolitionists, whose demands include divesting from prisons and policing and reinvesting in community carework, name Wages for Housework as an influence. At the 2011 International Labor Organization Conference that successfully passed Convention 189, known as Decent Work for Domestic Workers, recognizing the rights of domestic workers as workers and the home as a workplace, one of the advocates who took the stage was Ida LeBlanc, daughter of Clotil Walcott, founder of Wages for Housework in Trinidad and Tobago. In my own neighborhood, activists are organizing for a more just and healthy food system in my son's public school, starting with revaluing the labor and skill of cafeteria workers, most of whom are economically marginalized women. I am delighted, and unsurprised, to learn that Wages for Housework is one of their guiding lights.

Despite its influence, the Wages for Housework campaign itself was small, with never more than a few dozen members. They were multi-racial and international. Many of them were lesbians. Some were disabled. They included sex workers, welfare mothers, and nurses. Few of them were "housewives" in the conventional sense. They were seen by many as quirky, even cultish. They appear often in oral histories of second-wave feminism as a kind of curiosity. A commonly told story recounts how someone would stand up at a public meeting and identify themselves as part of the Wages for

Housework campaign, eliciting a collective groan from audience members, who knew they were in for another long lecture about capitalism and housework. A 1975 article in the *Guardian* compared them to Jehovah's Witnesses.[4] People often didn't know what to make of them.

If in the 1970s their ideas seemed outlandish, today they seem less strange. I assign Silvia Federici's essay "Wages Against Housework" to my undergraduate students, and though they are nineteen and twenty years old, mostly unburdened by housework in the traditional sense, they immediately find themselves in Federici's analysis of capitalism. My students question the constant demand for productivity. More than my generation, they grew up aware of the looming threat of climate catastrophe and are primed to see what relentless economic growth and "productivity" has done to the planet and to human thriving. Most are starting out their adult lives saddled with debt and wonder why they are cast in the role of debtors to our society, rather than as contributors to our collective wealth. If my generation believed that the upward escalator toward education and a career would set us free, I find that many of my students are decidedly more skeptical.

My fascination with Wages for Housework arose out of a desire to understand my own life, but it has led me to much bigger, more ambitious questions. What would it be like to live in a society that rewarded the care of people and their environments as much as the production and consumption of commodities? What kind of relationship to the natural world could we have if, rather than emphasizing productivity and growth, we uplifted maintenance and repair of environments – in other words, housework? What new experiences of love, kinship, desire, and pleasure would be possible if we were not pressed into isolated nuclear family units, each responsible for its own housework? What if our cities and towns were designed to nurture vibrant intergenerational communities, rather than centering on the mobility of the able-bodied "productive" worker? How would geopolitics and the global distribution of wealth be transformed if governments had to recognize their indebtedness to the unpaid work of women with the same gravity with which they recognize their debts to financial institutions? Perhaps most basic: what would the women of the world do with their lives if they had more time?

This book explores the ideas and work of five women: Selma James, Mariarosa Dalla Costa, Silvia Federici, Wilmette Brown, and Margaret Prescod. Admittedly, by choosing this format, I contradict a feminist principle held dear by many members of this movement: that political ideas are the products not of individual "geniuses," but of collective action and struggle. It's true that none of these women worked in isolation, and I hope that this book offers a glimpse of what is possible when women work together across various boundaries, devoting their effort and imagination to a common purpose. At the same time, Wages for Housework is not monolithic. I chose to write about these five women because each of them contributed something intellectually distinct and formative to Wages for Housework as a feminist political tradition.

Selma James was in her 40s and had been involved in revolutionary politics for decades by the time the feminist movement of the 1970s arrived. As a child in 1930s radical Jewish Brooklyn, she was politicized by men like her father, who organized labor unions, but also by the neighborhood women like her mother, who staged rent strikes, protested rising food prices, and struggled with the painful experience of having to foster out their children in times of financial strain. As the wife and comrade of C. L. R. James, she spent her 20s and 30s witnessing and participating in working-class and anti-colonial struggles in the US, UK, and Caribbean, all with her young son Sam in tow. A working-class housewife and mother, a self-taught Marxist, and a charismatic, provocative orator, James insisted that housewives were the key to working-class struggle. While the left fixated on the white male factory worker, in the kitchens of the world were millions of unwaged workers, waiting to be organized.

"Let us remember," wrote Mariarosa Dalla Costa, "that capital first made Fiat and THEN the canteen." A meticulous scholar and committed militant, Mariarosa Dalla Costa was politicized in the crucible of radical student politics that swept Italy in the late 1960s. Growing up in rapidly industrializing postwar Italy, she saw a world in which human needs seemed to be subordinated to the demands of industry; a twisted logic in which the point of human life was to serve the interests of capitalism, rather than the other way around. As a young woman in a Catholic country, she encountered a patriarchal culture that pressed women of childbearing age into producing children, and then all but discarded them in old age, when their bodies no longer served that purpose. In the 1970s, as she and her feminist sisters, on the cusp of adulthood, confronted the incongruity between societal expectations and their own desires for free and meaningful lives, Dalla Costa saw clearly that women and their labors were at the very heart of capitalism. Their bodies gestated future workers. Their homes, where they worked in isolation cleaning and caring for workers and future workers, were not a refuge from the world of work, but extensions of the factory system. "And that," she wrote, "is where our struggle begins."[5]

To Silvia Federici, a philosophy PhD student living in Brooklyn, the myth that housework and caring were natural to women amounted to a violent distortion of the body and soul. Having grown up in Italy in the aftermath of fascism and its patriarchal cultural directives, she described the nuclear family as a prison, where people disciplined each other into rigid gender roles. In speeches and writings, she is relentlessly, methodically critical of the capitalist social order, yet she is also deeply idealistic, suggesting glimmers of other possible worlds. She provokes us to ask: what kinds of sensual pleasure and love, and community, would be possible were bodies and souls to be untethered from the nuclear family and the capitalist workweek? A lover of art and music and literature, she pondered a world in which creativity was a mass condition, and not just a privilege reserved for those who could buy themselves out of housework.

When asked by a journalist in 1987 to identify herself, Wilmette

Brown told him: "I am a Black lesbian woman cancer survivor struggling for Wages for Housework for all women from all governments."[6] In Wages for Housework, Wilmette Brown saw more than a feminist demand: she saw a continuation of the Black freedom struggle. She radically expanded the concept of housework. In place of the housewife laboring in the heterosexual nuclear family home, in her writings and speeches we encounter Black women fighting off cockroaches in dilapidated public housing; women caring for those made sick by toxic waterways and polluted air; mothers struggling to protect their children from racism and police violence. To the insight that housework is the work that creates profit for capitalism, Wilmette Brown added: housework is the work thrust on us BY capitalism in the form of repair work for its harms. It is the work of survival.

"How dare they tell us that we're scroungers or we're beggars and that our life is worth nothing," Margaret Prescod said to a group of Black women in Bristol in 1986. "We have helped to create practically everything that exists on this planet!"[7] Prescod, who emigrated to Brooklyn from Barbados as a teenager, saw connections between the struggles of welfare mothers and her own experience as a West Indian immigrant, in a country that portrayed both as undeserving beneficiaries of American largesse. Prescod saw in Wages for Housework an intimate standpoint from which to comprehend the violent sweep of global history. The vast stores of wealth that made European and North American countries prosperous had been created through the unpaid work of women of color. When she and other immigrants came to New York and London and Paris and Amsterdam, they weren't begging for charity: they were reclaiming what was rightfully theirs.

At the same time as my fascination with Wages for Housework grew, several founding members of the campaign were also thinking about their history and putting their papers and ephemera into archives. At first, my task seemed simple: I would visit these archives and, like an archaeologist assembling the scattered shards of an ancient vase, I would reconstitute the story of Wages for Housework. But I soon learned that telling the story of this movement would be more complicated than I had anticipated. There is pain and internal struggle in this history. Frequently, while speaking to former members of the campaign, I would blindly stumble into arguments I did not know existed. I would mention a name and be met with a facial expression making it clear to me that a former comrade was now a sworn enemy. I would sometimes be grilled about my loyalties even as I was trying to figure out what the grievances were about. At times, it seemed as though the archives themselves were assembled, curated, and organized for the sole purpose of settling scores.

The recollections of different members of the campaign are shaped, in part, by where they stand in relation to it now. For Silvia Federici and Mariarosa Dalla Costa, though they carry on the work of Wages for Housework in their activism and writing, the campaign itself is nevertheless in their past, and they have some critical distance from it. For Selma James and Margaret Prescod, the campaign never ended. The archive (and, they hope, this book) is an instrument of their ongoing movement, now updated into a demand for *Care Income Now!*

Wilmette Brown is a different story. She left the campaign in 1995. Her essays are long out of print and, unlike the others from the early days of the campaign, she no longer publicly identifies herself with Wages for Housework. At the time that I am writing this book, she has not republished her work nor documented her years of activism in an archive. To me, it is clear that she is a singular intellect, creator of some of the foundational ideas of this feminist tradition. She has acknowledged, but neither endorsed nor objected to, my writing about her work, nor has she tried to shape or influence what I write.

The main disagreement about the history of Wages for Housework is this: Prescod and James (and, to an extent, Brown) have publicly stated that, in the late 1970s, there was a split in the movement based on race. Dalla Costa (and others, who don't wish to be named) deny this, and say that the split was over questions of leadership and control – that James had a top-down vision about how the movement would operate, and that this drove people away. This book might provide context for these competing accounts, but cannot resolve them.

The internal struggles could have taken over and become the subject of this book, if I let them. I decided not to. In these pages, I try to sit with the messiness, exploring the disagreements that have political stakes, providing clarification when evidence allows, and, at times, letting contradictory accounts exist side by side.

"To be a member of our movement, there is only one requirement: you have to want Wages for Housework for yourself," Selma James told me one day in early 2022 over Zoom. She was ninety-two years old at the time. Her white hair was pulled tight into a twist behind her head, and she looked small, birdlike in her chair. She leaned forward and pointed her finger at me: "Do you?"

I was caught off guard.

Until that moment, I had embraced Wages for Housework mostly as a thought experiment. Immersed in the archives, I thrilled to the promise of an unseen future catalyzed by the demand. But now, James' question put me in mind of what I might have to give up. Like many of my generation, and those before me, I have tried to definitively sever the link between my gender and my suitability for housework. How would identifying with housework change my sense of self, and how would it change my status in the world? To some extent, has my own sense of accomplishment relied on my ability to escape this kind of labor when I've wanted to? And what about my children: do I want to understand the time I spend with them as "work," and must I accept the premise that what I am raising them for is capitalism? (And can I deny it, without playing into the very ideology that exploits my unpaid labor?) Perhaps the part that makes me most uneasy is the centrality of productivity in their vision. Wages for Housework reveals how women's work creates economic value in a capitalist system, and, in that sense, they make a brilliant case for wealth redistribution on capitalism's own terms. But should we accept those terms? Do we have to be deemed "productive" to claim a share of the collective wealth?

I still don't have an answer to James' question. Thinking it through forces me to confront my personal investments in the very systems that I call unjust. Against my tendency to dwell in the abstract and idealistic, she calls on me to stay grounded in the materiality of housework and money as a place from which to envision a radically new world. This book is an invitation for you to do the same, wherever you are, whatever your relationship to housework.

Selma James

Selma James speaking in 1970 at the National Women's Liberation Movement Conference at Oxford's Ruskin College.

In 1969, Selma James appeared in a documentary called *Women Talking*. The film was an attempt to capture the zeitgeist of the emerging Women's Liberation Movement, and the format was simple: a number of well-known American feminists, including Kate Millett and Betty Friedan, were filmed sitting casually and speaking about their feminist visions. The film was shot in black and white, and the camera panned over the women's faces as they talked and smoked at a leisurely pace, musing on their experiences of womanhood. The topics ranged from girlhood experiences of Catholic schooling, to sexual assault, to gay rights, to the Miss Alaska pageant, to repressed sexual desire.

For the final ten minutes of the film, the floor is given to Selma James, who sits at the front of a room of well-coiffed audience members. She speaks quickly, as though her words cannot keep up with the speed of her thoughts. "We have to expand the conception of what a revolution is," she says. "We have to expand the conception of what socialism is. And we have to make ourselves into human beings who can totally participate in society. We are not going to be forced into the roles that the family lays out for us." As she speaks, her whole upper body is animated. Her dark hair is cut very short, accentuating dramatic facial expressions: she raises her eyebrows and tilts her chin as she poses a rhetorical question, and narrows her eyes when describing something unjust. She is colloquial, throwing in a "goddamn!" or "eh?!" for emphasis. Her pace quickens as she zeroes in on a point, and then slows for dramatic effect. She is making a joke one minute, and the next minute matter-of-factly promising the complete destruction of the capitalist social order.

Watching the film, you get a glimpse of her method. With her eyes and body and words, she surveys the room as though attempting to pull everyone in, trying to understand how each person might relate to the question of women's liberation. You get the impression of someone who is ardently interested in people. She speaks sympathetically about the hypothetical woman who might be on the fence about feminism: say, a young wife who adores her man and who might balk at any movement that seems to belittle or mock that relationship. James stays grounded in the practical challenges that must be overcome in building a movement: how do you go to a political meeting in the evening, if you are the one who is expected to make dinner and look after the children? And what happens after the argument you and your husband have about it? What little everyday rebellions are required on the way to a revolution? At one point, she asserts: a sensible man would not feel threatened by women's liberation. To emphasize her point, she does an impression of a "sensible man" responding to the Women's Liberation Movement: "You mean that *I* have been involved in the oppression?!?!" She widens her eyes in mock disbelief, puts her hand to

2

her temple, pinching her brow, as though wincing in pain at the discovery. "Good Lord! I have to really begin to rethink everything . . . If they want to have a meeting by themselves, I am the first to defend them because I have been involved in keeping their mouths shut!" That, she explains to the audience, is how a sensible man acts.

Shortly after making the film, James described the experience in a letter to her old comrade, Marty Glaberman. "I met Kate Millett when she was here," she wrote. "She told me that American working-class women were 'very reactionary.' So we didn't have much to say to each other. She didn't know she was speaking about me."[1] James and Glaberman had been friends since the early 1950s, when they had both been members of a small splinter group within the Trotskyist Socialist Workers Party. While, in the film, James seems barely able to contain her excitement about the growing feminist movement, her letter to Glaberman reveals another layer: Selma James did not see feminism as separate from the struggle of working-class people against capitalism, but as a radical expansion of it.

The film ends with James speaking these words: "We are going to start with the actual lives that people live. And anything that doesn't deal with that is outside the scope of the politics that we are trying to build." The room breaks into applause, and her face relaxes into a warm, wide grin.[2]

Selma James was raised on the class struggle. She was born as Selma Deitch in 1930 in Ocean Hill–Brownsville, a working-class immigrant Jewish neighborhood in Brooklyn. Her father was a Jewish immigrant from the Austro-Hungarian Empire, the region now known as Ukraine. Her mother was "five foot nothing"[3] and tough, had worked in a paper-box factory as a teenager, but had left waged work to raise three daughters, Edith, Celia, and Selma. They lived in a small house divided into four small apartments, with two families on each floor. James' mother was active in the neighborhood: James remembers her helping her neighbors defy their eviction notices by breaking the locks on the doors and dragging furniture back into the apartments. She organized housewives in the neighborhood to demand their "home relief": small government payments of goods and money distributed to families during the Great Depression. Her father, who drove trucks for a living, organized a branch of the Teamsters Union. As a child, James witnessed him beaten up, arrested, and carted off for a short stint in jail in the course of battling both the bosses and the mafiosi who tried to control the union.[4] Class struggle was not an abstract concept to Selma James.

For the people whom Selma James grew up with, there was no question of whether or not you were a socialist: the question was what kind of socialist. Both her parents were Communist Party sympathizers. "My father didn't know how to write," James recalled, "but he taught himself to read the *Daily Worker*," the newspaper published by the American Communist Party.[5] On Pitkin Avenue, the main drag through the center of Ocean Hill–Brownsville, the flyers of various organizations called passersby to action for various political causes – tenants organizing to protest evictions by landlords, mothers getting together to demand "home relief," or the Socialist Workers Party Youth Wing recruiting new members to their meetings. Stalinists and Trotskyists congregated on stoops and street corners to debate what was happening in Moscow. Among her neighbors were men and women whose fierce idealism led them to drop everything and go to Spain to fight alongside the Popular Front in the Spanish Civil War. "I remember being on my father's shoulders when the parade went by of nurses for Spain, and we all threw money into this big red banner that they held on the four corners."[6] As a child, James scoured the neighborhood with other children to collect tin foil from the insides of cigarette packets to make what she and the other children were told were bullets to fight Franco. Selma James grew up in a world where planning your life around the cause of revolution was not an unusual thing to do.

Though they lacked formal education, the adults in Selma James' world studied and debated politics and history with passion and urgency. Communist newspapers like the *Daily Worker* and the Yiddish language *Morgen Freiheit* gave working-class people direct access to world events. When they read about the struggles of the proletariat in other parts of the world, they felt themselves to be part of an international movement extending far beyond their neighborhood. To be a member of the working class was to be part of something real and urgent. By contrast, to be an "intellectual," in the parlance of the time, was to be frivolous, useless, bourgeois.

I made the mistake of describing Selma James as a "feminist intellectual" the first time I spoke with her. It was the height of the COVID-19 pandemic, and we were speaking on Zoom. James, who had recently turned ninety, leaned in toward the screen, listening intently as I tried to explain my intentions for this book. As soon as I uttered the word, I could see her visibly recoil. "Inte-*lect*-ual?!" She practically spat the word, as though it were sour in her mouth. She shot an incredulous look to her partner, Nina Lopez, who sat beside her. An intellectual, she corrected me, studies ideas for the sake of ideas. Selma James does not identify as an intellectual. She makes things happen.

As a teenager, James' older sister, Celia, joined the Workers Party – an offshoot of the Socialist Workers Party based on the ideas of Leon Trotsky, who, at the time, was living in Mexico City in exile from Stalin's Soviet Union. In contrast with Stalin, who placed Moscow at the center of the world revolution, Trotsky advocated a decentralized path, in which various peoples of the world could move toward revolution in their own way and time, rather than follow in lockstep the directives from Moscow. When James was thirteen or fourteen, Celia brought her along to a Workers' Party meeting to meet the great Trinidadian Marxist C. L. R. James.

He was over six feet tall, Black, charismatic, and brilliant. He had recently published a book called *The Black Jacobins*, a radical retelling of the history of modern democracy that cast Black slave rebels in Haiti, rather than white political elites in Europe, as the central protagonists. C. L. R. James was worldly. He could recite Molière and Shakespeare with ease. He was a committed Marxist, and a lover of culture without distinction between low- and high-brow. He had worked for years as a sports journalist, covering cricket for the *Manchester Guardian* in the UK. His acquaintances included literary stars like Leonard Woolf and Richard Wright. He had visited Trotsky in exile in his Coyoacán home in Mexico City. But in that moment, Selma James did not know any of this. What she knew was how he talked about working-class people like her. For C. L. R. James, working-class people were not backward or ignorant; not pawns waiting to be led by a party leader or educated into the correct political consciousness by intellectuals. He believed that workers of the world, from sharecroppers in Missouri to autoworkers in Detroit, were creative and self-aware, capable of making sense of their own lives, and expressing themselves in their own words. He was building a movement not to speak on their behalf, but in order to uplift their voices, to discover their organic genius for making a better world.

Selma James was hooked. Nothing she could learn in a classroom would compare with being part of this. After graduating from high school, she declined an offer to attend Brooklyn College.[7] For many generations of working-class New Yorkers, enrolling in one of the free public city colleges was a stepping stone into the middle class. But James did not aspire to a middle-class life. Instead of going to college, she married Norman Weinstein – a factory worker and fellow movement member – moved to Los Angeles, went to work in a factory, and joined the movement.

C. L. R. James had come to the United States from the UK as a spokesperson for Leon Trotsky's Socialist Workers Party. But he soon became frustrated with the Trotskyists. He found their political party model hierarchical, still based on the idea that workers needed to be told what to do by an enlightened cadre of party leaders. Moreover, despite its critique of the Soviet Union, their economic vision was still based on increasing production and consumption and squeezing profit out of workers. Crucially, C. L. R. found that the Trotskyists did not have anything relevant to say about Black people and racism. This called for a new kind of politics.

His two main collaborators were women. Raya Dunayevskaya, a Ukrainian militant and political theorist, had been the personal secretary of Leon Trotsky in exile before defecting. Grace Chin Lee – later to become Grace Lee Boggs – was the daughter of Chinese immigrant restaurateurs, a young political rebel who had a PhD in philosophy and could read Marx and Hegel in the original German. C. L. R., Dunayevskaya, and Boggs became a trio. Boggs recalls the three of them walking the streets of New York arm in arm, reading and discussing Marxist theory in each other's apartments.[8] In writing, they addressed each other with pseudonyms – C. L. R James was J. R. Johnson, Raya Dunayevskaya was Freddie Forest, and Grace Chin Lee was Ria Stone. They did not consider themselves to be a political party – they had, after all, come together on the premise that political parties were unnecessary and inherently hierarchical. Instead, they named their group the Johnson–Forest Tendency. Selma James – at the time Selma Weinstein – became a member of the Los Angeles chapter.

The Johnsonites were small. At their peak their members numbered around seventy, and they were spread across the country with groups in New York, Detroit, and Los Angeles. In Detroit, the movement was largely made up of labor organizers in the auto industry, including Martin Glaberman, Nettie Kravitz, and, eventually, Jimmy Boggs. In Los Angeles, Selma James' circle included her sister Celia and brother-in-law Pete, and her close friend Filomena Daddario, a young Italian-American woman from Queens who loved jazz. It also included Lyman Paine – a successful and well-to-do architect who acted as financial patron of C. L. R. James for many years – and his wife Frances, known by friends as "Freddy." Though scattered across the country, members remained connected through letters, their annual meetings, and their newspaper, *Correspondence*. As James recalled years later, they chose the name *Correspondence* because in letters to each other they spoke the truth, whereas writing articles invited a level of detachment and performativity that distorted the truth. They wanted to keep each other honest, rooted in working-class life, rather than abstract ideas.

They believed that the path to a better world was to be found not in the theories of university intellectuals or grand plans of political party leaders, but in the lived experiences and spontaneous rebellion of everyday people. Often, their pamphlets and newspapers consisted of direct transcriptions of the words of working-class people, such as a group of sharecroppers in Missouri, or an autoworker in Detroit, as dictated to members of the group. James recalled: "Our phrase in the fifties to sum it up was 'to record information about the new society.' You record the daily strivings of people for something new, that was a basic part of your job as a Marxist. And you can point to what you record of this subversive reality and say, yes, there is an alternative . . . here it is, this is the evidence."[9] This was an idealism that looked toward the possibilities of the present, the unrecognized talent and potential in people as they are, right now. This was both a political ideology and a way of being in the world.

James moved to South Central Los Angeles in the late 1940s, as the city was growing into a hub of the electronics and defense industries. She settled in a neighborhood that, until recently, had been mostly white, but was quickly changing as Black and Mexican families moved in. Her and Norman's marriage was, in her words, "over before it began," but while it lasted, she gave birth to her son Sam Weinstein.[10] She was eighteen years old at the time. When Sam was two years old, James went back to work. At one factory, she packaged marshmallows, while at another, she wired and soldered radios and radar sets for the military. She waitressed. She did housework. She looked after Sam. And all along, she worked for the movement, attending meetings, writing to comrades around the country, and contributing to *Correspondence*. Once a week, she would spend several hours standing on the same street corner selling the party newspaper and getting to know the neighbors.

Selma James' writings and notes from those years give the impression of someone with irrepressible curiosity and a clear sense of purpose. From literature to popular culture to everyday interactions with her neighbors and co-workers, everything seemed to be potential fuel for political insight. "I have just finished Pearl Buck's *Of Men and Women* and thought you might like a few comments," she announced to her comrades in 1951. Buck, who had recently been awarded the Nobel Prize in Literature for *The Good Earth*, had written the 1941 treatise about the plight of middle-class women who were bored at home, excluded from the world of men and, therefore, never given the opportunity to challenge and improve themselves. James was unimpressed. "Buck does not pose the question of women sharply and clearly . . . because she is too busy revealing her own problems as an intellectual or 'exceptional' woman. She is absolutely writhing." Yet James quickly pivoted from her criticism to pose more practical questions of how to organize middle-class women of the kind Buck describes: "It is true that, in one sense, the middle-class woman is even more degraded than the working-class woman. Even less is demanded of her. So she feels that she is even more obsolete . . . Yet these are the women who became abolitionists and suffragettes . . . They must ally themselves with the working-class women, but how?"[11]

More often, James sought political clarity through observations about the people around her. She expressed annoyance at generic platitudes about proletariats and capital and urged her comrades to look for and record the creativity and rebelliousness of working-class people. In one of her dispatches, she described how, beneath the loud grind and hum of machinery in the electronics factory where she worked, the women amused each other by loudly singing the commercials of their company's competitors.[12] Elsewhere, in an article in *Correspondence*, James pondered the spectacle of the Miss Universe pageant, which her neighbors were eagerly following on television. She noted the lack of Black contestants, and the way that the competition projected the impression of an America that was open to the world at a time when McCarthyism was at its peak. For those who were not contestants in the Miss Universe competition, US immigration was far less welcoming. "When I saw them [the contestants] smile continually, not because they wanted to but because it was part of their job, it made the word smile lose its meaning," she wrote. But she does not judge her neighbors or the participants: "I can understand women doing all this to be different, to get away from just a routine existence, to have a little excitement."[13] She also observed how race operated in her segregated factory workplace, where white women worked the assembly line and Black women were lower-paid janitorial staff, and how race shaped her political organizing activities. Her Black co-workers, she noted, were more likely than white workers to buy their newspaper and talk about the ideas, but they were less likely to sign up as members of the organization. She asked her comrades: what does this tell us about how experiences of racism intersect with class politics? Why are we failing to reach them?[14]

The Johnson–Forest Tendency divided members into three categories, or "layers" – the leaders were the first layer, the bourgeois intellectuals were the second layer, and the working class were the third layer. In a meeting they called the "Third Layer School," they flipped the hierarchy by having the rank and file members of the group (the third layer) teach the "intellectuals."[15] As a housewife and worker, Selma James was a member of this third layer, and in 1952, she traveled to New York to educate Grace Chin Lee, Raya Dunayevskaya, and other movement intellectuals about the everyday lives, desires, and revolutionary potential of working-class housewives.

C. L. R. had never heard anything like it. Like many on the left, C. L. R. was not accustomed to thinking of housewives as political. The conventional party line of the Socialist Workers Party had been that housewives were politically backward and needed to join men in the workforce in order to become politically conscious. C. L. R. asked her to write a pamphlet about the "woman question." As was his typical practice, he instructed that nobody was to interfere or offer their input: this young comrade was to write it on her own, in her own words. "I don't know how to write a pamphlet," she remembers protesting, but he told her it was easy: you get a shoebox and put a slit in the top, and any time you have an idea, you write it down on a piece of paper and put it in the box. Then, eventually, you open the box, put the slips of paper all together, and you have your pamphlet. (Years later, she concluded that he likely invented the "shoebox method" on the spot, to encourage her to trust her instincts.) She followed his advice. The day that Selma James opened the shoebox to put her thoughts together, she took a day off work, dropped her son off at school, and went to her friend's house where she could write, undisturbed by all of the housework that needed doing in her own house. By the end of the day, she had drafted her first political pamphlet.[16]

In "A Woman's Place" James described the drudgery and isolation of housework, the joys and stresses of motherhood, and the feeling of utter powerlessness that came from being materially dependent on not just one man, but two: a husband and his boss. She wrote about the maddening experience of having no access to money. She wrote about how the nuclear family arrangement of breadwinner and housewife destroyed romantic love, taking two people who had been lovers and dividing them into different roles so that they had little in common. It wasn't just women who suffered: men, forced to make all the money for the family, were deprived of the rewards of really knowing their children. But James was not interested in portraying working-class people as victims. She looked for beauty, promise, and political creativity. She wrote about the close bonds between women in the neighborhood and the brief window of joy when, on a Friday afternoon, they scrambled to finish their housework early so they could share a glorious beer in each other's company before the men got home from work. "The best time of the week in my court is Friday," she wrote.

> Everyone cleans house on Friday so they will have less to do on the weekend. After they are finished, in the afternoon, someone will run out for beer and we will sit around and talk and relax and compare notes. The sociability is at its highest and we all feel most relaxed when the work is done. There is a feeling of closeness and kidding around that you can't get anywhere else except with these people that know you and accept you on your own terms. This is how women are organized.[17]

James wrote and edited "A Woman's Place" in conversation with her neighbors, sharing her drafts and making changes based on what they said. She co-signed the pamphlet with her friend and comrade

Filomena Daddario, James signing her name as Marie Brandt and
Daddario signing as Ellen Santori. She sold copies to co-workers at
the factory where she worked. It was the most popular pamphlet
ever published by the Johnson–Forest Tendency, and the only one
to ever sell out.

After the success of "A Woman's Place," James began writing
a bi-weekly column on women for *Correspondence*. The intention
was to document the ideas of the women in her neighborhood,
even though she did not agree with everything they said. Her
work method was collaborative. She would visit women in their
homes, take notes, and then bring what she had written back to
the women so they could make edits. "It was one of the most
remarkable days I have ever spent," she wrote of a day she spent
in conversation with neighborhood women. "I have never been so
grateful for the movement as I was that day. It was said in a letter
that we *make* people, not like the old organizations, which broke
them . . . That day I could see that it was the paper itself . . . which
brought them something they had never had, and in turn brought
out thoughts they had never spoken . . . It was a thoroughly successful 9 hours."

"I *knew* these women," James told her comrades. In women who
fantasized about ending housework; who sold their own children's
clothes just to earn a bit of money of their own; in women who desperately wanted new drapes just to break the monotony of being in
the same home all day; in women who worked extra hard just to carve
out a few minutes of the day to have a beer with their girlfriends – in
these women, James did not see backwardness or triviality. She saw
herself, and she saw political potential. "The closest the radical movement has ever come to this type of person was to ask them to make
coffee for party functions," James wrote. "We have only begun to
touch the surface of their demand to enter the world."[18]

Some members of the Johnson–Forest Tendency complained about
the demands of life in the movement; how it took all of their free
time and made it impossible to have a "normal life." But James saw

things differently. She described an experience of friendship and love that was inseparable from political work. As she wrote in a report addressed to her comrades, her political striving to bring forth a better world was inseparable from who she was, not just when she was selling newspapers for the movement, but all the time. In James' description, the joy experienced in the movement was not about a promised future utopia: it was about *right now*, being alive to the political possibilities and creative potential of the present moment. She wrote:

> The people who want friends are making a separation between what they want and what the organization needs. You can't be happy that way, in or out, and you tear yourself between what you want to do and what you have to do for some abstract idea that you feel the intellectual compulsion to carry out. That will ruin you. You must feel no conflict between what you want and what the movement needs. You have to feel that life in the movement is for YOU, not for some abstraction.[19]

By the time she wrote those words, C. L. R. James was living in self-enforced exile in London, and she was preparing to join him there and marry him. The Johnson–Forest Tendency did their political work in the shadows of McCarthyism, and in 1952, after years of surveillance, the US Immigration Department arrested C. L. R. James, rejecting his application for citizenship because of his political activity, rendering him in violation of his visa. He was detained on Ellis Island, which by that time was operating exclusively as a detention center. Suffering from stomach ulcers, he was in and out of the hospital throughout his six-month incarceration and, on his release, he asked Selma James to come out from California to read and comment on a book he had drafted during his time in prison: a Marxist interpretation of *Moby Dick* called *Mariners, Renegades and Castaways*. He admired his young comrade as a writer and editor, and came to trust her for her ability to take his dense analytic prose and express it in an engaging, narrative form that readers could understand. She had never read *Moby Dick* herself but found that she quite enjoyed literary criticism.[20]

Selma and C. L. R. James had a deep connection. They had become romantically involved several years earlier, in 1951, in Los Angeles.[21] They were also both still married to other comrades in the movement, and both soon began the process of divorcing their spouses. James was nearly thirty years his junior, but, when reflecting on their relationship, it was their different class backgrounds rather than the age gap that she found to be a source of creative tension between them.[22] C. L. R. was a cosmopolitan man of letters. He saw no contradiction in fighting imperialism while loving and frequently quoting British literature. He had traveled the world and written books, bridging scholarship and literature and activism. He spoke with authority, power, and experience. Selma James, by contrast, had been a teenage mother from Brooklyn who never went to college. She had spent most of her adult life shuttling among various factory jobs while raising her son. She was not schooled in the highbrow literary lexicon of C. L. R.'s world. Her education had happened through devotion to a political movement. In their collaborations, C. L. R. often asked James to offer a more grounded, working-class perspective. Increasingly, he relied on her as his intellectual partner, to the irritation of some of his comrades. When he started asking her to read and rewrite Raya Dunayevskaya's dense theorical writing so that it would be more accessible to readers, the latter was reportedly deeply offended.[23]

By summer 1953, facing the prospect of deportation, he decided to leave before being forced, so as not to be permanently barred from the United States. He returned to the United Kingdom and set up an apartment in Parliament Hill. Selma James arrived in London with her six-year-old son right at the start of 1955 to join him. A photo taken before their departure shows a smiling Sam Weinstein, cheek to cheek with his mother.

They arrived in London in January. The dampness and cold of the London winter shocked their bodies after years of warmth and sunshine in Southern California. Even the crowded housing blocks of

Brooklyn where James had grown up had central heating, but most buildings in 1950s London did not, and so she was constantly shoveling coal into the furnace to keep their small apartment warm. C. L. R.'s incarceration at Ellis Island, compounded by his continuing anxiety over his legal status, had been punishing to his body, making his ulcers far worse, and James nursed him back to health, while she and her little boy adjusted to life in a new country.

At first, it was not easy. James wrote to her friends back in Los Angeles that she missed dancing. She complained that the British radio only played classical music and stilted operettas. In the early days of their courtship in the United States, James would jitterbug circles around C. L. R., her older, gentlemanly dance partner. She vowed that, any day now, by God, she was going to go out dancing. Any day now.[24]

For all of his deep, genuine intellectual connections and friendships with women, by most accounts C. L. R. was accustomed to Victorian gender roles in his domestic life. He had been raised in a middle-class Trinidadian family in which his mother and sisters had taken care of all of his material needs. Though his intellectual equal and comrade, as his wife James was the one who did the housework. At the same time, C. L. R.'s devotion to his writing and activism did not always result in steady income, and to support the family, she went to work in a West London factory, once again soldering radio sets. At first, she wasn't thrilled about it, but the experience connected her with working-class British life. Now a member of the workforce, she got to know working-class women, many of whom were immigrants, and how they felt about their work, the unions, the political parties.

A mixed-race household in 1950s London, the Jameses made an unconventional family. Sometimes they were joined by Nobbie, C. L. R.'s son from his previous marriage. In letters home to her Johnson–Forest friends, James described moments of contentment, the three of them traipsing across Hampstead Heath together, Sam and C. L. R. a few steps ahead of her, chatting on their way to watch the cricket match. An audio recording that C. L. R. James made in

1957 to send to his Los Angeles comrades offers a glimpse of the trio. He began: "Hello Lyman, Freddy, Filomena and everybody else, but first of all here is Selma to say hello."

> Selma James: Hello everybody. It is a long ways to talk and it is very hard to talk into a tape machine, but it is also very nice.
>
> C. L. R.: Alright, Selma has run dry. Now enter, you will have heard him giggling already, Master Samuel Weinstein. Go ahead, Sam, enter Sam.
>
> Sam: Hello everybody. I hope you've had a very happy new year and a good Christmas and hope it will be a prosperous New year.
>
> C. L. R.: Well, I think that is good enough. Sam has held forth nobly. You want to say something more?
>
> Sam: No.[25]

And with that, C. L. R. launched into his political analysis of recent geopolitical events. Exciting things were happening all over the world. In October 1956, in Hungary, workers' councils had risen up against the Soviet state, and though they were soon crushed, their act of rebellion affirmed their belief in the self-activity of workers and rejection of Soviet communism. In West Africa, Ghana became the first country in sub-Saharan Africa to declare its independence from British colonial rule, under the leadership of Kwame Nkrumah, a socialist and pan-Africanist. Nkrumah invited C. L. R. to attend the Independence Day celebrations in March 1957. James saw him off at the airport, a smart suit packed in his luggage for the historic occasion. It was there, in Ghana, that he met Dr Martin Luther King Jr and his wife Coretta Scott King. When the couple passed through London on their way back to the United States, the Jameses invited them to their apartment. Selma James remembers the Kings telling them about the bus boycotts while she served them fish for lunch. It seemed the whole world was rising up in revolution, and that the politics that Selma and C. L. R. James had devoted their lives to were now blossoming everywhere.

Then, in 1958, on their way toward independence from British colonial rule, Trinidad and several other former British colonies organized themselves into the West Indies Federation, uniting into a single bloc to fight colonialism and pursue their own interests. Eric Williams, a former student of C. L. R. James, was poised to become Prime Minister of an independent Trinidad and Tobago, and he invited C. L. R. to come home to participate in the creation of a liberated West Indies. Selma, C. L. R., and Sam pulled up stakes once again and moved to Trinidad. While Sam enrolled in the local schools, C. L. R. and Selma James devoted themselves to the cause of building a postcolonial future for the Caribbean. C. L. R. edited the *Nation*, the newspaper of the People's National Movement – the party of the independence movement – while James worked on editing and proofreading. West Indian politics infused their family life. James recalled how, at all hours of the day or night, Eric Williams would come to their household to discuss matters of state, from the education system to control of the police force.[26]

For Selma and C. L. R. James, national sovereignty was never the aim: they were interested in the West Indian Federation. C. L. R. James and Eric Williams had originally shared this vision, but the two men eventually fell out over the issue, and when Trinidad became an independent nation in 1962, C. L. R. did not remain to be part of it.

Those four years in the West Indies made a deep impression on Selma James. She loved the culture, eagerly absorbing the calypso, carnival, the food, and the literature.[27] Even as most of her time was devoted to C. L. R. and to her work at the *Nation*, she gravitated toward women. She was often invited to meet with women's groups, where she asked them about their lives, their housework, their income-earning activities, and their political involvement.

In 1961, near the end of their Caribbean sojourn, Selma and C. L. R. James were in a car accident in Jamaica. Though knocked unconscious, Selma soon recovered, but in the aftermath C. L. R. was severely concussed and remained in a coma for three days. Afterward, he would become dizzy whenever he tried to stand. James threw herself fully into his care, tending to his health, writing and speaking to doctors and hospitals to coordinate medical treatment, and updating devoted comrades around the world about his condition.[28]

When their family of three returned to London in 1962, C. L. R. was still recovering from his injuries. He was working intensively on two major projects – *Beyond a Boundary*, a book that he had been working on for years using cricket as a lens into global history and politics, and a new edition of *The Black Jacobins*. This meant that James was spending a lot of time typing and retyping his manuscripts. Both books came out in 1963 to great acclaim, launching him into public life once again. Now white-haired and in his sixties, he was embraced as a beloved elder statesman of the Black left.

After years of preparing her husband's manuscripts, James had become a skilled typist, and when in 1965 C. L. R. returned once again to the West Indies, she remained in London and supported herself and Sam by getting a job as a freelance audio typist for the BBC, transcribing television interviews. That same year, she co-founded the Campaign Against Racial Discrimination (CARD) – an organization devoted to naming and addressing the virulent racism of British society. Inspired by a 1964 visit to the UK by Dr Martin Luther King Jr, Trinidadian activist and writer Marion Glean convened the group, together with other activists, including Grenadian doctor David Pitt, Indian anti-colonial activist Ranjana Ash, and a Jamaican law student named Richard Small. They shared a deep disillusionment with Britain's political parties' lack of action on racism – the Tories were a nightmare, actively hostile toward immigrants, but they found the Labour Party utterly inadequate to the task as well. CARD criticized the Labour Party for defining racism as a kind of moral flaw that could be addressed by banning acts of overt discrimination, rather than a systemic problem to be addressed with the active involvement and leadership of the immigrant community. Within the group, Selma James was one of a number of vocal members who tried to steer them toward becoming a grassroots organization to amplify the demands of the immigrant community.[29] It was through her work as a spokesperson for CARD that she became a confident public speaker.

Meanwhile, scholars, revolutionaries, writers, musicians, cricketers, pan-Africanist politicians – all kinds of creatives and idealists – gathered in C. L. R. and Selma James' first-floor flat on Staverton Road, finding a seat among the clutter of books and papers while C. L. R. reclined in his armchair. West Indian novelists, including V. S. Naipaul and George Lamming, passed through for discussions about literature. The playwright Stanley French brought drafts of his plays there to share with C. L. R. and Selma James. The great Guyanese anti-colonial theorist and revolutionary Walter Rodney recalled being schooled by the couple during weekly Friday night meetings at their place. Frequent guests included Ian Macdonald, an anti-racist activist who would later become an accomplished barrister, known for his role in numerous civil rights and human rights cases. Italian radicals from the workers' group Potere Operaio described the Jameses' apartment as their unofficial London headquarters.[30]

In one of the opening scenes of Steve McQueen's film series *Small Axe*, we are taken into a fictionalized recreation of the living room of C. L. R. and Selma James. The decor is late-1960s earth tones, and every available surface is piled high with books. A multi-racial group of activists gathers around a stately gray-haired C. L. R. James, who sits comfortably in his armchair across from his younger wife, who is seated on the couch. C. L. R. raises his glass to toast James for her work convincing the powers that be at the BBC to air a documentary about racism and police violence in the United Kingdom. She raises her glass to toast her husband for his love and support. And Barbara Beese, an outspoken freedom fighter and member of the British Black Panthers movement, also raises her glass from her seat on the floor in another toast: "To change!"[31]

Though fictionalized, this brief scene of C. L. R. and Selma James convening a community of young activists in their North London flat captures something about their place in the collective memory of London political and intellectual life in the 1960s and 70s. McQueen's five-part series conjures an intimate, loving portrait of the lives and struggles of West Indians in London in the 1970s and 80s. Throughout the series, young Black activists are seen carrying dog-eared copies of *The Black Jacobins*. In her brief appearance (played by the actress Jodhi May), Selma James is portrayed doing the behind-the-scenes work of anti-racist organizing. A few years after the fictionalized living-room scene, Selma James testified on behalf of Black protesters in the Mangrove Nine trial – the first trial to successfully challenge police violence against people of color in the United Kingdom. A few days before she was to testify, she wrote to a comrade: "They [the prosecution] are going to try to tear me apart. But that is not the problem. The problem is that as a white person I must try to get the jury (10 white, 2 women, 2 black) to identify with me and thus with the defendants."[32]

By the late 1960s, the couple's years of intense collaboration were coming to an end. They gradually began to live autonomous lives, him spending most of his time abroad while she worked full-time as a typist, activist, and mother. Sam Weinstein, now a teenager, was stepping in to do some of the cooking.[33] By 1969, C. L. R. took up what became a series of residencies at American universities. Sam, who was getting ready to enroll in university at Sussex, was getting into his own trouble as an anti-war activist, much to the delight of his proud mother.[34] Selma James remained in the apartment on Staverton Road. After years of being C. L. R. James' wife and closest collaborator, her time became her own. Looking back on those early years of separation a few years later, she wrote, "After I left Nello [C. L. R.'s nickname], I spent literally years questioning every one of my assumptions to find out if they were the result of my relationship with him, or they were what I wanted to assume, or what came from my interpretation of my own experience. Strange that today even after all the years I still hear myself saying things which I no longer believe."[35]

By 1970, her fortieth birthday was approaching, and she told her friend Marty Glaberman how she wanted to mark the occasion. First, after years of appreciating Marxism through the mediation of other comrades, she would finally read Karl Marx for herself. She convened a study group to read and discuss Volume I of *Capital*.[36] Second, she would pick up the great political question that had been on hold all these years: she would turn her attention again to the liberation of women.

When she described her feminist vision in the documentary *Women Talking*, Selma James had said, "We are going to start with the actual lives that people live." A year later, she made good on that promise, this time in her own film, *Our Time is Coming Now*.[37] On January 21, 1971, it aired on the BBC, opening with the image of hands moving over a typewriter, the sound of clacking keys, and the zing and whir of the paper roller at the end of each line. The camera zooms out to reveal Selma James, in an orange turtleneck sweater and hoop earrings, her dark hair cropped short, headphones in her ears as she transcribes what she hears onto the page. She is focused, the muscles in her face straining slightly with the effort. Then she looks into the camera and speaks: "Who am I? Like millions of women everywhere, I am a typist. I'm a housewife, a mother, and I've been a factory worker. For twenty-five years I've been involved in revolutionary politics, concentrating on the liberation of women, in the US where I grew up and later in the West Indies and England. I am one of those people who have always listened to women, assuming that what they are is not necessarily what they can be."

The camera cuts to a woman on a break from her job at a grocery store; then to a woman outside the gates of a factory after her shift. The women recount their daily schedules, from when they wake up until when their heads hit their pillows at night. What they describe is a nonstop series of work tasks, both at their jobs and in their homes looking after their families. As the camera cuts from woman to woman, we hear James' voiceover: "Women have two jobs: the one they get paid for, and the one they don't."

The film weaves together the lives of British women of various backgrounds and circumstances. We hear from factory workers and housewives. We hear from single mothers on public assistance, as well as educated middle-class feminists theorizing patriarchy in their consciousness-raising group. The central protagonists of the film are three young housewives from South London who were members of the Peckham Women's Liberation Group: Janet Williams, Hazel Twort, and Ann Bachelli. The film crew goes with them into their homes, where they work the washing machines, cook dinner, mind their children, scrub dishes, bundle kids into their coats and shoes. The women describe a deep sense of disappointment with their lives. They had high hopes for marriage and motherhood, having always been told that this was their purpose in life. "When we got married, when I was twenty-one, I really wanted to wear a ring," Janet told the other two. "I used to sit on the tube train coming home from work and thinking, it itches, this finger, I can't wait to get a wedding ring on it." In the end, instead of a source of joy and self-realization, her role as housewife felt isolating, boring, grueling. Ann recalled: "My father . . . puts his teacup down on the table, and just sort of looks, and if you don't catch his eye then he will make a noise to say that he wants another cup of tea." Now mothers and housewives themselves, the three women were surprised and frustrated to find that they were unable to escape these same dynamics in their own households. "It's very bad for children to just see these women doing all this sort of mopping up all the time. You know, they must just get the idea that women are for that," Janet said. "I've been fighting against it all my life, my sort of conditioning from my mother for that, and here I am, I am still trying to fight against it but I am doing the very same thing to my two daughters here and now." "The dream life," James narrates, "the myth of fulfillment through marriage and motherhood is shattering to bits. The modern individual, if she is a woman, is cramped and stifled by the institution of the family as we know it."

Our Time is Coming Now presented James' distinctive approach to the emerging feminist movement, starting from the mundaneness of housework. The film captured what it feels like: the endless sequence of repetitive tasks, and what laboring in this way, day in and day out, did to one's sense of self, to love, to a mother's relationship with children, to her place in the world. James' film expanded on many of the themes she had begun exploring twenty years earlier in Los Angeles, speaking with housewives about their lives. There were echoes of her earlier musings about Pearl S. Buck, and her annoyance with the idea of the "exceptional woman." "We want to make it clear," she said, looking directly into the camera. "We are not concerned about the few women who make it in this society. We are not concerned that there be more members of Parliament who are women . . . We are concerned with redefining politics."

Selma James was inspired to make the film after attending the Ruskin Women's Liberation Conference: the famous gathering held at Oxford University in late February 1970, which inaugurated the British Women's Liberation Movement. She recalled hearing about the conference from a friend and thinking: "I'm going if I have to crawl. This is a women's conference. All my life I've been waiting for something like this."[38] She was thrilled but also trepidatious. Having come of age politically in the Black movement, she found some attitudes puzzling: for example, the belief of some white women that the police would protect them from men. From her experience with anti-racist organizing, and as a member of an interracial family, she knew about the brutality of the police, especially toward Black people. She also questioned some of the attitudes of middle-class women toward poor and working-class women, speaking on their behalf while neglecting to ensure that any of them were actually in the room to speak for themselves. And as a working-class woman herself, she resented what she saw as the implicit assumption of the mostly middle-class gathering that their struggle was distinct from the working-class struggle. Women were working all the time, even if their work conditions varied: work was something they all shared. When she stood at the front of the room to speak, wearing two Black Panther Party buttons pinned to her jacket, she proclaimed to the assembled women: "We ARE the working class!"[39]

In the months following the Women's Liberation Conference at Ruskin, more and more women, most of them middle-class and white, assembled in Women's Liberation workshop groups across the UK and in different neighborhoods of London. The workshops were deliberately small, designed as such to facilitate frequent meetings and discussions. Together, the network of groups took turns publishing their writings in the Women's Liberation Movement journal *Shrew*. James joined the Notting Hill group. When it came time to publish their issue of *Shrew*, rather than print their own writings, they interviewed four women about their lives and filled the pages of the journal with the transcripts. "We wanted to know the relation of a primarily middle-class movement to working-class women," they explained in an editorial note. "Did university education or trendy clothes or a Hampstead way of life or status jobs inevitably separate us from each other? Can we ever bridge this gap?" In the issue, we hear from Babs, a housewife reliant on government support for her children, who described herself as "poor but proud"; Muriel, a factory worker active in the union but frustrated by her mostly male union comrades, who expected her to be subordinate; Ros, a middle-class professional woman and a member of the Notting Hill group trying to figure out what to do with her life; and Gerlin, a Black bisexual mother who emigrated from Jamaica to work as a nurse, who was interested in women's liberation, but felt excluded from it. Gerlin archly referred to the Ruskin conference as a "white women's liberation conference."[40]

Though published collectively by the group, one can't help but notice a very Selma Jamesian approach in the Notting Hill issue of *Shrew*, reflecting her training with the Johnson–Forest Tendency, printing the words of women themselves, rather than attempting to speak for them. They asked: could a movement made up mostly of middle-class educated white women make common cause with women like these? Such were the kinds of questions that James had been asking for twenty years, since her days recording the "daily strivings" of people in the new society for *Correspondence*. She brought this approach to the feminist movement.

James' vision did not always go over well with others in the British Women's Liberation Movement. But she found a comrade and friend in one of the Italian sojourners who visited her Staverton Road apartment – Mariarosa Dalla Costa.[41] Dalla Costa was thirteen years her junior and was a new faculty member at the University of Padua, where she taught political science and law. Like James, she identified as a Marxist. The two women came from very different backgrounds. Dalla Costa grew up in a middle-class family, had gone straight from being a student to a university professor, and was gaining a reputation in Italian academia as an important political theorist. In contrast with James' worldliness, Dalla Costa's political frame of reference was more localized. She had spent almost her entire life in the northeast of Italy. Her understanding of race politics and imperialism was largely based on academic study, rather than first-hand experience. Yet despite their different backgrounds, both women shared the conviction that, in a capitalist system, work was a form of exploitation, and this primed them to reject the liberal feminist premise that the workplace would be the site of women's liberation. Theirs was a vision of feminism which aimed at liberating women, but with the ultimate goal of overthrowing capitalism and dismantling ALL systems of oppression.

James and Dalla Costa began corresponding and visiting each other regularly. In June 1971, James traveled to Milan to join Dalla Costa and a group of Italian feminists in a conference. The speech she prepared for the occasion was called "When the Mute Speaks." We women, she argued, suffer from a lack of radical traditions of our own to draw on. As women, we have never been asked our opinion about our own lives. "When the mute speaks for the first time," she cautioned, "someone will try to put words in her mouth. Our major responsibility is to see that the women who have never spoken, even if we think what is coming out of their mouths is nonsense – that when they speak, no one is to tell them what to say." She applied what she had learned from years in the Johnson–Forest Tendency: the downtrodden of the world did not need to be told what to think. The housewives and sex workers and mothers and caregivers of the world knew their own lives and their own desires. They were capable of making revolution without anyone else's input; the job of the feminist movement was not to speak for them, but to listen and join together with them. James ended with this: "No political group can tell us, 'You have a wrong political line.' What we have to tell them is: we will work out our political line among ourselves. In short, fuck off."[42]

2.

Mariarosa Dalla Costa

Mariarosa Dalla Costa in Toronto in 1973.

There is an audio-cassette reel held in the Lotta Femminista Archives at the Padua Civic Library, dated 1970. During a visit there in 2018, I sat in a windowless interior storage room and played the tape on an old reel-to-reel player. First, a crackle of static, then a nasal, adolescent-sounding male voice tentatively begins: *"*1 . . . 2 . . . 3 . . . 4 . . . 5 . . . 6 . . . 7 . . . Hello Selma!*"* A young woman's voice chimes in: *"He-lloooo!!!!"*

The voices belong to two young Italian radicals, Ferruccio Gambino and Mariarosa Dalla Costa. In 1970, Dalla Costa and Gambino were the two youngest members of the Political Science Department at the University of Padua. Dalla Costa, at twenty-seven years old, was one of the only women on the university faculty. Photos of her show her in the simple Army and Navy surplus-style fashion of the time, in plaid shirts and sweaters and bell-bottom jeans, her face framed by a cloud of black curls. Her friend Gambino was a gregarious, extroverted world traveler. Both were militant Marxists and organizers with a group called Potere Operaio, or "Worker Power." In the mid-1960s, a Fulbright scholarship had taken Gambino to New York, where he eagerly sought out other Marxist intellectuals, especially those connected with one of his heroes, C. L. R. James. Ferruccio's political passions led him to C. L. R. and Selma James' apartment on Staverton Road in London, and he soon became a frequent guest and friend. At the time of the recording, Gambino and Dalla Costa had recently returned from a summer trip to London they had taken with a group of their Italian comrades. On that trip, Mariarosa Dalla Costa and Selma James became fast friends.[1]

Back in Padua a few weeks later, Dalla Costa and Gambino sat down with a tape recorder to continue a conversation they had started in London. They were pondering: how did housework fit into an analysis of capitalism? On the recording, Ferruccio Gambino, confident and fluent in English, gets right to business. "Let us start with the passage in Tronti's book *Operai e Capitale* that Mariarosa couldn't find because she hadn't a copy of the book in London. Now, on page 169 Tronti says, 'The characteristic element of the productivity-worker is that he does not produce commodities for his own . . .' Now, what has to be added . . . "[2]

When I had first requested that recording from the archivists, there was no device on hand on which the tape could be played. But then, on my last day, in the final hours before my flight home, a librarian excitedly ushered me into a back room, where he had set the tape up on an old reel-to-reel player he had procured. After a week of immersing myself in her writings and collected ephemera, I was eager to hear the voice of a young Mariarosa Dalla Costa. I wanted to hear the unedited thoughts and feelings of a woman on the cusp of her intellectual epiphany. But instead, I heard her male comrade examining passages of *Capital*. At first, I was charmed by the passion and excitement of the young professor holding forth. But twenty minutes in, I started to get bored, and then impatient. I had come to Italy to visit Mariarosa Dalla Costa's archives, leaving my partner to parent our one-year-old son alone for ten days. Only after arriving in Padua did I discover that the archives were only open to the public a few hours during the week. Dalla Costa had to intercede on my behalf to allow me special access throughout the week, surely an inconvenience for the library staff. Then there was the trouble of finding obsolete technology on which to play the recording. All of this effort was expended so that I could hear Mariarosa Dalla Costa speak. Had I done all this, only to listen to a man talking over her?

Young 1970's Ferruccio Gambino held forth cheerfully in pro-fessorial mode for nearly two hours on that tape. Throughout the exegesis, Dalla Costa remained silent. Only in the final seconds of the recording did she at last approach the microphone. Shy, self-conscious in her halting and thickly accented English, she addressed Selma James slowly: "Kisses, first of all, and our greetings!" She told James that she was excited to be talking with her but confessed that she still felt unclear about her ideas. "Ferruccio is making continu-ally a mess in my brain!" she exclaimed, and then giggled. "I am not always sure that the intention of this man is good!" Gambino, now in the background, laughed and shouted out in good-natured protest.

Dalla Costa paused. Her voice dropped into a more serious, even-toned register: "Selma, I continue to be really convinced that these men of Potere Operaio – and Ferruccio in the middle of them – continue to prevent me to understand deeply and deeply and deeply. They prevent us from a complete understanding. Selma, Goodbye.' The tape clicks off.

I met Mariarosa Dalla Costa roughly fifty years after she made that recording, in her apartment in Padua on a cobble-stoned block right at the heart of the ancient university city where she has spent her adult life, first as a student, and then a professor. She and I sat across from each other in her living room, me apologizing for my halting, awkward Italian, and she apologizing for her out-of-practice English. Her demeanor was businesslike. Her time was precious. We filed into the phone-booth-like elevator, descended to ground level, and walked around the corner to a cafe for a drink. She listened with stern interest, or maybe just politeness, as I described the book I wanted to write. She told me that, as a policy, she never gives interviews. Everything there was to know was in the archives, but I could ask her a few questions now if I wanted. I asked where she grew up, and she seemed to relax as she waxed lyrical on the beauty and natural abundance of Treviso, her hometown. I asked her about a 1976 photograph I had seen earlier that day in her archives depicting thousands of women marching for Wages for Housework on May Day in Naples, and she became animated as she explained the complicated mechanics of coordinating thousands of young women around the country who didn't have access to telephones except through their fathers and landlords. When I asked her what Wages for Housework has meant to her personally, I was surprised by her curt answer: "It wasn't personal," she told me: through study and political struggle, she concluded that it was the correct analysis of capitalism.

Mariarosa Dalla Costa was born in 1943 and has lived her entire life in the Veneto, the northeast region of Italy encompassing the foothills of the Austrian Alps to the north, flattening out to the foggy plains of the Po Valley in the south, and spreading east along the tributaries of the Po River that empty out in the Venice Lagoon and the Adriatic Sea. Dalla Costa grew up in Treviso, an ancient walled city of canals and bridges about twenty miles north of Venice, with cobblestone streets and the sound of the rushing water that turns the old watermills.

As Italy emerged from the shadow of World War II and the aftermath of fascism, economic modernization became an obsession of its politicians. Compared with the rest of northern Italy, the Veneto was seen as a kind of backwater in need of development, and at the center of these efforts was the industrial zone at Porto Marghera. Located on the Venice Lagoon on the mainland across from the island of Venice, Porto Marghera invoked both the promise of modernity and the environmental horrors of industrialization. Initially built in 1917 as a port to serve Italian efforts in World War I, from the 1940s onward, Porto Marghera became home to dozens of petrochemical factories. They transformed the Venice Lagoon, clouding the waters with chemical effluvia, rendering the surrounding soils infertile, and releasing toxic fumes into the air. Though it would be years before the public would learn the extent of the environmental damage, people knew early on that it wasn't good. In Venice, a particularly noxious-smelling breeze was known by locals as "Margherina."

The Veneto remained largely rural into the second half of the twentieth century. To the west, in the cities of Milan, Genoa, and Turin, hundreds of thousands of migrant workers from the south packed into the massive factories of Pirelli and Fiat and SIT-Siemens, returning each night to crowded urban squats, far away from their families. By contrast, the Veneto was made up of smaller factories, employing around 200 or 300 workers each, rather than tens of thousands. Many workers continued to live in their rural homes, commuting to work each day on bicycles and commuter trains and buses. The young men who entered the workforce remained enmeshed in the world of their family farms. Some of the factories of Porto Marghera recruited workers through local parish priests.

Compared with the rest of postwar Europe, Italian women did not enter the waged workforce in large numbers. In 1969, they made up only 25 percent of the labor market, and by 1973, that percentage had fallen to less than 18 percent. The numbers were even lower in the Veneto. But these statistics tell only part of the story. Many women worked for income, often in industries based in the home – small-scale agriculture, food preparation, sewing, knitting, mending, laundry, and craft production. Textile factories hired women to do piecework on their own sewing machines, on their own time. Many of them worked late into the night, squinting into dim lamplight when their children were sleeping, or at dawn before their husband and children awoke, or during the day between household tasks. For someone who left the home to work an eight-hour shift at a factory every day, there was a clear division between housework and waged labor, but in households like these the boundaries between housework and wage labor were less clear.

The Catholic Church infused the social worlds of the Veneto, and the conservative Christian Democratic Party held electoral majorities throughout the postwar decades. One of the cultural legacies of fascism was the upholding of patriarchal gender roles. From the pulpit on Sunday, Catholic clergy urged women to have children and refrain from using birth control. "Don't deny a soul to the Lord!" The refrain repeats like a haunting chorus through Cecilia Mangini's 1965 film *Essere donne*, evoking the pressure many women felt.[3] But by the 1960s, young women started to envision different kinds of futures for themselves. One of the catalysts for this change was the expansion of the education system.[4]

Dalla Costa studied at the University of Padua, one of the oldest and most prestigious universities in Europe, dating back to the thirteenth century. She studied with Enrico Opocher, a well-respected philosophy professor and a former member of the Italian Resistance. When Dalla Costa graduated in 1967, he hired her to assemble the archives of the Venetian Institute for the History of the Resistance. Each day she'd go into the Palazzo del Bo – the magnificent fifteenth-century palace at the heart of the old campus – to read and catalog the clandestine reports, diaries, correspondences, and ephemera of the men and women who risked their lives fighting fascism.[5]

She began to teach as a faculty member at a time when the Italian university system was changing rapidly. In 1962, secondary education was made compulsory for the first time in Italy, meaning there were far more students eligible for university than in previous years. Between 1950 and 1970, the student body at the University of Padua grew from 5,000 to 30,000. Yet the universities struggled to keep pace with the growing enrollments. The historic campus, with its courtyards, collonaded walkways and frescoed lecture halls, was crowded with more students than it could accommodate. There were not enough full-time professors, and many syllabi were hopelessly outdated.

In Padua in the 1960s, it was hard to avoid politics. Though historically a conservative provincial city, Padua was caught in the crosshairs of militant fascists and Maoists, both of whom had operatives in town and both of whom periodically detonated explosives in public places.[6] At the same time, the global movements against the Vietnam War and colonialism in Southern Africa inspired students to rise up and occupy campus buildings. Italian students soon turned their attention toward their own universities, rebelling against the traditional elitism of the higher education system. Initial student demands for better student housing and more professors and updated curricula were replaced by a deeper questioning of the very relationship between the university and modern Italian society. Students looked to the workers' movement for inspiration.[7]

As a student, Dalla Costa joined Potere Operaio, an organization of students and workers inspired by a new philosophy called *operaismo*, or workerism. Potere Operaio arose out of Italy's hot autumn of 1969, when wildcat strikes rocked factories across the country. Many workers and activists were frustrated with the inability of unions and the Italian Communist Party (PCI) to adjust to rapidly changing work conditions, and union membership had dropped to its lowest in decades. Traditionally, these older workers' institutions idealized the figure of the male proletarian – defined as a skilled worker in a trade, proud of his work and the wife and children he supported on his wages. Yet the economic boom of the postwar years brought another kind of worker to the factories of northern Italy. Each morning, the *Treno di Sole* – the Sun Train – pulled into the stations at Milan, Turin, and Genoa, packed with migrants arriving from their twenty-four-hour journey from the south to work in the factories of the north. These unskilled workers were not the proletariat; they were peasants. They did not identify with a trade. For them, work was a means to a paycheck, rather than a source of identity. In this new world of mass production, employers offered low base wages supplemented with productivity bonuses.[8] A worker's wages would increase incrementally the faster he worked, the more he punished his body, the more profit he handed up to his boss. As Rachel Kushner succinctly puts it, "a worker whose wages are tied to productivity . . . collaborates with the bosses against himself."[9]

The *operaists* rejected this premise. Mario Tronti, the most influential theorist of *operaismo*, argued that it had been a mistake for the labor movement to accept the inevitability of capitalist development as a starting premise and to carve workers' demands out of that broader aim of productivity. "Now we have to turn the problem on its head," he wrote, "and start again from the beginning. And the beginning is the struggle of the working class."[10] In other words, workers' self-realization would no longer be secondary to capitalist development – it would become the central aim of political action, productivity be damned.

One of the rallying calls of the *operaists* was "Less work, more money!" Or, as the writer Nanni Balestrini – himself a member of Potere Operaio – titled his novel about the hot autumn, *Vogliamo Tutto* – we want everything! Unlike the traditional union strategy of negotiating with bosses on behalf of workers, these workers were not interested in building union institutions, recruiting members, and getting recognition as a bargaining partner from the bosses. Instead, they wanted to change the workplace through direct action, unmediated by a lobbying body.

Operaismo resonated deeply with Dalla Costa. In particular, Dalla Costa was drawn to the idea of autonomy: of the powerless defining their lives on their own terms, rather than on the terms of those who held power over them. This language of autonomy became central to Dalla Costa's politics.

For the Padua branch of Potere Operaio, the focal point of struggle was Porto Marghera and Mestre, the neighborhood across the railroad tracks from the factories where many workers lived. Here, the *operaists* extended their gaze beyond factories to include the surrounding environment and the health of the people living in the vicinity of the factory. In the early 1970s, a number of workers were hospitalized with poisoning from breathing in the gas phosgene. In a move to contain growing concerns about worker safety, Venice's labor officer ordered all the Porto Marghera's factories to issue gas masks for their workers. At one of Potere Operaio's biggest protests, they held up the effigy of a crucified worker wearing a gas mask.

The factories of Porto Marghera produced various petrochemicals. Some factories manufactured PVC – synthetic plastic polymer used to make hard white plastic pipes. In others, they made chlorine and industrial solvents, pesticides, and refrigerants. The work was physically intense, and the equipment and safety standards did not keep pace with the latest engineered chemical products. Some workers unloaded vats of heavy raw materials from the ships in the port and lugged them into the factories. Others worked the furnaces and autoclaves, boiling and extracting chemicals, exposing themselves to extreme heat that burned the clothes and skin. Leaky valves and substandard equipment led to gas leaks and exposure to toxic substances.

At stake for the *operaists* at Porto Marghera was not just salary, but the seeming expendability of workers. The pay scheme that tied wages to productivity squeezed workers, making them work faster and more dangerously, trading their health and safety for money. Their work conditions contrasted starkly with those of the chemists, engineers, and other white-collar workers, who drew a regular salary with health benefits and paid vacation. One of the campaigns of the workers' councils, inspired by Potere Operaio, was to reject the offer of a 1.5 percent productivity bonus and instead demand a 5,000 lire increase for all factory employees, regardless of job classification. It was a relatively trivial amount and some objected to this – what difference could 5,000 lire (roughly $65 in today's terms) possibly make in people's lives? As one former worker recalled, it was the mindset that was important – it changed the conversation; rejected the logic of the factory by asserting workers' worth as distinct from productivity.[11]

"Where were you in 1968?" a journalist for *L'Espresso* asked Mariarosa Dalla Costa in 1978.

"I was waking up at four in the morning to leaflet at the petrochemical plants in Porto Marghera in a cloud of industrial miasma and mosquitoes," she answered.[12]

Dalla Costa found intellectual satisfaction in Potere Operaio. "This is my home," she told a reunion of former *operaist* comrades in 2002. "This is where my thinking fits. Here I find the people who speak my language." But the work was not easy. "I can't remember even a single moment of joy," she recalled. "I do not by any means remember that period as a time of convivial living, as others claim to. It was rather a period of great learning, of very austere living, of much sacrifice and commitment, and of much determination."[13] The student militants expected total commitment from each other. They studied the factories intently, learning each detail of the production process along with the health hazards and physical ailments of workers. They were expected to read and study the texts of Marx and Tronti, along with the *operaist* journals, and to discuss them in study groups. Leaders in Potere Operaio (Potop) imposed discipline so that all members shared the same "correct" analysis. To open your mouth, or put pen to paper, or create a leaflet without authorization was a serious affront to one's comrades.

Life in the movement was grueling. Dalla Costa recalled waking up in her apartment in Padua at 4 a.m., making her way to the train station while it was still dark, and beginning the commute east to Porto Marghera, the fog of the Venice Lagoon mingling with the smoke of the factories as the sun rose.[14] She would walk to the gates of the Montedison petrochemical factory to encounter the first shift of workers on their way to the all-male locker rooms to suit up in their protective gear for a day at the furnaces and shipping containers and autoclaves. Picture her, the young scholar confronting the crowd of working-class men gearing themselves up for a day of body-punishing physical labor. She would distribute the leaflets that she and her fellow militants had composed the night before. Then, the sun now up, she would return to Padua for a day of work at the university – teaching classes on Marx and Rousseau, marking papers, attending various meetings. In the evenings, she would meet with her comrades to discuss that morning's efforts at the factory gates and create new materials for the next day. They would compose and print up new leaflets. Then to bed, only to rise early the next morning and do it again.

"Perhaps the most beautiful thing," Dalla Costa said, "was the immediacy of relations, finding ourselves active in the same cause, and the blooming of this great community to which we belonged. It was not necessary to fix appointments in order to meet, we all knew where the others were, it was a life in common."[15] At any point in the day, you knew where to find your friends – they were either at home, in class, on a shift leafleting at Porto Marghera, or at Caffè Pedrocchi, an old Padua establishment where activists and student groups hung out. The cafe was divided into three rooms with different colored upholstery in each: the Red Room, the White Room, and the Green Room, after the colors of the Italian flag. In the Green Room, members of the public were allowed to sit without purchasing anything, making it an ideal space for penniless students to gather. A former student militant described her beloved former hangout to me years later: in one corner, you'd find the PCI youth; in another, the Christian Democrat youth members; in another area, the Potere Operaio comrades, and so on.[16]

Yet alongside this conviviality, Potere Operaio was also riven by hierarchies. One division was between workers and students. Former workers at Porto Marghera recall taking inspiration from the ideas of the student members, while simultaneously feeling wary of them as comrades. At worst, they saw the students as carefree agent provocateurs who had time on their hands and nothing to lose, whereas the workers had little free time and their livelihoods to lose if their rebellions failed. The worker members of Potop were careful to guard their autonomy and did not allow the student militants to sit on the factory councils and participate in decisions or planning.[17]

They were also divided by gender. Alisa Del Re recalls being sexually harassed by workers as she approached the gates at Porto Marghera to hand out leaflets.[18] Accepted wisdom among comrades was that such sexist treatment was simply part of the struggle – to complain about it was to impose bourgeois ideals of respectability on the working class. But sexism was not a working-class affliction – it threaded throughout the ranks of Potere Operaio's intellectuals. Self-assured Potop men assumed their role as the thinkers of the movement – the writers of leaflets, the makers of speeches. By contrast, the women were nicknamed: *angeli del ciclostile*, angels of the mimeograph – the helpers, the women who would work the mimeograph machine copying and printing and distributing the manifestos that men had written.[19] They would type up the stencil, insert it into the giant roller, and then turn the handle around to push ink through the stencil to print. They were expected to support the efforts of the men, not to work beside them as intellectual equals. Stefania Sarsini, a former member of Potop, recalls:

> Lucia, despite her militancy, always remained Scalzone's woman, as I was Verità's woman, and Grazia Zermann was Daghini's woman: we were all "the woman of." Our identity as persons didn't exist and this made militancy all the harder. No documents were elaborated by women. And the "gratification" of cyclostyling [mimeographing] leaflets until late at night, or of cleaning a branch office soiled by the [remnants of] sandwiches and cigarette stubs smoked by dear [male] comrades intent on staying awake so that they could elaborate revolutionary theories, was certainly rather minimal for a revolutionary militant![20]

Some women of Potop grew dismayed by the hypocrisy of their male comrades. Dalla Costa recalled that, when she joined Potere Operaio, she had high hopes that it would offer emancipation from the straitjacket of family life; that in her political relationships, she would be treated as an equal and trained for revolution, rather than marriage, motherhood, and homemaking. "Seen from a woman's viewpoint," according to Dalla Costa, "that experience undoubtedly represented a decisive emancipation from one's family of origin and its expectations. It meant finding free and friendly territory from which to discover the world, without being forced to marry soon, a territory for learning things other than those necessary to be a good wife."[21] This promise of dignity made the sexism of her comrades feel all the more like a betrayal. "We felt split," she recalled, "between the imperative to be like men, to be capable of being and acting like them, and the feeling that we belonged to another world, one where men would also ask different things of us and expect us to be different."[22]

A political cartoon made by feminists in Florence, which Dalla Costa clipped from a newspaper and saved in her archives, captures the sentiment. The cartoon depicts a man, long-haired, mustachi-oed, smoking a cigarette like a stylish 1970s politico. In the first panel, framing only his face, he says: "Until there is a revolution, and, consequently, the abolition of class, the liberation of women is not possible." In the next panel, framing his entire torso, he says: "Don't you agree, Puffina?" and we see that he has a girl under his arm, limp like a rag doll, subordinate. *Until there is a revolution . . .* This was the maddening refrain of so many leftist men the world over, whenever their female comrades brought up the subject of their own liberation. This ever-moving horizon of revolution cut off any discussion.

Soon, Dalla Costa took the concept of autonomy – that cherished ideal that *operaismo* had given her – and applied it to her own life.

After Dalla Costa's trip to London in the summer of 1970, she began corresponding with both C. L. R. and Selma James. With C. L. R., she exchanged notes about her academic research on French and Italian working-class history, and she appreciated his advice that she consider the role of colonialism as part of the history of European class politics.[23] But it was her relationship with Selma James that endured. The two women began writing to each other frequently. They compared notes about Marx and Lenin and Tronti. They commiserated about men: their shortcomings as lovers, and their uselessness as comrades. They edited and translated each other's political writings, shared news of their respective political groups, and schemed about the future. They complained about what they saw as the trivial bourgeois trend of consciousness-raising and psy-choanalysis among other feminists. James' letters are searingly intelligent, but also playful. She signs a letter "Love from your autonomous friend ☺." She often takes a sisterly tone, urging Dalla Costa to take better care of herself – to get enough sleep, to eat proper meals, to enjoy herself, to forget about men who disappoint her and find herself a feminist boyfriend.[24]

As intellectual misfits, caught between Marxists who ignored women and feminists who, in their view, paid insufficient attention to class, James and Dalla Costa agreed that capitalism needed a new origin story. For Marx, exploitation began the moment when men were separated from the products of their labor and forced to work making profits for someone else. Dalla Costa began theorizing a new version. When wage labor outside the home became the organizing principle of the economy, she argued, the home became a feminized ghetto, walled off from the life of the community. No longer collaborators in a complex household economy, women became materially dependent on men's wages. Able-bodied wage-earning men became the protagonists of public life and politics.

In her writings, Dalla Costa asked: where do the rest of us – women, and for that matter children, the elderly, the disabled – fit into this great human drama of capitalism? If factories were the place where exploitation happened, why didn't women who stayed at home feel free? To understand capitalism, rather than start with the male worker, nailing bumpers onto Fiats or lugging vats of chemicals from the ports into the factories, Dalla Costa instead looked at his wife and mother – the women who raised him, fed him, gave him shelter and care. She began to rethink the entire history of capitalism from the standpoint of the housewife.[25]

Her Marxist contemporaries argued that women create use value, but not surplus value – that is to say, they perform work that is useful, but not transformed into profit. Their work is, therefore, outside the boundaries of capitalist relations. Dalla Costa thought that this was completely wrong – not only do women produce, but they produce the single most valuable thing, without which capitalism could not exist: *labor power itself.* Before a worker appears in the factory to have profit wrung out of his body, he must be gestated, fed, nourished, clothed, socialized, educated in school, provided with a home. By cooking, cleaning, caring, breastfeeding, nurturing, and teaching, women create and cultivate workers for capital to exploit, and they do so for free. An employer gets not only the benefit of the worker he employs; he gets the benefit of all that unpaid work as well.

Dalla Costa took her analysis further. Just as capitalism distorted the body of the worker, bulking certain parts of the body unevenly to serve the repetitive motions of the assembly line, the female role in capitalism distorts women in mind and body. The wife becomes a dependant of her husband, and the receptacle of male frustration. She is told that she is naturally suited to housework and mother-hood, and that it will bring her joy. She makes herself submissive, soothing her husband against the harshness of his workday, submit-ting to his demands rather than exploring her own sexuality and desires. She is made to find self-worth in meaningless tasks like iron-ing and cleaning the pavement outside her house and maintaining the few square meters of the world that make up her household. Told she is outside the realm of real productive work, she is made myopic, directing her frustration at her husband, rather than her true oppressor: her husband's boss.

Dalla Costa's initial writings on the subject reveal a vision of healing, bringing back together what capitalism had severed. If women were isolated in the home, the first step toward liberation was to somehow bring women together and make the struggle against housework collective. She imagined the remaking of neigh-borhoods. "We demand communal canteens," Dalla Costa wrote "– and the canteen should serve OUR needs, not just become like the lunchrooms of factories, which shuttle workers through only to make them more productive. Let us remember that capital first made Fiat and THEN the canteen."[26] She envisioned cooperative childcare centers where mothers and fathers would work, in which the boundaries between biological parents and community caregiv-ers was blurred. She wrote about neighborhood elder-care facilities that would allow the elderly to be integrated into the community, not separated from it. In her vision, everyone would partake of col-lective wealth and social life and caregiving.

In spring of 1971, Dalla Costa sent her written reflections in a letter to James. James replied with line by line comments.[27] In June, James came to Padua, and, at a meeting of twelve women – mostly former Potop members – Dalla Costa read a version of her essay aloud for the first time and took notes on the discussion that ensued afterward.[28] Over the summer, she continued to work on it, and, that September, Dalla Costa shared another draft at a meeting of women, which once again included Selma James.[29] Her essay became the founding document of a new group: Lotta Femminile – Women's Struggle. She made mimeographed copies to share, and from that moment it began to make the rounds in feminist and *operaist* circles in Italy. Selma James introduced it into feminist circles in the UK, where it was translated and sent around through her networks.[30] It made its way to the United States.

That summer, Dalla Costa, together with the women of Lotta Femminile, composed a manifesto, the "Programmatic Manifesto of Housewives in the Neighborhood," a utopian vision of what a post-capitalist neighborhood could be. In this new world, everyone who performed housework, whether men or women, would be paid for it by the government. The neighborhood would have communal kitchens, laundry rooms, nurseries, and elder-care facilities, all free of charge and high-quality so that those who performed housework would not do so isolated in their homes but in each other's company. Everyone would receive a guaranteed income as a basic entitlement, affirming that the right to exist and thrive was not dependent on wage labor. The houses in the neighborhood would be "free and beautiful", surrounded by open-air spaces for children to play. Finally, given that truly communal living that put carework at the center would require a lot of time, they called for a twenty-hour workweek so that everyone would have time to participate in the raising of children, the care of the elderly, the nurturing of the community.[31]

That autumn, Dalla Costa resumed teaching at the university with a new focus. Though it was true that women were entering university in unprecedented numbers, it seemed to her that nothing they were learning was supporting their liberation. Instead, women were concentrated in high numbers in the education school, where they were trained to become elementary-school teachers. Curricula across the humanities and social sciences accepted uncritically the idea that women and men had different natures, rather than looking for the historic and economic roots of patriarchy. Dalla Costa made space to study such questions. "To everyone interested in exploring [women's] issues from an historic, economic, and psychological point of view," proclaimed a leaflet distributed on campus, "we invite you to join the seminar 'La Liberazione della Donna.'"[32] Mariarosa Dalla Costa led the seminar every Monday and Wednesday afternoon. Together, students and faculty in these sessions would meet to study and demystify what had been cast as "natural" gender roles. The seminar also became a place to break down the gender politics of the university, in which women workers did the lowest-status work – cleaning and secretarial work – while the men were professors and administrators. Mariarosa taught the seminar on her own time, for free.

Dalla Costa and her Lotta Femminile comrades, including Leopoldina Fortunati and Maria Pia Turri, worked off campus as well. They set out trying to connect with women in the neighborhoods of Guizza and Paltana, the suburbs of Padua south of the Bacchiglione River.[33] Unlike Potere Operaio, which could meet at the factory gates and expect to encounter all of the workers in the same place on their way to or from a shift, organizing women who worked in the home, separate from each other, was difficult. They approached women at grocery stores, laundromats, schools when children were being dropped off. They distributed a questionnaire to the women in the community, with the goal of both gathering information and provoking discussion.

> *Which chores do you find most odious?*
> *Do you have money at your disposal?*
> *Do you have access to birth control?*
> *Did you know that dishwashers and washing machines were invented*
>   *a century ago?*

42

Do you think it is fair that you don't get a pension for all the years you spend working in the home?[34]

They also wrote leaflets and manifestos addressing housewives directly: "Women, do you know how much work you do in a day? In the factories, they are fighting for fewer hours, but what about you? How much work do you do without being paid? How much are you paid? NOTHING!"[35] At the end of each manifesto was a time and place for a Lotta Femminile meeting.

Throughout autumn 1971, Dalla Costa continued to labor over her essay. She worked straight through the winter holidays. On New Year's Eve, as she completed the edits alone in her campus apartment, her Lotta Femminista comrade Pia Turri stopped by with panettone and Spumante to encourage her and celebrate the new year.[36] By the end of the night, Dalla Costa's manifesto was ready. She called it "Women and the Subversion of the Community."

The essay contained the core ideas of earlier drafts, but it was sharper in its analysis. In it, she explicitly rejected the demand to be paid for housework, arguing that a wage would further tether women to housework, institutionalizing "women's work," when the point was to abolish it. Dalla Costa wanted to transform the home into a place of political struggle; the place from which to seize the machinery of global capitalism. She called on her sisters to "challenge the whole structure of domestic work . . . to smash the entire role of housewife."[37] She drew inspiration from rent strikes in working-class Milan. She cited the great anti-colonial thinker Frantz Fanon, who argued that, under the colonial policy of indirect rule, colonial subjects were ostensibly ruled by their own people but were really under the thumb of a larger system of imperialism. Dalla Costa extended the argument to women in the home: ostensibly ruled by their husbands but really ruled by global capitalism.

Perhaps the most significant change in this new version was a more expansive understanding of housework. The feminist "we" of

Dalla Costa's address had now widened dramatically. It was not just about housewives. Instead, it was about how all women's work was exploited and undervalued. "We have chopped billions of tons of cotton, washed billions of dishes, scrubbed billions of floors, typed billions of words, wired billions of radio sets, and washed billions of diapers by hand and in machines," she wrote. In this version, she includes the work of plantation slaves and domestic servants, as well as women in the wage labor force. Her reference to typing billions of words and wiring billions of radio sets clearly refers to her friend Selma James, who had spent years making money doing exactly that. Whereas the scale of her earlier argument was the kitchens and the factories of a quintessentially Italian city, now she also referred to "the kitchens of the metropolis and Third World." She implored women to leave their homes and discover what they shared in common as comrades. "And this," she concluded her essay, "is where our struggle begins."[38] It was worldly and powerful, breathtaking in its ambition, embracing all who lived and labored under capitalism.

In March 1972, "Women and the Subversion of the Community" was published alongside an Italian translation of Selma James' 1953 essay "A Woman's Place" and a text by Lotta Femminista about abortion. Published by Marsilio Editore with the title *Potere femminile e sovversione sociale*, the book was a beautiful object. The paperback cover was a deep, vibrant indigo blue with white and yellow lettering, all lowercase letters, and "Dalla Costa" appeared in bright yellow letters on the spine.[39]

That summer, Selma James and Mariarosa Dalla Costa met in Padua along with members of Lotta Femminista to discuss what to do next. They were joined by Silvia Federici, a philosophy PhD student visiting from New York, and feminist Brigitte Galtier, visiting from France. At the meeting, they took the opportunity to declare themselves the International Feminist Collective, and to write a statement establishing their shared aims. "We identify ourselves as Marxist feminists and take this to mean a new definition of class . . . based on the subordination of the wageless worker," they wrote. Their struggle was not, they emphasized, merely a negation of the left, but rather a "positive expression of the level of female struggle." The position of women and their unwaged work offered a unique position from which to mount a challenge against capitalism, and while they could act in concert with the male-led class struggle, they could not be subsumed within it. They ended their statement by proclaiming their autonomy as a feminist movement and declaring their intention to coordinate "mass actions transcending national borders." They signed their statement "International Feminist Collective, Padua, Italy, July 1972," and then participants went back to their respective countries. Though "Wages for Housework" appears nowhere in their declaration, and though the "International Feminist Collective" seems to have scarcely been mentioned again afterward, the conference launched the collaboration that would become the International Wages for Housework campaign. Galtier did not remain part of the network, but the other three participants became key nodes in the international movement: Mariarosa Dalla Costa in Italy, Selma James in London, and Silvia Federici in New York.

The necessity of their declaration of autonomy from the male left became evident the following month. Lotta Femminista had been planning a conference for July 7 at the Faculty of Education in Rome on the theme of women and the university – a topic the women of Lotta Femminista in Padua had been thinking about for months. In study groups on campus they had been discussing the different kinds of work that made a university function, the denigration of the work of secretaries and cleaners, and ways the university funneled women into low-paid caring professions and reproduced the gendered capitalist system. Only women were invited to the meeting. The conveners knew from their experience as student activists that men would try to dominate the discussion and the agenda, and that an open discussion of the matters at hand would not be possible with men present.[40]

A group of men proved them right almost immediately. On the day of the conference, about fifty women who had come from across Italy to attend were met with violent resistance from a group of "self-styled comrades," young men from Potere Operaio.[41] An article in *L'Espresso* recounted:

> Rome. A lightning-fast assault, doors and windows broken, punches, kicks, the throwing of chairs and condoms filled with water on the part of some bold extra-parliamentary leftists against a group of militant feminists in a classroom . . .[42]

Letters appeared in the Italian left-wing press throughout the month, from the PCI newspaper *Manifesto* to *Lotta Continua*, the magazine of Potere Operaio. Some were self-described Marxists, scandalized at Lotta Femminista's claim that unwaged women, rather than just male factory workers, could be considered "the proletariat." Others drew on more well-worn misogynistic stereotypes about feminists, caricaturing Lotta Femminista as castrators, and as navel-gazing perverts, obsessed with masturbation and artificial insemination. Others attacked them for being bourgeois. "Suffice it to say," a group of women from the ranks of Lotta Continua and the PCI asserted, "this group supports the absurdity that every woman is exploited by every man, and therefore even the wife of Agnelli (or Nixon) is exploited." Potop's leadership itself responded in more measured tones: they condemned the attack, but at the same time asserted: "We consider it politically serious to have a unisexual assembly, without men."[43]

"It gives an idea of what the times were like," Dalla Costa recalled years later. "Just the fact that women chose to meet by themselves provoked a violent reaction. That episode is indicative of how hysterical the male response could be when faced with the new fact: women analyzing and discussing autonomously."[44]

3.

Housework in Global London

In London, Selma James saw the untapped potential of a vast, diverse working class, waiting to be organized. There were unemployed Black young men, whose parents and grandparents were recruited to England as workers, but who were written off as separate from the class struggle, and were instead seen as a social problem. Throughout the 1970s, clashes between striking miners and the government appeared on the front pages of the papers and on the evening news, but just off camera you could find miners' wives protesting price increases that made their work in the home far more difficult. There were mothers defending the Family Allowance against government cuts. There were rent strikes and squatters movements. None of these groups made their protest at the point of production – that is, in the workplace – yet their struggles were surely about class. For James, the daughter of a Teamster and for whom there were few sins more odious than scabbing, the initial critique that she addressed to the unions was not that they were harming those that they excluded but that they were harming themselves, and the working class as a whole, by missing all this potential. Instead, what she found in London in the 1970s was a labor movement that was inflexible and stuck in its ways, determined to define the working class as "white, male and over thirty."[1] James was eager to explode open this narrow definition and build a more robust and powerful working-class movement, starting with women.

She had like-minded allies in her Women's Liberation group. In January 1972, during one of the standoffs between striking miners and the Conservative Heath government, the Notting Hill Women's Liberation workshop made and distributed leaflets in support of the unions, but their statement included a caveat. "Support must work both ways," they wrote. "Men workers have to understand the special exploitation that women struggle against, in jobs and at home, and join that struggle."[2] In another leaflet they pressed further: "Women in industry have almost no representation on the shop floor. They have always been ignored by men who call themselves militants. Now that we are all attacked these men expect us to join in defense of our class. And we will join. The question is, are they going to join with us?"[3] James and her fellow feminist sisters tried to convince the unions that organizing with women was in their interest: when women are financially dependent on male breadwinners, the bosses have leverage against those men. When women are paid less, it puts downward pressure on men's wages, incentivizing bosses to replace male workers with lower-paid women. Women's financial dependence on men was bad for everyone. By supporting women's struggle for economic power, they invested in working-class power.

Soon, James grew impatient and struck out on her own. She published a pamphlet in her own name right before the third Women's Liberation Conference in Manchester in March 1972. "This is perhaps written as an open letter to women attending this Manchester conference," she wrote. "It is impossible any longer to sit in the protection of a group and see the potential of the movement squandered."[4] The Notting Hill group printed James' pamphlet and distributed it on the buses of women on their way north for the conference. The title was *Women, the Unions and Work, or What Is Not To Be Done.* To those in the know, the subtitle referenced Lenin's 1902 pamphlet *What Is To Be Done*, which argued that revolution was advanced through the spread of "trade union consciousness." James argued the opposite: in the current context, she wrote, unions do not raise working-class consciousness but maintain the status quo, especially with respect to women. James accused the unions of suppressing women's organizing: they accepted the pay grades that shunted women into lower-paid jobs and assigned men to the highest-paid ones in a given workplace. They ignored opportunities to organize women workers. She referenced the recent Nightcleaners campaign, in which the low-paid women who cleaned office buildings at night tried to form a union and struggled to get unions to support them, as a case in point. Unions, she wrote, collaborated with bosses to make workers more productive. They ignored the realities of women's lives and all the unwaged work they did outside the workplace. They negotiated for a marginally better spot for working men within an exploitative capitalist system, rather than challenging that system altogether. If women wanted to organize against their economic exploitation, James argued, joining the unions was not the answer. They needed their own organizations.

At their inaugural 1970 conference, the UK Women's Liberation Movement had endorsed four demands – equal pay, equal opportunities for education and employment, free contraception and abortion, and free twenty-four-hour nurseries. To James, these demands were unambitious, unimaginative, and narrowly focused on middle-class white women. Equality in the workplace maybe made sense for the narrow subset of the population that had the possibility of good, well-paid, satisfying work, but for many working-class women like herself, a job was anything but liberating: it was the money that was liberating. More importantly, it ignored the fact that women already worked an indispensable job in the home, for no pay. As for access to contraception and abortion, this too was necessary but limited: it excluded women who wanted to have children but were prevented by poverty from raising them in a safe and nourishing environment, or who might find themselves coerced into sterilization or invasive contraceptive implants when they claimed their welfare benefits. Free state-run nurseries might sound appealing to those whose encounters with the state were generally positive, but what if the state and its representatives were systemically racist toward you and your children? James countered the four demands issued at the conference with a revised list of six demands.

1. We demand the right to work less. A shorter workweek for all. Why should anyone work more than 20 hours a week?
2. We demand a guaranteed income for women and for men, working or not working, married or not. If we raise

kids, we have a right to a living wage. The ruling class has glorified motherhood only when there is a pay packet to support it. We work for the capitalist class. Let them pay us, or else we can go to the factories and offices and put our children in their fathers' laps. Let's see if they can make Ford cars and change nappies at the same time. WE DEMAND WAGES FOR HOUSEWORK. All house-keepers are entitled to wages. (Men too).

3. WE DEMAND CONTROL OF OUR BODIES. If even birth control were free, would that be control? And if we could have free abortions on demand, would that be control? What about the children we want but can't afford? Give us money and give us time and we'd be in a better position to control our bodies, our minds, and our relationships . . . WE DEMAND THE RIGHT TO HAVE OR NOT TO HAVE CHILDREN.

4. We demand equal pay for all . . . Whoever works deserves a minimum wage, and that minimum must be the rate of the highest grade.

5. We demand an end to price rises.

6. We demand free community-controlled nurseries and childcare. We are entitled to a social existence without having to take another job out of our home. Mothers too have a right to work less.

Of those six demands, it was demand two – wages for housework – that exploded into the feminist movement.

That summer, Selma James and Mariarosa Dalla Costa traveled together to Stromboli, a small island off the north coast of Sicily, famous among Italian tourists for its black sand beaches, the product of pulverized lava rocks from the island's active volcano. There, several hours by ferry from the mainland and with no electricity, the two women talked, typed, and cooked while working on the English version of their book *The Power of Women and the Subversion of the Community*, which combined their writings. From the island's one post office, James posted their revisions to Suzie Fleming, co-founder and editor of Falling Wall Press in Bristol.[5]

Fleming had started Falling Wall Press a few years earlier with her partner Jeremy Mulford when he unexpectedly inherited £500 at his grandmother's death. A socialist, poet, and lover of literature, Mulford used the money to buy an offset litho Gestetner printing press, which they then put in their basement and used to launch Falling Wall Press. In an oral history interview with her daughter in 2018, Fleming recalled that Falling Wall Press was a labor of love, and a time-consuming affair, taking over the Fleming-Mulford home. They were a small operation. Fleming and Mulford distributed their publications hand to hand, through networks of friends and at radical bookshops, and at feminist conferences, where Fleming would set up her literature stall.

They started with pamphlets. "In Jeremy's mind," Fleming recounted, "we were in a sort of pamphleteering tradition from the 1920s."[6] Some of their first publications were reprints of older socialist-feminist pamphlets, including writings by the Bolshevik feminist Alexandra Kollontai and Member of Parliament Eleanor Rathbone, who had envisioned and successfully campaigned for Britain's Family Allowance in 1945. Fleming met Selma James at the 1970 Ruskin conference and went on to publish all of the English-language publications of the Wages for Housework movement, starting with the English version of *The Power of Women and the Subversion of the Community*. "That press has impressed me deeply," James wrote to Dalla Costa. "You will see that although we do not have the facilities of the ruling class, we are more careful in production than they are. I hope it has not one typo."[7]

An introductory text by James presented the two essays – "Women and the Subversion of the Community" and "A Woman's Place" – as discrete moments in a single revolutionary feminist trajectory. "The two articles which follow were written 19 years and 7,000 miles apart," she wrote. "What was posed by the struggle of so-called 'reactionary' or 'backward' or at best 'non-political' housewives and factory wives in the United States 20 years ago is taken by a woman in Italy and used as a starting point for a restatement of Marxist theory and a reorientation of struggle." The original Italian version of the Dalla Costa essay had argued against wages for housework, warning that it would institutionalize women in the home, rendering them servants of the state who paid their wage. But in the English version, James added a footnote, explaining that since the original publication of the essay, the demand had been getting traction. "It is clear in any case that the demand for a wage for housework is only a basis, a perspective, from which to start . . . "[8]

The text ended with a short open letter written by James, to women in the Eastern Bloc. One member of the Notting Hill Women's group, Hungarian filmmaker Esther Ronay, agreed to take copies of the book with her on a visit home to distribute to a women's group there, and James took the opportunity to address them directly. "Dear Comrades and Sisters," she began. "The Socialist governments have claimed that we are victims of our state and nothing more, and have hidden our subversive power. The western governments have told us the same about you. We have never believed them." Cold War ideology, she argued, prevented women on either side of the Iron Curtain from seeing what they shared as unwaged workers. The letter concluded: "Our best hope is that our sending you this Marxist Feminist book is stage one of an inevitable process. Stage two will be when you send us yours. Stage three may be further away but it is just as inevitable, when we meet to talk and act together." She signed off: "Power to the sisters and therefore to the class, Selma, Mariarosa, and many others." Falling Wall Press released the English version in October, just in time for the Fourth Women's Liberation Conference in London. "I set up my literature stall, and we were literally selling it hand over fist," Fleming recalled.[9] Almost immediately, translations were in the works in French, German, and Spanish, and there was talk of additional translations in Portuguese and Danish.

The following spring, James and Dalla Costa went on a speaking tour of North America. In Toronto, Cleveland, Detroit and New Orleans, and other cities, they attended potlucks and spoke to women's groups on college campuses and in community centers. James was the more talkative of the two – Dalla Costa's English was not as strong – and she increasingly narrowed in on wages for housework as the core demand, rather than one of several demands. In a speech in Detroit in May, she called it "the perspective of winning." In explaining what she meant, she told the audience a story. "When the women at the Chesebrough-Pond's factory in London began to organize themselves, the union man stated his case and ours: 'The union only represents people who want to work.' The young woman from Ireland who jabbed the woman next to her in the ribs and said 'He must be joking,' had other ideas about why she was spending her precious time away from work going to meetings." This overworked woman, Selma said, did not want more work: she wanted to get more of her time, more of her life, back. "And when she looked around to find the power to do that, standing opposed to her was the union, ready to defend her, but only if she was ready to continue to accept exploitation as her natural destiny." The unions, she reiterated, have made common cause with capital by agreeing to squeeze as much work out of workers as possible. "The perspective which we counterpose to trade union gradualism is the perspective of wages for housework. It is the demand of women for power, for autonomy against capital. It is the perspective of winning."[10]

Selma James offered Wages for Housework as a theory of working-class power, which started from women. As James saw it at the time, unions were limited to acting as vehicles for getting power for waged workers within capitalism: by contrast, Wages for Housework was a means for attacking capitalism by ending the unwaged work on which it relied. "Our feminism finally grasps the totality of exploitation, in the home and out of it, and therefore grasps the totality of working-class struggle, in the home and out of it. No working-class organization has ever done that before. Our struggle against the factory is not only to get out but never to go in."[11]

That summer, after returning to London, James acted on the new focus of her politics by dissolving the Power of Women Collective and convening the Wages for Housework campaign in its place.

At the same time, she turned her attention to race. Her ties to the Black movement predated the feminist movement of the 1970s, and it was there that so much of her political education had taken place. This gave her a different perspective than most women she encountered in the Women's Liberation Movement. "I was in the Notting Hill women's group for years," she recalled.

> We did a lot of good work . . . but I was never able to speak about my relationships with men, because I knew that women might seize the opportunity to slam Black men. They were lovely women . . . but one thing they almost all shared, and that was they were too frightened to oppose the State. If you are too frightened of bucking the State, you cannot get to the bottom of racism. A Black woman may or may not be very clear about men, white or Black, but if the police come after a Black man, she'll usually know what side she's on.[12]

When, for example, James would address a feminist conference with the words "All prisoners are political prisoners," taking an expression from the Black movement and using it to talk about incarcerated women, some stood up and applauded but others were uneasy.

By August 1973, she addressed the Black movement directly with an essay she called "Sex, Race and Working Class Power," an eloquent, impassioned distillation of her definition of class and her vision of social change. She began, as in her earlier writings, by challenging the common wisdom conflating male white waged workers with "the working class." The narrowness of this vision, she contended, quashed the creative potential of a far more capacious working class that she considered herself to be part of. She extended Marx's concept of the division of labor – the way that a capitalist society distributes discrete, specialized tasks among its different workers – to an analysis of race and sex. "Racism and sexism train us to acquire and develop certain capabilities at the expense of all others. So planting cane or tea is not a job for white people and changing nappies is not a job for men." She argued that everyday experiences of identity can teach us about where we fit into capitalism. We are encouraged, she wrote, to think of identity as separate from capitalism and class. "In our view," by contrast, "identity is the very substance of class." To label the Black struggle as "race issues" is to divide the working class: "When Black workers burn a city, everyone sees race and not class." This, James believed, was a way of preventing people who have common interests from making a common struggle. For her, Wages for Housework was the common struggle.

> It is here in this strategy that the lines between the revolutionary Black and the revolutionary feminist movements begin to blur. This perspective is founded on the least powerful – the wageless. Reinforcing capital's international division of labor is a standing army of unemployed who can be shunted from industry to industry, from country to country. The Third World is the most massive repository of this industrial reserve army. (The second most massive is the kitchen in the metropolis.)[13]

In other words, housewives and immigrants were selectively incorporated, and then abandoned, by employers and the state to meet the needs of capital. During times when labor is needed to build the economy, immigrants are brought in; when they are no longer needed, the walls go back up and immigrants are vilified as a drain on collective resources. The same is true of housewives: they are asked to fill in men's jobs during a war or a strike or labor shortage, but then they are paid less, the first to be sacked, their wages called frivolous, "pin money." Her aim was not mutual sympathy, or a conflation of their struggles, but power. She believed that workers of all kinds, waged and unwaged, gain strength from each other by first identifying their place in the capitalist order, and uniting to fight a common enemy: the capitalist class that profited off their labors.

Her essay was the cover story of *Race Today* in 1974. She was speaking to her fellow activists, but they were also friends and family. The *Race Today* Collective was formed by Darcus Howe, C. L. R. James' younger relative, and a group of young Black activists in the wake of the Mangrove Nine trial, in which Selma James had testified. They occupied a squat in Brixton and published their journal along C. L. R. Jamesian lines, seeking to capture the expression and "self-activity" of Black Britons. They embraced the idea of "political Blackness," defined by one's subordinate position in a racist world order. In his introduction to that issue of *Race Today*, Howe wrote: "if any single document has informed the theoretical perspective of *Race Today*, 'Sex, Race and Working Class Power' has." When James later published her essay as a pamphlet with Falling Wall Press, Barbara Beese and Mala Dhondy, both members of the *Race Today* Collective, wrote the introduction.

In this sequence of James' early writings, it's as if she is constantly moving, pivoting to address different audiences, trying to unite them into a single struggle. Each of these texts was meant to do more than make an argument: they were carefully honed political tools, meant to build relationships across different communities. It's not that she was seeking diversity for its own sake, but rather, as she put it, "We are together because we have something to *do* together."[14] By 1973, James saw Wages for Housework as the political project that would connect them all. "It is not Wages for Housework or lifestyle, health groups, or squatting. Wages for Housework is all these things, not as an umbrella or abstract solidarity, but as organizational practice and organizational connections in the process of getting power. We are not choosing between the 'working class' and ourselves, and sacrificing ourselves for the 'working class.' We are the working class."[15] For Selma James, in the 1950s as in the 1970s, revolution was a holistic way of life.

Not everyone in the Notting Hill Women's Liberation Workshop embraced Wages for Housework. Those who did split off with James to form their own group, which they called the Power of Women Collective. They published a journal, *Power of Women*, and from their first issue they began making their case for Wages for Housework. Her early collaborators included Priscilla Allen, an American comrade from her Johnson–Forest days, a playwright and literary scholar who had worked with C. L. R. on the script for a theatrical version of *The Black Jacobins*, and Esther Ronay, from her old Notting Hill group. Also present were Bernadette Maharaj, a Trinidadian immigrant who worked as a nurse and was mother of three children, and Anne Neale, who saw linkages between her work as a waitress, pleasing male customers for tips, and housewives who had to be pleasing to their husbands in exchange for a bit of money.

Wages for Housework groups assembled in Bristol and Cambridge. The Bristol group, convened by Suzie Fleming, included a number of women from Claimants Unions: single mothers who received government benefits and organized to support each other, share information, and advocate for themselves politically. Among the Claimants Union organizers was Norma Steele, a Jamaican immigrant.[16] "When I say these politicians are racists I am not talking about their personal preferences or bad attitudes," Steele said in a speech at the House of Commons in March 1978, on the subject of the Child Benefit. "Racism is about money."[17] The Wages for Housework campaign saw themselves as heirs to the struggles of the Claimants Unions, and several of their members were active in both, though James criticized their "low level of organization."[18] In her view, they lacked a broader anti-capitalist strategy. In "An Open Letter to All Women in the Claimants Unions," the campaign urged the claimants to demand wages. "By demanding money rather than wages," they argued, "claimants have been more easily isolated as special cases asking for kindness from the government rather than what they actually are: part of the working class and part of its universal struggle for wages and against work."[19] The response from Claimants Unions themselves was mixed. Some joined the campaign, but others found members of the campaign condescending, more concerned with ideological conformity and future revolution than day-to-day struggles for survival.[20]

The launch of the Wages for Housework campaign in the UK coincided with a major public battle concerning mothers and money. The Family Allowance was a payment from the British government to each mother, calculated on the basis of the number of children she had. First introduced by MP Eleanor Rathbone after World War II, women collected their payment each week at the post office. In 1972, the Conservative government proposed a Tax Credit System to replace the Family Allowance, making it so that it would be paid through a man's employer, linked to a man's paycheck. Crucially, under the new system, the payment would go directly to the male worker, rather than to his wife. A mass movement formed in protest.

In Bristol, Suzie Fleming was active in the campaign, organizing petitions, convening groups of women to educate themselves, reading through the dense policy jargon and preparing each other to testify before Labour MP Barbara Castle in 1973.[21] Across Britain, thousands took to the streets to defend the Family Allowance. The Wages for Housework campaign had their own take on the issue. They objected to the way the new proposal tied benefits to waged work outside the home. As they saw it, the Family Allowance was a form of wages for housework. They rejected the language of charity, which framed the debate as a matter of government largesse, rather than simply a wage that was owed for the work of mothering.[22] Some in the Family Allowance campaign favored language that challenged the assumption that childrearing was the natural role of women by framing it as a benefit for children, so that anyone who cared for a child could get it, regardless of gender. By contrast, the Wages for Housework campaign framed the Family Allowance Campaign as a fight for financial autonomy for women. For many women, the Family Allowance was the only income they had access to. James recalls:

> We all went with a petition to post offices, which is where women collected it on Tuesdays, some cities on Thursdays. I went up to a woman and I said, "Can you sign our petition?" and she said, "I don't sign anything that my husband doesn't read first." That was 1972, you know! And I said, "But madam, they want to take your Family Allowance!" and I'll never forget what she said. She said, "But this is the only money I can call my own! Where do I sign?!" I said to myself: *This is a winner. Wages for Housework is a winner.*[23]

The Wages for Housework campaign argued that the Family Allowance was a source of autonomy and freedom for hard-working women, and should be unabashedly claimed as such, rather than wrapped in the virtuous, self-sacrificing language of children's well-being. As James wrote: "Money for us is autonomy from men, the right to choose what we eat and when, how much we work and where, where we live, whether or not we have children and under what circumstances and with whom." For Wages for Housework, the Family Allowance, paid directly to women as wages for the work of mothering, was not simply about alleviating poverty: it was about freeing women to have choices, including the rejection of heterosexual marriage or of "shit jobs for shit wages" outside the home. It was leverage against capitalism. They collected it not as wives of workers but as workers themselves.

The Family Allowance campaign succeeded. As Priscilla Allen said in a speech in 1974, on the day that they delivered a petition with 80,000 signatures to their MP, "If this is the climax and the end of our campaign on family allowances, it is also the beginning of something bigger."[24]

For the first few years of their existence, the Wages for Housework campaign mostly met in Selma James' apartment on Staverton Road. In 1975, they opened their first women's center in a squat at 129 Drummond Street in Camden Town. They painted their storefront façade red with "Women's Centre" in white block letters over the top, and across the front window, they stated their intention in large black letters: "Wages for Housework for all women from the state." It was a tiny space, with a desk and a few chairs, crammed with books, pamphlets, posters, and tea cups. At meetings, there were sometimes more attendees than chairs, so some women sat together on the rug. Women from the neighborhood were invited to drop in and discuss their problems during open hours, Tuesday, Wednesday, Friday 1:30–6:30 p.m. If part of the problem of organizing with women and unpaid workers was that they did not all work in one centralized location, the women's center was meant to bring them together. Early visitors included single mothers and immigrants struggling to access their benefits, lesbians seeking to keep custody of children, squatters facing eviction, women of color threatened by coercive sterilization, and sex workers harassed by the police. The center workers were practical, supporting women in their daily struggles, but they had bigger aims as well. Here is how they described their work, in a petition to the Camden Town Council a few years later to protest their impending eviction:

> The Women's Centre aims to change women's views of themselves and their possibilities. Firstly, as a Wages for Housework Women's Centre, it stands for recognition of the often invisible work women do at home, and has come to stand for that in the eyes not only of the local women but of the whole community. The discussions at the centre often give women a new estimation of their own worth and the confidence to confront their problems themselves. The Wages for Housework literature, tea towels, pot holders, balloons, etc., on sale at the centre provide on the one hand a source of revenue for the centre and on the other give women something to take home with them that supports this view of a woman's worth.[25]

London Wages for Housework Committee storefront, circa 1976.

To go into the various archives of the UK Women's Liberation Movement is to encounter intense disagreement over Wages for Housework. Some questioned the practicality of it. How do you quantify the value of housework? Who would get the wages? How much would it be? Would everyone get the same amount, or would it be calculated based on how much housework you do? And in that case, would you have to report all your activities to the state? Wouldn't that just invite more state surveillance and control into the private lives of women? The most common critique of Wages for Housework was that it would reinforce the link between biological sex and housework. At a time when many in the Women's Liberation Movement were seeking to break away from their role as housewives, Selma James was seemingly asking them to do the opposite: to identify with that prescribed role. How they got from there to liberation was unclear, and a common response was earnest confusion. In a radio interview with Selma James, you can hear New York radio host Nanette Rainone struggling to understand. She asks: "But *how* does getting paid for housework allow you to refuse housework? Doesn't getting paid for a job mean that you actually have to *do* it?"[26]

In London, feminist Zoë Fairbairns didn't know what to make of it. She could see both sides of the argument. She wrote: "That no one should have to be a full-time housewife, but that women who choose to should not be penniless dependants, seems to me elementary." Wages for Housework made sense to her as a metaphor, "but I think we are meant to take it literally."[27] To figure out what she thought, Fairbairns wrote a novel playing it out. In *Benefits*, published by Virago in 1979, she attempts to follow Wages for Housework to its most extreme conclusion: a future in which the government pays women to produce children for the state. Because the state paid the wage, the state could control women's reproduction, and the result she envisions is something akin to industrial-scale livestock farming.[28] It was a dystopian literary depiction of what many feminists feared: that wages for housework would institutionalize women in the home, render them permanent housewives, tethered to their reproductive roles.

For others, it was not the demand that was the problem, but the single-pointed focus of the people in the campaign. The feminist journalist Amanda Sebestyen, who had been a member of the Notting Hill group and who had helped to publish and distribute *Women, the Unions and Work*, later found their focus reductive. In an article for the magazine *Spare Rib* covering a conference on rape, she described how members of the Wages for Housework campaign took the floor over and over again, reducing rape to a metaphor for economic exploitation, as a problem that could be solved by Wages for Housework. Sebestyen found them insensitive and bullish, silencing and speaking over women who had actually been raped and were attending the conference in the hope of working through their trauma.[29] Dale Wakefield, a lesbian activist who founded Bristol's Pride parade and launched Gay Switchboard – an anonymous support hotline for gay people – lamented the effect their presence had on queer spaces in her city. Wakefield had devoted her life to creating places of support and safety and fun for lesbians at a time when these were rare in Britain. In an oral history interview, she recalled that when Wages for Housework members started to dominate those spaces, steering every conversation to their struggle against capitalism, it wasn't fun or inclusive anymore, and people stopped wanting to come. "We were utterly destroyed by it," she said.[30] Lynne Segal, in a recent memoir of second-wave feminism in the UK, described the approach of Wages for Housework as "vanguardist hectoring," which made open conversation and communication impossible.[31]

One of their most outspoken critics was Sheila Rowbotham. In her recent memoir, she recalled that *Women, the Unions and Work, or What Is Not To Be Done* sparked debate and discussion, including in the Arsenal Women's Liberation Workshop, of which she was a member. She agreed with critics that it shoved women back into the home, right as they were trying to break free of it, and disregarded the desires of many who derived satisfaction from their jobs. She thought that the demand was vague, conflating housework and childcare when there were important differences between them: it's one thing to refuse to clean the dishes but another to refuse to feed a child. Rowbotham was troubled at the possibility of bringing even *more* areas of life into the commodity relation. She criticized James' call to separate their struggle from that of the unions, which she saw as counterproductive. Most of all, she found Wages for Housework unrealistic as a strategy for fighting capitalism. How would you actually get the government to pay for housework – women can demand it, but why would the state agree? In the end, she saw Wages for Housework as little more than a gimmick. She wrote: "Many of Selma's demands are based on the desire most of us feel to find a short cut out of capitalism."[32] After all, who doesn't want to work less? Who doesn't want more money?

Wages for Housework was not always easy to explain. Priscilla Allen tried to respond to their critics this way: "A Ford worker would like to destroy the production line that dehumanizes him, but he knows he cannot destroy it by refusing wages and working for nothing. Indeed his main weapon is to demand more wages. So too a housewife, if she wishes to destroy housework, must first gain that minimum leverage that a wage provides."[33] In letters to the editor and in leaflets and pamphlets, James and Allen and their comrades explained their perspective: that housework needed to be waged so it could be brought out into the open and contested; that as long as women did it for free, capitalism would continue to exploit them.

When an interviewer mistakenly characterized the campaign as "Wages for Housewives," James clarified: "We phrase it as a demand of wages for housework rather than housewives for two very specific reasons. If men want to do the housework, that's fine with us. Let them get paid. Housework is work, that's the second reason. We want to drive that into the mind of every member of society . . . that when we are working in the home, we are doing work."[34] The first step, even before demanding a wage, was to bring women together to make their work visible, to themselves and others: to make them aware of how they fit into capitalism. In their films, newsletters, and anthologies published with Falling Wall Press, and at public conferences and events, the Power of Women Collective gathered testimonies of women, describing in detail their daily waged and unwaged work.

For an issue of the *Power of Women* journal, Esther Ronay described working all day as a film editor alongside her male co-workers.

> The crunch came for me every night when we eventually went home. All the men would ring up their wives to announce their imminent arrival and ask what was for dinner. They would go home after a hard day's work to hot meals, clean houses, clean clothes for tomorrow, and lots more understanding. I on the other hand would go home hoping to find a shop still open to grab some food, to a flat I hadn't had time to clean, to dirty clothes, to unanswered correspondence and no time to deal with any of it till my day off.

She went on to say: "Housework is productive work which is unpaid. In a nuclear family the wife produces and reproduces labor power (both her own and her husband's). In the case of the single person . . . the person who reproduces the labor power is the same person who sells it."[35]

A woman who identifies herself as "Helen" loathed her dull, monotonous, stressful job as a typist, and reflected on how her life would be different if she were paid for the housework she did: "I could give up that shitty job and just begin to enjoy my time a bit . . . I want wages for housework so that I can get out of the house for forty hours a week, not to bash a typewriter for capitalism but to be part of the struggle to get rid of capitalism altogether."[36]

Rose Craig, an Irish Catholic woman from Belfast, spoke about taking care of her three young children in poverty and in occupied territory. She recounted how some of her fellow mothers had protested cuts in their benefits: they dropped their children at the welfare offices, telling the state, "You look after them, we can't afford to anymore." Faced with children on your doorstep, how can anyone deny that to look after them is work? Craig noted that, at the time, it cost the government £8.15 per week to look after a child in a foster care home: "You picture one family out of every street in a mining village, every week, bringing their whole family down and leaving it there. How much is it going to cost the government after about four or five weeks? You'll break the government quicker this way. They'll have to give in to you, so they will." In other words, the state already puts a price on the work of caring for children. Wasn't that an acknowledgment of the core premise of Wages for Housework: that caring for children is work?[37]

In a feature entitled "Interview with a Shoplifter," someone identified as "E.W.", from Glasgow, said:

> those people who own Tescos and all those shops can so easily afford to lose the odd two or three things which it takes all my ingenuity to take. When you get home at the end of a little spree you flop down in the chair and think to yourself, "Well, what have I got after all that work?" And you look in the bag and you know it's peanuts and for it you have probably risked prison.[38]

In a subsequent issue of *Power of Women*, the collective discussed shoplifting further, admitting: "We can't really go round with leaflets suggesting that women shoplift, because in the present circumstances, that would amount to suggesting to women that they do something they can get caught and fined/imprisoned for, and we couldn't even help defend them."[39] The approach they favored was supporting women who HAD shoplifted, removing the stigma, and letting them know they weren't alone. Shoplifting, in other words, was a legitimate response to rising prices, stagnating wages, and women's lack of independent income: it was reclaiming wealth that was denied to women.

The Power of Women Collective also published a series of conversations with two teenage girls, Gaye and Karen, who demanded wages for schoolwork. Due to recent policy changes, students were now required by law to stay in school until the age of fifteen; the girls argued that, if the state was going to make them stay in school rather than work for wages, they should be paid for their time. When asked if it should be paid through parents, Gaye said absolutely not: "Like, if we was naughty, they'd say, oh, you're not getting your money today, and all things like these. Like, if we had our own wage, we'd be independent."[40] Selma James, who, in her earlier pamphlet *Women, the Unions and Work*, had written about the liberation of children from the capitalist nuclear family, took them seriously. In her view, struggles against school, often cast as delinquency, were legitimate rebellions against the plans of capital. She quoted a West Indian mother observing how Black children like her seven-year-old son were trained at school for their future role as an economic underclass: "They're choosing the street sweepers now."[41]

The campaign connected housework with the work of nursing. "The hospital worker is a waged houseworker," the Power of Women Collective wrote in a special issue on nursing. "Hospital work is socialized, industrialized housework."[42] The hierarchies within the hospital mirror those of society: those paid the least and whose working conditions were worst tended to be immigrants and women of color. They saw hospitals as an extension of the social factory: like mothers in the home, workers in hospitals are essential to capitalism, repairing labor power that has been damaged. They saw connections between the vulnerability of mothers and of nurses: both roles were lauded as exemplars of female virtue and selflessness. Both faced the blackmail of not being able to refuse work because of not wanting to harm those they care for.[43] They wrote: "When the nurses shouted on their demonstrations, 'We can't put dedication in the bank,' they spoke for every woman."[44]

To go into the archives of Wages for Housework in London in the 1970s is to be immersed in dozens of women's stories: women in abusive relationships afraid that they don't have enough money to leave; women bored to death and lonely working in the home; immigrant women who send remittances home for the women who look after their children abroad. Rachel Smith, the pseudonym used by an African lesbian immigrant associated with the campaign, concurred: "While we are working over here, we leave behind a whole community of women caring for the children; grandmothers, sisters, aunts . . . the money we send back circulates

66

among all these women."[45] In the process of showing their work, they revealed unexpected connections. Dodie Seymour, a housewife from Bury, a working-class town on the outskirts of Manchester, joined the campaign in part because of her frustration trying to manage her own unpaid work as a mother and the caregiver of disabled relatives, including her husband.[46] On behalf of the campaign, she lobbied her Labour Party MP to support the rights of immigrant mothers to collect the child benefit even if their children were overseas: as it stood, only mothers whose children were resident in the UK were eligible. Seymour, though a white housewife from the north, felt she shared something important in common with Rachel Smith. As an unpaid caregiver, she was saving the government money doing work the NHS might otherwise be expected to provide. In the case of the immigrant woman, family members back at home in the Philippines or Bangladesh or the West Indies were caring for children so their mother could work low-paid jobs in London, saving the British state the cost of supporting them. Those women back home "in effect also work for Britain," Seymour said in her testimony before the House of Commons.[47] In both cases, Seymour argued, the government was freeloading off the work of women, at home and abroad. (Their campaign, alas, was not successful.)

The Wages for Housework campaign inspired coalitions of lesbians, single mothers on benefits, and women trying to escape domestic violence. They came together as women who cared for children but who were vilified by the state, which tried to ensure that the work of mothering was confined to the heterosexual nuclear family, with women dependent on wage-earning men. Anne Neale, an early member who was part of the autonomous sister group Wages Due Lesbians, recalled how one of their early struggles was to protect lesbian women who were threatened with loss of custody of their children if they came out. They shared this fear in common with poor mothers and single mothers. In one testimonial, a woman describes a maddening plight to regain custody of her children from the state foster-care system. She recounted how, when she was with her abusive ex-partner, she was blamed by social workers for staying with him and exposing her kids to the violence, but how, when she left, she was then blamed for subjecting her kids to poverty, and, as a result, lost them to the foster-care system. The struggle to get them back was Kafkaesque: she could not qualify for public housing deemed suitable for children because she didn't have custody of her kids, and in order to get custody of her kids, she needed to prove that she had housing suitable for children.[48] "Black, immigrant, lesbian, we are all called unfit mothers or treated as unfit mothers," she wrote. By demanding wages for housework, and support for mothering, they were demanding the economic power to raise children in circumstances of their own choosing, and not as the appendages of wage-earning men in nuclear families.

By collecting testimony about housework in its various forms, the Wages for Housework campaign made visible a new kind of working class, made up of women with different experiences but who all agreed on the common enemy: the capitalist system that exploited their unpaid labor. A few years after James set out to document the working lives of women in her BBC film *Our Time is Coming Now*, she collaborated with her fellow campaign members on a second film, *All Work and No Pay*.[49] It aired as part of BBC's Open Door series: a program that invited community members to make their own episodes, with technical assistance from a BBC film crew. Their episode begins with Bernadette Maharaj's morning, sped up through jump cuts, as she makes breakfast for her two little boys, coaxes them into drinking their juice, bundles them in coats to meet the school bus, cleans up the dishes and table, puts away toys, sweeps, and gets herself ready to leave the house. The scene ends as she arrives at the storefront on Drummond Street, picks up a ringing phone and says, "Wages for Housework campaign." While the first film raised the problem of housework, this one directed the viewers toward a solution: wages for housework. We hear Selma James' voiceover:

> Housework. Feeding and cleaning. Comforting and mothering. Smiling and pleasing. Suiting yourself to the needs of others. Working to

their time clocks. Housework. The work that produces workers. The basic ingredient of all industry and all profit. Housework. The work all women do. The only work that isn't considered work. The only work you don't retire from. The only work you don't get wages for.[50]

The film included news footage of the women's strike in Iceland, a wildly successful one-day event in October 1975 in which women took a day off from all forms of work and instead met together in the city center to protest, bringing the whole economy to a halt. They showed footage of the Italian Wages for Housework campaign marching through the streets in Naples. They spoke of a rent strike in Northern Ireland. The impression they create, from their small Women's Centre in a squat in Camden, is of a worldwide movement, a spontaneous uprising, connecting women together in a struggle to make a new world. At the end, they give their address and phone number and invite women to stop by.

In the film, Selma James appears once again with a microphone, approaching people on the street, young and old, of different races and classes, in front of their workplaces at factories and grocery stores. This time, unlike in her earlier film, she doesn't just ask about their work but also provokes them to consider wages for housework. She asks a stout, jovial white-haired woman in an old-fashioned hat, out with her gentleman companion: "Don't you think we should get paid for the housework that we do?"

The woman, who does not stop walking, laughs a jovial, throaty smoker's laugh:

"Then I've worked for nothing for fifty years then, love!"

"Would you like to get some back pay?"

"I don't suppose the government would give me any money now."

"Not by yourself, but if millions of us got together all over the world and demanded it, what would you think about that?"

"Oh, if we all stuck together we might get something."

"Are we entitled to it?"

"I should say we are!"

4.

Potere, Baci e Soldi!

On a cloudy chilly Saturday in March 1974, a crowd gathers in Piazza Ferretto in Mestre, the working-class neighborhood of mainland Venice across the railroad tracks from the factories of Porto Marghera. Power lines crisscross the gray sky and paint peels off buildings. A stage is erected in the square. Behind it, an advertisement promotes a bitter liqueur with the image of a Hollywood cowboy: *"L'uomo forte beve Petrus"* – "the strong man drinks Petrus." Loudspeakers hang from the windows of a shabby building. From behind the curtains of a window, a face furtively peaks out at the gathering crowd, and then hides itself again. Old men in fedoras and thick eyeglasses congregate at newsstands and page through the daily papers. A young man wearing a smart suit, tie, and sunglasses strolls with hands in his pockets. A pair of hunched elderly women in headscarves and calf-length black winter coats shuffle arm-in-arm across the piazza. A well-dressed family walks together – a man in a tie and jacket holds a baby girl in a white winter coat and bonnet while his tall, slender wife, hair neatly coiffed in an updo, attends to a little boy in a red winter hat.

Young women in bell-bottom jeans and winter coats mill around the stage. Some wear their hair in bandanas. Some sit casually on the edge of the stage smoking cigarettes. Others hold megaphones, occasionally speaking into them: "Men! Go home and look after your children so your wives can come to the piazza!" Some hold placards with slogans: *"Non più per l'amore, ma per i soldi"* – "No longer for love, but for money!" and, more simply, *"Soldi alle Donne"* – "Money to the women." Tables are set up with pamphlets and books for sale.

On the stage, Mariarosa Dalla Costa approaches the microphone.

Her dark curls are cropped short and she is wearing jeans and a dark brown peacoat. Her jaw is set, her tone steady, as she announces the launch of a new campaign, Salario al Lavoro Domestico – "Wages for housework." "The demand for wages for housework is the demand for power, for it unites millions of women," she says. Wages for housework gets to the true source of women's powerlessness: their lack of money. This, she insists to the crowd, is the most revolutionary of all demands – the true working-class struggle.[1]

It was International Women's Day, but in organizing the rally, Lotta Femminista drew on the symbolism of the workers' movement instead. The location was intentional, for it was in Piazza Ferretto where the Italian Communist Party (PCI) had held its annual May Day demonstrations, where men marched, handing out flowers to the women. Piazza Ferretto had also staged the various strikes and protests of Potere Operaio militants at Porto Marghera. "We remember well the processions of workers leaving Porto Marghera, crossing the Mestre bridge and arriving here in this very plaza," Dalla Costa reminded the crowd. "But let us be clear: no strike has ever been a general strike! When half the population of workers are in the home, in the kitchen, while others are out on strike, it is not a general strike. We've never seen a general strike. Today in this piazza we start our moment of mobilization for wages for housework, for *our* work schedules, for *our* holidays, for *our* strikes, for *our* money. Only then can we speak for the first time of a general strike of the [working] class."

Following Dalla Costa's speech, women from various newly formed Salario al Lavoro Domestico (SLD) committees in Padua, Venice, Milan, and Trieste came to the stage to speak. One of the speakers was Leopoldina Fortunati. She was dressed up for the occasion, her hair curled, wearing a large fur coat. She spoke slowly and steadily, at times closing her eyes and pausing for dramatic effect. Years later, she described the tension and power of that moment. "A man, maybe a trade unionist, tried to interrupt me," she recalled. "I raised my voice and didn't allow him to interrupt. A great silence filled the crowded square." She explained to me that part of the struggle that was being played out on that day in the public square was over communication: who had the right to speak, and on what terms. Men accustomed to controlling the terms of the debate were now being told it was their turn to listen. Fortunati ended her speech by leading the crowd in a chant: *"Stato, padroni / Fatevi i conti! / Perchè le donne / vogliono i soldi!"* ("Government, bosses / Time to pay up! / Because women / Want money!")

Then Laura Morato, another Padua SLD member, came to the stage with her guitar, cheeks rosy with the cold and hair held back in a bandana, and she and several comrades led the singing of a song: "Government, bosses, / Time to pay up! / Because women / want money! For years, for centuries, / we have worked, / for years, for centuries, / you have exploited us . . ." Some members of the audience may have recognized her words as a reworked Potere Operaio chant that went like this: "State, bosses, / Take care. / The party of insurrection / is being born. / Workers' power and revolution! / Red flags and communism / are on the way!"[2] This was not a women's day that would hold women up on a pedestal, or offer them flowers. With the Mestre demonstration, the Wages for Housework Committee called to assembly all women of the world, united in their shared exploitation as unpaid workers.

The Wages for Housework campaign marked a new focus for the women of Lotta Femminista. Their earlier demands had been more elaborate: a twenty-hour workweek, communal nurseries and elder care facilities, neighborhood canteens, a blurring of the boundaries between biological parents and community caregivers, and, underpinning all of these demands, free abortion and contraceptives. For several years, Lotta Femminista tried to make common cause with working-class women, housewives, and prostitutes on these issues. But neighborhood women, when asked what they wanted, were often more practical. They wanted more teachers, free daycare, public parks, affordable housing. A Lotta Femminista group in Venice wrote to their Padua comrades to express their frustration: "We are no longer willing to tire ourselves out continuing from Venice to Mestre to participate in meetings in which every woman of the neighborhood poses her problems and asks us for directions on how to move forward, to participate in the drawing-up of pamphlets which then only we mimeograph and distribute."[3] The work of fighting for better social services, neighborhood by neighborhood, engaging local government, building coalitions, was uninspiring. More importantly, it was reformist. Better social services could make women's lives easier, but it would not challenge the fundamental problem: capitalism ran on the unpaid carework of women, rendering women powerless and dependent.

For some, wages for housework was a frustratingly vague, unrealistic proposition. Alisa Del Re was on the faculty at the University of Padua and was a committed, outspoken Marxist feminist. Like Mariarosa Dalla Costa and Leopoldina Fortunati, she had been a member of Potere Operaio in Padua in the early 1970s. But the demand for wages for housework was where she parted ways with her former comrades. "It was difficult to understand who was demanding these wages," she recalled. "It was nonsense." Instead, she devoted her political energies to campaigning for social services, such as free nurseries and better schools. "The issue of wages was perhaps more 'revolutionary,'" she admitted, but "I needed these things because I started having babies and felt very justified in demanding things that I immediately needed. Maybe it was not revolutionary, but I had to put the babies somewhere!"[4]

Wages for Housework was not a program of social reform. It was, in Dalla Costa's words, a "lever of power."[5] "If I have 120,000 [lire] for the work I do at home," she told the crowd gathered at Mestre, "I will never again sell myself for 60,000 in a textile factory, or as someone's secretary, or as a cashier."[6] Wages for housework was bargaining power for the working class. It was the unshackling of female sexuality – for, despite all of the consciousness-raising groups and their discussions about sexual liberation, how could women truly explore their desires when they were economically dependent on the men they were sleeping with? Wages for housework was the ability to create kin based on love and connection, rather than on material desperation. Across Italy at the time, feminists were fighting for the right to divorce – but what good was the legal right to divorce if women did not have the economic power to live independently of marriage? With money in her hands, a woman could choose, refuse, or leave a marriage not just in theory but in reality.

The Wages for Housework campaign put the fight for abortion rights into a new light: if the home was a workplace, unwanted pregnancy was a work-related injury. Pregnancy was yet another kind of unpaid labor, and the work of gestation and childbirth was followed by decades of unpaid work caring for children. In this respect, the fight for access to abortion was essential to Wages for Housework: to criminalize abortion was to force women into a lifetime of unpaid servitude. In Italy, the struggle for abortion rights brought thousands of women out into the streets and public squares. They held mass "auto-denunciations," in which women publicly recounted their own experiences, to make abortion visible and to express solidarity with women who were prosecuted for it. Wages for Housework embraced the fight for abortion, demanding "Abortion, free and free of charge!" as part of the larger struggle to reclaim bodily autonomy and to refuse unpaid work.

Juxtaposing "wage" with "housework" provoked questions. It sounded, at first, almost like a joke, or a bit of political theater. The home is the opposite of the workplace, and housework, by definition, is not waged. But the campaign countered with a question: Why not? Why is a loaf of bread baked for people outside the home a commodity that can be sold, while a loaf of bread baked for the family must be done for free, out of "love?" Why was it scandalous to demand pay for looking after your own children, when women routinely were paid to look after other people's kids? How are we, as women, persuaded to do such work without pay? What would happen if women refused to do it anymore? What would happen if women were paid for housework? What kind of society would that be? This provoked people to look at their lives with fresh eyes and ask: What kind of society do we live in NOW?

*

The Padua Wages for Housework Committee rented a small storefront in a one-story brick building on Piazza Eremitani. In their headquarters, they read and answered correspondence, organized leafleting campaigns, published newsletters, and made posters. They held open office hours two afternoons a week – Wednesdays and Fridays – and invited women from the community to come in and discuss how Wages for Housework related to their own lives.

Padua's committee grew and shrank over the years, as people joined the movement and then drifted away. Leopoldina Fortunati – Polda, as she is called by friends – was, like Dalla Costa, a former member of Potere Operaio. The child of an affluent Veneto family, when she arrived in Padua as a student she was determined to give up the privileges of her upbringing, rejecting her parents' money and working part-time jobs to get by.[7] Over lunch in 2019, she told me how she had loved her time as a militant, letting the urgency of her political convictions, rather than domestic duties, dictate the rhythms of her life. Sometimes, she recalled, her mother would come into town to visit, bringing plates of delicious home-cooked food to feed her daughter and her feminist comrades.[8] Another core member of the Padua group was Maria Pia Turri. Turri was a schoolteacher and one of her main interests in the campaign was the education system and the ways it conditioned children into gendered roles as workers. She was also a musician, and she wrote and performed protest songs for the movement along with another member, Laura Morato. Giovanna Franca Dalla Costa was Mariarosa's younger sister and Fortunati's roommate, and she, like her older sibling, was embarking on a career as an academic.

Mariarosa Dalla Costa was at the center of the Padua committee. Her meticulously detailed and organized archives, a true labor of love, convey her devotion to the cause. Dalla Costa worked at such a pace, and with such single-pointed focus, that letters from her friends often implored her to slow down, take care of herself, take a rest, delegate tasks to other comrades, remember to eat, look after her health. Sometimes, in her intensity, Dalla Costa came across as blunt, forgoing social niceties to give directives or criticisms. In letters and reports, she painstakingly delineates correct from incorrect analyses of Wages for Housework.[9] Though some seemed to chafe at her exacting perfectionism, her closest comrades loved her for it. Once, after Dalla Costa apologized in a letter to Federici for having criticized her over a minor planning detail, Federici responded: "Don't worry about the tone you use when you write to me. I find it impossible to use 'half-terms' or to speak with finesse when I'm talking about politics."[10] Fortunati admired Dalla Costa's clarity of vision. "She had a specific and rare political capacity," she told me: in every situation, she seemed to intuitively know what to do. Other comrades – and Fortunati included herself in this category – may have had the conviction and passion, but it was Dalla Costa who had the political instincts, and could translate their ideas into action.[11]

The Padua committee, with Dalla Costa at the helm, published a magazine called *Le operaie della casa* – "The Workers of the House." A review of various feminist issues, presented through the lens of housework and money, *Le operaie della casa* featured personal essays, editorials, political cartoons, short stories, poems, photographs, song lyrics, and news about struggles from other groups around the world, from Germany to Iceland to Canada. Some features were silly and irreverent, like the short story written from the perspective of an anthropomorphic IUD – a Queen, sending away all the sperm who tried to enter her kingdom. There were cartoon caricatures of bullying and idiot men – leftist activists, priests, and doctors. They published testimonials from women about the brutality they endured from sexist doctors when undergoing a gynecological examination, and offered advice about how to resist – whether through going to appointments in groups for moral support, or seeking care at a *"contro-informazione* health center," run by women, where they could bypass the medical establishment and get health information and advice from fellow feminists. There were drawings and poems. Gleeful stories, told in narrative and in cartoons, of women refusing housework, smashing dishes, walking out of their homes.

Le operaie della casa published dispatches from Wages for Housework groups around the world – updates from the Italian groups in Milan, Rome, Ferrara, Modena, Bologna, Rome, Varese, Trieste, Naples, and Udine, as well as from various locations abroad: New York, Ireland, London, Germany, Switzerland. It was published by Marsilio and sold in bookshops and on newsstands and through informal feminist networks around Italy, each issue beginning with a print-run of around 8,000 copies.[12] The effect was to present Wages for Housework as a global movement, and a space for imagining what was possible.

There was also music in the campaign. Laura Morato, a member of the Padua branch, wrote songs for the movement and performed them with her folk music group Il Canzoniere Femminista. She drew on protest songs and traditional Italian lullabies for inspiration and refashioned them with feminist lyrics. Il Canzoniere Femminista would provide the soundtrack of the Italian Wages for Housework movement, and I often listened to their songs as I wrote this book. In 1975, they recorded their first album with Dischi dello Zodiaco (Zodiac

Musical performance at a Salario al Lavoro Domestico / Wages for Housework demonstration in Mestre in 1975.

Records), titled *Songs of Women in Struggle*. The cover shows women marching with a Salario al Lavoro Domestico banner, and the liner notes read: "Women the world over are presently struggling for the right to have their own money and their own time, for the possibility of living a different life, a life in which they can, for instance, also make music. These songs are born of that struggle and for that struggle."[13]

The album opens with satire. We hear a church organ, as though in a Catholic Mass, and a woman's voice is heard reciting a biblical text: the letter from Paul to the Ephesians: "Man should not live alone; I will make him a suitable helper . . . "and so God creates Eve out of Adam's rib. The songs consist of four women's voices in harmony, accompanied by an acoustic guitar and an occasional snap of the tambourine. "We are tired of making babies, washing dishes, changing the diapers, having a man who acts like he's the boss, and stops us from using contraceptives . . ." So begins the song "Siamo Stufe" – "We Are Fed Up." The tracks on the album ranged in subject matter from housework, to abortion, to domestic violence, to divorce, to the annoyance of being expected to smile for random strangers, ending with the rousing "Stato, Padroni," which they often chanted at protests. The Canzoniere Femminista performed at protests and concerts, including a tour of France to promote their album.

Meanwhile, every day, Dalla Costa received letters at her home address from across Italy and the wider world. Socialist and feminist publishers in other countries asked about translations of her work. Feminists in far-flung locations wrote to her requesting more information about Wages for Housework and sending her updates about their own experiments with the idea. A young woman in Naples who started an SLD committee after reading Dalla Costa's work explained that she felt the poverty and underdevelopment of southern Italy made Wages for Housework even more relevant there than in the north. A young woman from the Milan SLD committee wrote to her to coordinate a protest, but emphasized that, when Mariarosa replied, none of the letters should have the phrase "Wages for Housework" or "Lotta Femminista" on the envelope, as the landlord was hostile to feminism and would harass his tenants if he suspected anything. Her correspondents included feminist groups in the United States, such as the Furies, Radical Feminists and NOW (National Organization for Women). Valerie Solanas, author of the SCUM (Society for Cutting Up Men) Manifesto who famously shot Andy Warhol, wrote to Dalla Costa from jail. Dalla Costa received letters and invitations from a feminist commune in Denmark. She corresponded with a group called Stewardesses for Human Rights. She responded to letters from women in Sweden, Germany, France, Switzerland, Jamaica, Mexico, the US and Canada, and Japan. Her apartment became a pilgrimage site for feminists from all over the world. Miriam Abrams, from a Wages for Housework group in Oberlin, Ohio, joked on a postcard: "You know, Dalla Costa's house is due to be put in with the Piazza San Marco on the American Express tour of Italy of things to see."[14]

Inspired by the creative militants in Padua, women across Italy began forming Wages for Housework committees of their own. They gathered in Milan, Naples, Sicily, Trieste, Venice, Florence, Ferrara, Modena, and Udine. They staged protests and street theater. They published their own zines, and interviewed their mothers. They wrote thousands of letters to each other and signed them "*Potere, Baci e Soldi*" – "Power, Kisses and Money."

In Udine, a small northeastern city close to the Italian borders with Austria and Slovenia, around 800 workers punched in each day at the Solari factory. About half of them were women. The Solari family had been making clocks since the eighteenth century. In the 1960s and 1970s, they became the world's premier manufacturer of industrial timetables for railroad and airport terminals. Solari is famous for a design innovation called the split-panel display. Whereas a traditional mechanical clock shows the time by turning a second-hand around a circular clock face, in a Solari split-panel clock, the mechanical gears instead turn a roller with a row of flaps that display the time with a sequence of numbers, letters, dashes, and dots. When a train or flight leaves the station or terminal, a great flurry can be heard as the panels flip through to the correct positions, the next scheduled departure appears in the top row and a new one appears at the bottom. Solari "Arrivals" and "Departures" displays could be found in all the major transportation hubs of the world, from New York's Grand Central Station to London's Heathrow Airport, Singapore's Changi Airport, and everywhere in between. A paragon of modern Italian design, Solari of Udine called themselves "The time factory."[15]

In 1974, as Solari displays synchronized the movement of bodies through transport hubs across the globe, a group of women who worked soldering, wiring, and assembling the displays in the Udine factory were having their own revelation about the nature of time in a modern capitalist society: namely, that women didn't seem to have any. Working eight-hour shifts at the factory had not made them the equals of men, for it did not replace or lessen the work they were expected to do in their homes. When their male co-workers clocked off the job, they could expect to go home and be cared for, fed, and rejuvenated, but when women workers got home, they resumed the job they did for free.[16]

The injustice of this arrangement became especially clear when it came to the matter of their health. Even though a health center was located about 100 meters from the factory, attending even routine medical appointments required the women to take several days off work, without pay. First, they had to go to a government health center and book an appointment with a general practitioner, waiting hours in a queue before being interviewed by an intake nurse who collected their health data. Then, they came back for the actual appointment, which, due to long waiting lists, was often months later. If anything unusual was found at the Pap smear or breast examination, they would have to return and book a follow-up appointment with a gynecology or oncology specialist. Then they lost another half-day to that appointment. Finally, if the doctor pre-scribed anything, they would have to attend a separate appointment to have their prescription filled. All of this was only possible during work hours, as those were the only hours the clinics were open. In total, the routine attending to women's health could result in losing pay for four days of work.

Anna Gottardo, a social worker, had been hired by the Solari company to work in the factory addressing the complaints of workers. She chafed at the implicit paternalism of her role, which she saw as placating workers rather than helping to mobilize them against their bosses; nevertheless, she was determined to use her position to advocate for working-class women. In her conversations with the women, she found that the matter of healthcare came up over and over again.

Gottardo had read and taken to heart Mariarosa Dalla Costa's analysis of women in capitalism. Through reading *Le operaie della casa*, she learned about counter-information health sessions and discussions held at Lotta Femminista headquarters in Padua, and began coming on the weekends to meet with Dalla Costa, Fortunati, and other activists to discuss the plight of the Solari women. Their strategies included women accompanying each other to appointments, rather than confronting the system alone, and making space for discussions and information-sharing among women, rather than relying on doctors, reframing the care of their bodies as a powerful political act, rather than as a passive experience of humiliation and powerlessness. Anna went back to Udine and led the women of Solari in forming their own independent Women's Factory Council.

The women of Solari began to meet regularly. They sent testimonies to be published in *Le operaie della casa*, and composed a manifesto breaking down their situation and setting forth some demands. In the process, they started to see their seemingly mundane logistical conundrum – how to find the time to get to their gynecology appointments without losing pay – as the symptom of a larger structural problem.

It came down to this: everyone seemed to have a claim on a woman's time. Families required women to care for bodies, feeding, clothing and sheltering them, healing them when they were ill, preparing them for work. But society set aside no time or resources devoted to caring for women. When a doctor or nurse spent time caring for bodies and ensuring they could function, nobody questioned that this was valuable, necessary work and that they should

81

be paid for it, but women were expected to do it for free. The factory paid women a wage in exchange for their work, but that was where the obligation ended. When a piece of factory machinery breaks down, the Solari women observed, the company must repair it and keep it in good condition, yet if women became ill or needed routine maintenance, it had to be at their own expense and on their own time. Meanwhile, the unions, whose job it was to advocate for workers, saw women's unpaid work and women's health as a "women's problem" and not a labor problem, and refused to address it. "One was resigned to not finding time even to cure herself," wrote the Solari women in a statement about their struggle. "What does it mean for a woman to fall ill? When can we permit ourselves to be ill? NEVER."[17]

This systemic denigration of women's work and time informed the very experience of a medical visit, where they were often treated with cruelty and condescension by male doctors, who were physically rough with them during examinations. Doctors and nurses were often unwilling to take the time to explain any of the diagnoses they gave, leaving women confused and alarmed – "How many women know what cervicitis is?" they asked in their manifesto.[18] Whatever diagnoses were given were often blamed on the women themselves, who were accused of being unhygienic or promiscuous.

This was more than a matter of the personalities of doctors. By presenting health and illness as a matter of women's individual pathology, doctors were hiding something more profound: the systematic exploitation of women's time and energy and bodily vitality by all sectors of society. This also hid the fact that healing the body *was* work. "To cure ourselves is not a pleasure," they wrote, "it is work. It is housework in so far as we have to spend those hours in order to try to put our body back into a fairly good condition that others abuse each day in the factory and at home." As they wrote in a dispatch to *Le operaie della casa*, "Confronting a struggle on health means confronting a struggle on the organization of labor, in the house and outside."[19]

In spring 1975, in a meeting convened with representatives from the Udine branch of the Italian National Health Institute, the Udine hospital, the union, and the Solari company, the women presented their demands. They requested that various medical procedures and examinations be combined in a single session. They also requested longer appointments so that medical personnel could answer women's questions, rather than leaving them with a diagnosis they could not understand. They demanded that all of this happen on company time. Most of their requests were denied. They were granted some concessions, though, including the right to make an appointment with a gynecologist without having to first make a separate appointment to request a referral. They were offered block appointments on company time, allowing them to go for their Pap smears and breast examinations together and skip the line, without losing a day's wages. They were granted an education session, also on company time, in which a medical professional would come to the factory to meet with them in a group and answer their questions.[20]

The victory was partial. In particular, the group appointments on company time raised concerns. On the one hand, these company-booked block appointments were efficient. The women of Solari noted cynically: when health visits are on women's time, nobody cares if hours and hours are wasted in the waiting room, but when it's on company time, a way was somehow found to be more efficient. This was a blatant lesson in whose time was considered valuable. Yet the Solari women noted the annoyance of the other women in the waiting room, and realized that their own block appointments were discriminatory toward housewives, for whom waiting times in the health center would be made even longer as a result. As Wages for Housework converts, they saw themselves in solidarity not just with factory workers, but with all workers – including those who worked in the home for no pay.

The following year, in 1976, they gained more concessions: paid leave for medical visits, the extension of group preventive medicine sessions on company time, and free contraception following a consultation with a gynecologist. Perhaps the most radical of their victories was the extension of these health benefits to the wives of male workers, in recognition that they too were part of what made the Solari "Time Factory" – and by extension, all the airports and train stations of the world – run on time.[21]

The novelist Maria Rosa Cutrufelli was born in 1946 in Sicily, where she spent much of her childhood. Her father was from a small town on the coast near Taormina, but, when she was young, her family moved north. Years later, she was radicalized by the student movement of the 1960s and participated in consciousness-raising sessions with her feminist sisters at each other's apartments.[22] She read Mariarosa Dalla Costa's *Power of Women and the Subversion of the Community* and became one of the founding members of the Bologna branch of Lotta Femminista.[23] Cutrufelli had long hoped to return to Sicily, to reconnect with her southern origins and think about how they fit into her changing sense of herself and the world. When in the early 1970s her husband, an engineer, was offered a job at a new oil refinery in Gela, a small city on Sicily's southern coast, she encouraged him to accept. They rented a small house by the sea. Cutrufelli found work as a teacher, and soon she assembled a Lotta Femminista group.[24] The context was different: in Bologna, Lotta Femminista members had taken turns hosting meetings in their apartments, but in Gela, where women lived with their parents and extended families until they married, this was not possible. Lotta Femminista Gelese met each week at Cutrufelli's home.

Sicily experienced Italy's postwar economic miracle differently from the industrial zones of the north. Instead of grappling with urban growth and an influx of migrant workers, Sicily sent its young men to emigrate for work, leaving behind towns populated by the elderly, the young, the infirm, and, at the center of it all, "white widows" – the workers' wives left behind to hold communities together, relying on remittances from the men to keep their households going. The work of these women was grueling. Despite the riches of the industrial cities where the men worked, back in Sicily, most of them lived in houses without piped water or sewers, leaving them to travel to the communal water tap to carry pails of water back to their home for bathing, dishwashing, clothes washing. Many did not have refrigerators or gas stoves. They made their own bread, sewed their children's clothing, pressed their own olive oil.[25]

With the oil refinery came the promise of industrialization in Gela. Hastily built houses were thrown up on a grid for the workers, while larger estates were built for the white-collar managers and engineers. The only women who entered the industrial zone were a handful who were employed to clean the offices. But the women of Gela were pulled into the orbit of the factory in more subtle ways. The wives, mothers, daughters, sisters of male workers now organized their days around the rhythms of factory life. The environment was changing too, alarmingly. They could smell the acrid fumes of the chemicals, and in the evenings they could see the night sky red from the flames of the refineries.[26]

By the early 1970s, most of the women of Gela were dependent on one of two arrangements: a man who emigrated and sent back remittances, or a man who worked at the industrial zone around the oil refinery. Very few women – less than 10 percent – worked for wages themselves. But the expansion of the Italian university system in the 1960s brought more girls into higher education and with that came different life possibilities. It was from the ranks of these aspiring young women that Lotta Femminista Gelese was formed.

The group was mostly made up of young teachers and high-school students. They included Ninfa Schlegel, who was half Swiss and half Sicilian, and Cettina Brigadeci, who would later become a scholar of feminism and professor of history at the University of Catania. They invited girls like "Una," a student who had a reputation at school for being "grumpy" and resented having to go to school dances, waiting passively for someone to ask her to dance. Why, she wondered, did these occasions that were supposed to be "fun" produce such misery in her? To be able to talk freely about ideas in a group of women was an epiphany for her – a glimpse of freedom.

The group also included Angela, who chafed at her mother's well-meaning – even loving – attempts to prepare her daughter for a future as a wife and mother. Angela herself desired no such thing, and, in the group, she found the space to imagine a different kind of future. Nunzia, another member, was a serious student who wanted desperately to succeed at school and become self-sufficient, but struggled to balance study with endless housework. These obligations grew overwhelming when her mother became ill and was hospitalized, leaving her to run the household. Nunzia would wake up before dawn to prepare the house and the clothes and the food before going to school, and, upon returning home, would run all the errands and clean the dishes before finishing her schoolwork at night. Meanwhile her brothers' lives remained virtually unchanged by her mother's absence, and they even continued driving the family car while Nunzia schlepped between school and home and hospital on foot. When she informed her brothers she was going to attend a meeting at Cutrufelli's house one evening, they responded in outrage – *"What, with Mama ill in the hospital, all you can think of is yourself?"*[27] "In reality," she wrote, "I am a housewife first, then a student."

Lotta Femminista Gelese meetings followed the feminist practice of *partire da sè* – starting from one's own experience. The women talked about housework. They wrote down the lyrics to misogynistic traditional Sicilian folk songs and poems. "Boys go to school, women darn the socks." They recorded jokes, like the one about how the death of a wife is preferable to the death of a donkey because you have to pay for the donkey, whereas a wife is free labor. Drawing on Dalla Costa's analysis, they placed their everyday experiences as women in the wider context of Sicily's role as an impoverished labor reserve. What Sicily creates for capitalism, they understood, is the ultimate raw material: labor power – and it was women who made that labor power. Their mothers, grandmothers, sisters, aunts were not backward people left out of capitalism but in fact *central* to it. They looked in horror (and with youthful eyes) at what they perceived as the misshapen, overweight, prematurely aged bodies of the women in their neighborhood who, as they saw it, were confined to the house all day and were so overworked that they could not even participate in the evening *passeggiata*. They wrote their experiences in their newsletter, which they called *Adesso Basta!*, and sent accounts from Gela to be published in feminist journals like *Sottosopra* and *Noi Donne*, and the literary journal *Rendiconti*.[28]

They alternated their group meetings with "neighborhood assemblies," in which they trekked through the working-class neighborhoods and interviewed women about their lives. This raised the hackles of members of the local PCI. What were the young women up to in these working-class neighborhoods – the PCI's electoral stronghold? Often, members of the local branch would tail the women as they weaved their way through town, knocking on doors. For their part, the neighborhood women were skeptical of them, but no one slammed the door in their faces.

In their discussions with neighborhood women, they found that abortion was surprisingly easy to talk about. For many women in Sicily, this was simply a fact of life – a sin, perhaps, but a necessary sin that you could confess at church and be forgiven for. The right to divorce, on the other hand – a core demand of the Italian feminist movement – was far more controversial. While, for middle-class women on the "continent," the right to divorce was associated with freedom and self-determination, in Sicily the issue had a different resonance. In a place where less than 10 percent of women were in the waged workforce and most either lived off the remittances of men who had emigrated or the earnings of men in the petrochemical plants, what could women actually *do* with the legal right to divorce? The more terrifying prospect was of men divorcing them, leaving them destitute.

On the question of wages for housework, the women of Gela didn't need convincing. They knew that their work was both arduous and necessary, and believed that they should be paid for it. But by whom? Whose door should they be banging on, demanding their back pay? The local mayor's? That of the CEOs of the wealthy companies who employed their husbands in the north? The Prime Minister? The young feminists didn't have an answer for them.

In 1974, Cutrufelli moved on from Gela. She went on to become an acclaimed writer of novels and memoirs, many of them drawing on her experiences in Gela. With her departure, Lotta Femminista Gelese dissolved. Other members of Lotta Femminista Gelese eventually left town to study and work in bigger cities, such as Catania and Palermo.

The young women of Lotta Femminista Gelese knew, perhaps more intimately than their sisters "on the continent," that housework was inescapable. It was not a cultural preference or a lifestyle choice but an economic reality, structured into the very survival of a community.

In 1974, in the town of Varese, a small city about an hour northwest of Milan, a teenage girl named Manuela noticed that her mother was acting strangely. She had stopped doing housework. When Manuela and her brother Michelangelo were hungry, their mother sent them to the deli across the road to buy sandwiches. She allowed dust to accumulate on all the surfaces of the house, and demanded that nobody disturb it. Then, she used her finger to draw feminist symbols in the dust and photographed the images. She took the cooking pots that she had previously used for making rich pasta sauces and soups and painted them in bright colors, drilled holes in the lids and sides and threaded barbed wire through to bind them shut. She fashioned a colander that was useless, due to its having fake holes. She invited her friends Mirella and Mariuccia to come over to the house and use lipstick to scrawl on plates and serving trays while she stood aside and took photographs. Like a trickster, she prowled her house undermining all forms of housework, systematically rendering the tools of domesticity useless baubles, objects of play rather than work.

The artist Milli Gandini lived with her husband Tino and two children, Manuela and Miche. The couple had forged careers as artists during Milan's swinging 1960s. Manuela remembers growing up among her parents' artist friends who drank whiskey and smoked unfiltered Gauloises cigarettes, and listening to jazz records late into the evening. Milli styled her hair in a cloud of curls around her head, wore colorful patterned skirts that brushed the ground, and smelled of patchouli. Tino and Milli ran a design studio together, where they made lamps, jewelry, books, and other beautiful objects. But for all their free-spirited bohemian ideals, Tino's artistic identity came first. *"I'm the artist!"* his daughter recalls him screaming at his family, sometimes drunk, smashing dishes. Milli, like so many women artists before her, was trapped by her desire to make art and her obligations as a mother and wife. So wrote Manuela Gandini, nearly fifty years later, in the introduction to her mother's posthumous book.[29]

Gandini's life changed in 1968, when she met Mariuccia Secol. In her late thirties, Secol was raising her four teenaged children with her husband Angelino – a former partisan in the Italian Resistance and an active member of the Varese PCI. Secol worked as an art teacher in a local psychiatric hospital, where she taught the patients to paint and write poetry. Their home was a warm and boisterous place, filled with friends and family. She was a generous hostess to their various artist and writer friends, as well as to the friends of her children, many of whom, by the late 1960s, were activists in the student movement. Secol was particularly known for cooking sumptuous risottos for her guests. It was through her children and their activist friends that she encountered the radical politics of 1968.

Gandini and Secol became close friends. Gandini encouraged Secol to start painting again, and she turned the attic of their family house into a studio – freezing cold in the winter and suffocatingly hot in the summer but *hers*. The two friends shared a sense of frustrated creativity – trying to live lives that had room for art and motherhood. In the early 1970s, Gandini and Secol began attending consciousness-raising sessions. It was eye-opening, but it did not relieve them of the burden of housework. Gandini's daughter Manuela recalls that the mothers supported each other by more or less merging the two families to form one large family, lessening the burdens of domestic obligations by sharing them among two families and taking pleasure in each other's company. Seeing the two women begin to liberate themselves changed the entire family dynamic, she recalls, including among their fathers and brothers.

Introduced by a family friend – a former Potop member based in Padua – Gandini met with Dalla Costa, Fortunati, and the other

Padua Lotta Femminista women and proposed starting a Wages for Housework chapter in Varese. But theirs would be distinct. They would merge art with activism, using the visual image as their medium. They called themselves Gruppo Immagine di Varese.[30] And so, in 1974, Gandini and Secol staged their first exhibition, based on the photographs of dust drawings and rejiggered housework objects that had intrigued and disturbed Gandini's daughter. Recalling Mariarosa Dalla Costa's phrase, "to leave the home is already a form of struggle," Gandini called the exhibition *La mamma è uscita* – Mama has gone out. She recalled the thrill of the phrase: "Always a housewife, I decided to leave the role and repeat happily like a song, softly like a lullaby, solemnly like a hallelujah, terroristically like a scream: *la mamma è uscita.*"[31]

Gandini and Secol gathered together other artists, including sculptor Silvia Cibaldi and architect Mariagrazia Sironi. They began to send playful dispatches to their Padua comrades for publication in *Le operaie della casa*. Secol wrote a story called "Maria" about a woman who is raised to become an expert in only one thing: risotto. Day in and day out, she hovers over the stove slowly making the most exquisite risottos, first for her parents and brothers, and then for her husband and children. Her children, seeking to liberate their mother, thrust her out onto the streets, but all she knows how to do is make risotto. She is baffled by the bustle of public life, as vendors try to sell her everything from happiness to beauty to . . . risotto. Men offer her flowers. Defenseless and confused, she screams for help! Suddenly, all the women from all over town rush out into the piazza, overturning the stalls and coming together to free themselves.[32]

Another story tells of "Isabella," who spends her every day, from dawn until dusk, caring lovingly for her twelve brothers, and then, eventually, her husband. The men in her life adore her and call her Fata – "fairy" – for her seemingly magical qualities. One day, she decides to stay in bed and do no work. Next, she begins throwing plates, dishes, glasses from the window, watching with pleasure as they smash on the pavement. Finally, she sets the house on fire. "She danced around the magnificent fire, and sang, and then, she disappeared and nothing more was heard from her." Isabella, formerly called "Fairy", was now rumored to have become a witch. Her brothers searched the world for her, but could never find her among the millions of other Isabellas out there.[33]

Meanwhile, Sironi, an architect, started a project in her studio on the theme of women and household architecture. Even in the most well-to-do families, she observed, women rarely had a household space of their own. There were rooms dedicated to men and their work, rooms dedicated to children and their play, rooms dedicated to all sorts of activities and pursuits. As housewives, women were an invisible presence in every room in the house, yet had none to call their own. Sironi began looking into the history of urban plans in the ancient world, in matriarchal societies. As a thought experiment, she designed a conceptual model village, consisting of a group of small individual circles each representing household members and activities set around a large circle, representing the space where all services and carework were performed. In the model, women's work, rather than happening invisibly throughout every room of the house, would be made visible – the central activity of the household, impossible to ignore. Like the provocation of wages for housework, this effort to render women's unpaid work visible was meant to provoke and foreshadow new ways of living together.[34]

After several years of creative play on the theme of art and housework, in 1978 Gruppo Immagine wrote an artist's manifesto.[35] Was art work, they asked, given that it wasn't useful and no one needed it? Could art ever serve the purpose of women's liberation, or was it a mere safety valve, substituting for power they would never actually have as women? Women were inherently creative, they proclaimed, but were forced to waste their creativity on menial housework. *Fare della calzetta* – darning socks – became a phrase that captured their predicament, having to spend one's time and energy on details that men were freed from thinking about. The manifesto drew on Secol's observations from teaching art in a psychiatric hospital:

male patients felt free to paint, but women were inhibited, instead only expressing themselves in "useful" tasks like embroidery and knitting. Together, the Gruppo Immagine collective asserted and demanded their right to be artists – not to fit that role into whatever time was left after housework, using whatever resources were left over from the men's art world, but to be treated seriously, to have access to good art supplies and to galleries.

Clemen Parrocchetti attended the 1978 Donne Arte Società conference in Milan where Gruppo Immagine di Varese presented their manifesto, and she soon became the fifth member of the collective. Born into a noble family in Milan in 1923, she had been making art, mostly paintings, since the 1950s. She had raised five children and was in her fifties by the time she was swept up into the feminist movement. She announced her entrance into the world of feminist art with a short manifesto in 1973, sewn with red thread into a sheet of aluminum, entitled "Memoriam for an object of female culture," playing with the links between women and the domestic objects that absorbed their creative energies: *Sew and be quiet woman pin cushion woman punching ball woman ultimately object woman.*" Like Gandini, Parrocchetti manipulated the tools of housework, creating what critic Caterina Iaquinta calls "anti-trophies of domesticity."[36] She made sculptures and large tapestries, deploying the techniques of sewing and knitting, and using kitchen utensils, reels, spools, shuttles, and pin cushions, all assembled together into soft configurations of fleshy mouths, thick, curvy vulvas, eyes, sometimes in disturbing configurations, or pierced by pins and needles.

Her tapestries became a core element of the exhibition that Gruppo Immagine di Varese staged for the 1978 Venice Biennale, the theme of which was "from art to nature, from nature to art." The title of their exhibit was "From feminine creativity as maternity-nature to the control (counter-role) of nature." At the heart of the exhibit was a subversion of the idea of natural womanhood. Upon entering the exhibition space, the observer encountered a pool of water – suggested, by critics, to be reminiscent of amniotic fluid – and hanging from the ceiling, reflected in it, were five large tapestries created by the members of the group. One tapestry depicted the crudely rendered outline of a woman, made in stitches so big as to be completely useless for the purposes of domestic embroidery and sewing; another featured the embroidered silhouettes of pregnant women; another the distorted and bloated shape of lips. Sironi's tapestry recalled the origins of the modern city with a representation of the urban plan of the Ancient Greek city of Miletus rendered in embroidered lace – a symbol of housework. The intended effect on the viewer was to reverse the idea that women were controlled by "their nature" and their reproductive function, and show that women are naturally, inherently creative – that reproduction could be the jumping-off point for a creativity that was liberated from domestic work, usefulness, housework, and could instead become the life force of art.[37]

What is housework, really? For the factory women of Solari, housework is the care, healing, and maintenance of bodies. In Gela, young students saw that housework is the physically exhausting work of gestating and nurturing workers who were then offered up to an extractive global migrant labor economy. A group of middle-class mother-artists in Varese saw housework as the mind-numbing repetitive work of darning socks: the antithesis of creative pursuits such as painting on a canvas or writing a novel. Housework is what women give to their families in exchange for the bare right to exist, occupy space, survive. Housework is compulsory heterosexuality. Housework is the isolation of women from public life. It is the mass theft of women's time and wealth. By demanding wages for housework on that cold gray day in the piazza in Mestre, Mariarosa Dalla Costa shared with the crowd her vision of a feminism that could unite all women against what oppressed them. At least that was the intention.

But while housework is something we all share, it also is a telling measure of what makes women different from each other. This is clear, even in the differences between affluent artists in Milan and "white widows" in Sicily. That day in Mestre, one of the placards carried across the square proclaimed "To work for a wage is hard, to work for no wage is slavery." The women of Salario al Lavoro Domestico invoked slavery frequently in their attempt to politicize housework, in writings and posters and even in their songs. They adorned the tables where they sold their pamphlets with pictures of nameless Black and Brown women toiling in poverty in various regions of the world, with no explanation of who the women were, and exactly HOW they were connected to the women in Italy who were marching in the streets. Their use of the images suggested an equivalence between all women and the oppression they face – to show just how bad things were – but without any reckoning with the ways that the European women, while facing oppression, also experienced privileges that were connected to the oppression of others. In their zeal to forge a struggle that was universal, they focused on the forms of oppression that connected women while glossing over the global realities of racism, imperialism, and inequality.

It is difficult convincing people to challenge something assumed to be natural – in this case, that women perform housework and care for children out of love, and that they should do so for free. In making this case, Salario al Lavoro Domestico were up against the entire grain of their culture – the Church, their families, all the cultural canons, and the political parties – even the "leftist" ones. Emphasizing their victimhood, one former SLD activist told me, was the most effective way to get their point across. It is easy for later generations of middle-class feminists like me to object to a lack of nuance: we no longer have to convince the majority of people of our right to become something other than housewives.

But it matters that housework is not the same thing as slavery. The inability to understand that was where the unifying potential of the Italian Wages for Housework movement found its limit.

5

Silvia Federici

Silvia Federici at a Wages for Housework meeting in Brooklyn, circa 1976.

"They say it is love. We say it is unwaged work."[1] So begins Silvia Federici's 1975 manifesto "Wages Against Housework" – with love. What makes housework so exploitative is that women are supposed to "love" it. As women, capitalism doesn't just demand our free labor, but it also demands our love. Waged workers, Federici wrote, even in the most degrading of jobs, can separate themselves from their work. It is socially acceptable, even heroic, for workers to name their oppression and down their tools in protest, and to separate from their job when they clock off at the end of a shift. "To have a wage," Federici wrote, "means to be part of a social contract . . . exploited as you might be, *you are not that work.*'[2] By contrast, since housework is a labor of "love," a woman refusing her role is not seen as a worker sticking up for herself but is considered a bad mother, or a failed woman. What is more unsettling than a woman who withholds her love?

In November 2019, as I sat with Federici onstage at a public event at Brown University's Pembroke Library inaugurating the opening of her archives, the conversation turned to "Wages Against Housework" and particularly that phrase: *They say it is love. We say it is unwaged work.* She laughed, reflecting on how this sentence has unexpectedly become the most frequently quoted phrase she has ever written. She told us how, on a recent trip to Buenos Aires, she had been sitting in traffic when she looked out the window and saw those words spray-painted on a wall in Spanish: *Eso que llaman amor es trabajo no pago.* She later learned that the phrase had been part of a confrontation with police: feminist graffiti artists were spray-painting the words on walls, police would whitewash over them, and the artists then would respond by painting them again in even more places around the city.[3] In 2019, as now, and as in the 1970s, the words resonate, inspiring acts of protest, new political thinking, and works of art.

At first, it sounds like a complaint, but the underlying mood is hopeful, even joyful. With it, Federici conjures not just a world where the economy is different, but one where we have the capacity to *feel* different. "We want to call work what is work," she wrote, "so that eventually we might rediscover what is love."[4]

I first visited Silvia Federici at her Brooklyn apartment in 2021. She greeted me at the door, all energy and warmth, and ushered me into a space filled with books, artwork, political posters, and photographs of family. We sat down to talk and on the table between us she placed a small bowl of plums from the Prospect Park farmers' market, still wet with dew. She sent me into the kitchen for espresso cups, and I opened several cabinets stuffed with books before locating them.

Among the works of art on the walls are several of her own

paintings. I noticed one in particular and asked her about it. It pictures a woman lying on her side, face turned away from the viewer, the contours of her flesh rendered in rich earthy browns and mossy greens, the outline of her body illuminated in yellow, as though she were engulfed in flames. It is a woman retreating away from the viewer, turning inward into herself, searching for something. She is undergoing a transformation. It is a self-portrait, Federici told me, which she painted in 1971.

At the time, Federici was a PhD philosophy student, living in Brooklyn with her then-husband and working on a dissertation about the Hungarian Marxist literary theorist György Lukács. She had come to the United States a few years earlier, joining a cohort of philosophy scholars in the late 1960s who were devoted to bringing together Marxism with phenomenology and the study of human consciousness. For this community of scholar-activists, philosophy was much more than an intellectual pursuit: it was part of a struggle for social justice; a vehicle for imagining and bringing about a different world. Federici, a lifelong lover of art and literature, was studying Marxism and aesthetics. Threaded through her studies was an underlying question: could art lead to social change? As a student, she wrote rigorous, densely theoretical essays about the works of thinkers ranging from Louis Althusser to Antonio Gramsci to Lukács to Enzo Paci.

Meanwhile, the feminist movement was exploding across New York City in bookstores and apartments and squats. Federici was skeptical at first. "I would go to some meetings but with reservations, since to the politico I was it seemed difficult to reconcile feminism with a class perspective," she wrote. "Or this at least was the rationale. More likely I was unwilling to accept my identity as a woman after having for years pinned all my hopes on my ability to pass for a man."[5]

It was around that time that a friend, a fellow Italian expat, gave her a copy of Mariarosa Dalla Costa's "Women and the Subversion of the Community." She read it on a train from Boston to New York. She often describes that journey, reading Mariarosa Dalla Costa's words, as an epiphany: the moment when her political convictions connected with her own life. "It spoke to my personal experience," Federici recalled, "my refusal of housework; my contradictory relationship to my mother."

Federici grew up in a place that was saturated with political struggle. "My town – Parma – was the town of barricades," she said, referring to events that shaped the collective memory of her community. When fascist paramilitary groups led by Italo Balbo began attacking trade unions and workers' organizations throughout the region of Emilia-Romagna in the early 1920s, the militant working-class people of Parma – the *Arditi del Popolo* ("the people's shock troops") – successfully fought them off, digging trenches in the streets and erecting massive barricades using the very materials of their town – bed frames and vegetable carts and furniture, timber, iron girders, benches – anything they could find. Balbo's militia was forced to retreat, leaving Parma autonomous. In later years, Balbo would become one of Mussolini's most important air force pilots, celebrated as a national icon after his successful solo flight over the Atlantic Ocean, but in Parma, they remembered him as the fascist thug they defeated with scarcely more than their bare hands.

Federici, the second of two daughters, was born during World War II in a city that was under siege. Parma had been a strategically important depot on the tributaries of the Po River, and its ports and train lines were subject to frequent aerial bombings from Allied fighter planes. Frequently, during nighttime raids, Federici's mother would grab her two young children and flee out into the fields searching for safety, squatting in the dirt and waiting for dawn while the sky blazed overhead.[6] Federici was only three years old when the war ended, yet she grew up immersed in stories of war, listening to songs, and witnessing memorials celebrating the Partisan– the figure of the heroic resistance fighters who fought the Italian and German fascists, ultimately liberating the region. Even after the war was officially over, there was a sense that the struggle continued. Throughout her youth, fascist Blackshirts repeatedly attempted – unsuccessfully – to blow up the statue of the Partisan that stands in Parma's town center. "Everyday life was already politicized," she reflected.[7]

Postwar Italy was ruled by the Christian Democratic Party, a conservative political force supported by the United States as part of the Cold War fight against the influence of Moscow. But the north-central agricultural heartland of Emilia-Romagna remained a communist stronghold. In Parma, where the PCI had been the driving force behind the resistance movement, the party's identity merged with the heroic story of the partisans saving Italy from fascism. Unlike the great industrializing cities of Milan, Turin, and Genoa, Emilia-Romagna's smaller cities, like Bologna, Modena, and Parma, did not have vast proletarian armies working in massive factories. Instead, the region was largely dominated by agricultural cooperatives and small-scale industry. Most factories in the region had between ten to fifty workers, rather than thousands. Instead of modeling the party narrative as a struggle of workers against bosses, the PCI of postwar Italy forged alliances among artisans, small business owners, and farmers, building more on a tradition of rural mutual-aid societies and agricultural cooperatives than on a struggle of organized labor against bosses. Accordingly, it was rapacious capitalist outsiders, out to extract resources from the sharecroppers and landless agricultural workers, that were the force to be struggled against.

Within their communes, the PCI put their efforts into building social services and infrastructure, such as communal launderettes, public housing, and public transportation. They built *case del popolo*, houses of the people – community centers for community activities – which proudly flew the red party flag. On Sundays, party members would go door to door selling copies of the party newspaper *Unità*. On May Day, they marched through the streets waving red flags, handing out red carnations to the women, and singing the PCI anthem *Bandiera Rossa* ("Red Flag").

*

Like all families, the Federicis told their own wartime stories about surviving in the face of scarcity, and dramatic brushes with death. As a girl, Silvia would often hear these stories on Sunday afternoons, during long, leisurely family dinners. One of them went like this: during the Nazi Occupation, her father, a philosophy teacher, was stopped returning home on his bicycle from a private tutoring session by a German officer. The officer searched him and found him in possession of a kilo of salt – it had been his payment for tutoring, but it violated the rationing requirements. The officer held him up against a wall preparing to shoot him, but before pulling the trigger first asked, "What do you do for a living?" And when her father answered, "I'm a philosophy teacher," the officer let him go. In later years, he would often say: "Philosophy saved my life!"[8] Federici grew up talking about literature and politics and history with her father. "I think that my critical powers came partly from him," she told me. "He always defended my reading. I was reading everything, everything, everything. You know, even the papers. I was a voracious reader. And he defended that."[9]

Federici's recollections of her mother are suffused with warmth. She describes her as someone always in motion, lovingly taking care of the household, "making bread, pasta, tomato sauce, pies, liqueurs, then knitting, sewing, mending, embroidering, and attending to her plants." "Even today," she wrote, "the efforts that my mother made to develop in us a sense of our own value give me the strength to face difficult situations. What often saves me when I cannot protect myself is my commitment to protect her work and myself as the child to whom it was dedicated."[10] I copied those words onto a piece of yellow notebook paper and folded it into my wallet after my first son was born.

Federici wrote those words in 2011, when she was an established feminist scholar in her sixties. When she was younger, she had a more ambivalent relationship to her mother's work. In contrast with her father, her mother had not been formally educated. For Federici, that inequality between her parents was a silent undercurrent of family life. "When I was very young," she told me, "my father was the dominant figure because he was very interesting. He always had stories. Because he was a historian, after all. Whereas my mother was a housewife."[11] She described how much it bothered her mother to have no income of her own, despite all of her work, and to be financially dependent on her father even for basic necessities, like socks. Throughout her childhood and well into adulthood, Federici herself avoided housework at all costs. She described the possibility of becoming a housewife as "a fate worse than death."

Yet she credits her mother as a profound influence on her politics:

> I realized she was the one who first saw the question of economic crisis, and prices, and the injustice of inflation. And my father always dismissed that. She was the one who said, "I don't see why I don't get paid for my work." And my father would explain, "Your work is not productive." I heard that in my family first.[12]

Federici's mother, who came from a peasant family, also inculcated in her daughter an awareness of the land and the work of those who care for it. These insights would influence Federici's politics decades later, inspiring her activism and theorizing about communal gardens and the creation and protection of "commons." But in the political idioms of the 1950s and 1960s, when Federici was a teenager, it was the waged worker who was cast as the protagonist of political struggle. "When I was fifteen, sixteen," she recalled, "I was always talking about the working class and the proletariat and my mother would say, 'But you never talk about the peasants. And your aunt is a peasant. She works from four in the morning.' My mother was the first who saw the peasants. She was the first to tell me about housework."[13]

After finishing secondary school, Federici enrolled in the University of Bologna to study modern languages and literature, specializing in French and English. Foreign languages seemed to her like a pathway toward expanded horizons, and during the summer of 1962, she left Italy for the first time on a student trip to Paris. There, staying in a youth hostel, she met students from all over the world: Yugoslavia, West Africa, Morocco, the United States. Algeria was on the cusp of independence from French colonial rule after a protracted freedom struggle, and in the evenings all the students gathered around a large table to eat together, speaking in their different languages, talking about the anti-colonial struggle. For Federici, these encounters were life-changing.[14]

She had studied languages in order to connect with a wider world of ideas and politics and the struggle for social justice, and that summer she got a glimpse of where her studies might take her. Yet after graduating in 1965, the only job she could get was teaching English to rural school children in Emilia-Romagna. Each morning she rose while it was still dark, walked to the train station and commuted to a small village, where she taught English and French to children who were equally uninterested in being there. She enrolled again at the University of Bologna for her graduate degree, this time in philosophy.

Phenomenology is a branch of philosophy devoted to consciousness and the human experience of reality. For philosophers in this tradition, descended from German philosopher Edmund Husserl, there is no boundary separating the world from experience; no Cartesian plane of glass separating reality from the perception of reality. Subjective consciousness is more than the apprehension of reality: it is a constituent part of it. Phenomenology is perhaps best understood as a method for discovering the facts of human experience. A central part of Husserl's method was the eschewing, or "bracketing," of preconceived notions – for example, putting aside religious or cultural baggage or political ideology – and exploring how phenomena are experienced in the consciousness of human beings. All experience is experience TO someone, and, in this sense, human beings, rather than abstract conceptualizations of reality, are at the center of phenomenology.

In 1960s Italian academia, philosophers such as Enzo Paci at the University of Milan initiated a revival of Husserl's work. A former student of Paci describes the professor's enthusiastic enactment of phenomenology for his students: "He made his own body the vehicle and fulcrum for his lesson on Husserl's *Cartesian Meditations*, beginning with the theatrical entrance of the imposing figure of this man, with his Etruscan profile, into a crowded, expectant hall and ending with the infinite revolutions around a large ashtray: each movement accompanied by a descriptive, critical, unbiased, that is, phenomenological, observation."[15] For Paci and others, phenomenology was a vehicle for revitalizing Marxism in the wake of Stalinism and its brutalities by placing human experience at the center of social analysis. If, as Husserl had claimed, consciousness was inseparable from objective material reality, consciousness could change the material world. For Paci, art, literature, music, language itself were evidence of human consciousness and could therefore become tools of revolution.

Luciano Anceschi, a former student of Paci and a well-known literary critic at the University of Bologna, took up this task. In the mid-1950s, he had founded the literary journal *Il Verri* – "the boars," referring to the name of the cafe in Milan where he gathered with young creatives and intellectuals to talk about art and literature. Anceschi situated art as local, as connected with human relationships; as experimental and formally subversive; and, most importantly, as freed from political ideology. Because capitalism would absorb all forms of protest into itself, literature had to be ever changing, subversive, impossible to capture or commoditize. Through *Il Verri*, he became a mentor to a generation of young experimental writers, including Umberto Eco and Nanni Balestrini. About *Il Verri*, he would later say: "Literary journals are in crisis – we are the journal OF the crisis."[16]

This was the intellectual world that Federici entered into when she enrolled at the University of Bologna and became a student of Anceschi. She started off working on a thesis about T. S. Eliot. On a trip to Edinburgh for a summer conference on phenomenology, she met philosophers from across the English-speaking world. She learned that, for those interested in phenomenology, the place to be was Buffalo, New York.

Marvin Farber, an American philosophy professor at the University at Buffalo, had been a student of Edmund Husserl's at Freiburg in the 1920s, and was known for bringing phenomenology to North America. By the 1960s, Farber was beginning to turn his attention toward Marxism. Encouraged by her English-speaking colleagues, Federici received a Fulbright fellowship to spend a year studying philosophy in the United States, working with him at Buffalo.

Federici arrived at Buffalo right as the anti-war student protest movement was taking off on college campuses across the United States. As a border town, Buffalo became a way station for young men on their way to Canada, fleeing the draft. The university also became a flashpoint of protest for Project Themis, a research project funded by the Department of Defense for developing military technology for the US war effort in Vietnam. Protesters dismantled the temporary building where the research was being conducted, disrupting and delaying the project by several years. Police clashed frequently with students on campus. When a group of forty-five faculty members held a sit-in in solidarity with them, the university had them arrested.

Soon after arriving, Federici joined *Telos*, a journal edited by students in the philosophy department. Aristotle used the term *telos* to refer to humanity's purpose and potential – the ultimate ends of human existence and effort. The editor of the journal was PhD student Paul Piccone, who was frustrated by what he called "establishment philosophy" and who wanted to create a space to bring phenomenology and Marxism together. The early issues of *Telos* set forth their countercultural intentions, proclaiming on their masthead: "since ideas should be neither sold nor bought, none of the included material is copyrighted and can be used for any purpose whatsoever by anyone." From its first issue, with the auspicious publishing date of May 1, 1968, *Telos* was self-consciously global in scope. Articles and reviews from all over the world – Italy, Czechoslovakia, Hungary, France – were solicited and published, translated from multiple languages. The *Telos* collective was particularly interested in what was going on in Italy, which was in part why Piccone recruited the young Silvia Federici. She worked on *Telos* from its first issue.

Paradoxically, it was while working on *Telos* that Federici first encountered the ideas of *operaismo* and the Italian extra-parliamentary left. When she was growing up in Parma, the left was largely dominated by the PCI. She worked with Piccone on commissioning and translating the work of thinkers on the Italian left to bring them to an American readership. In 1969, after a year in Buffalo, she returned to Italy, intending to remain. But she couldn't find a job and, forced to earn her income doing the dreary work of translating English medical textbooks into Italian, by fall, she decided to return to Buffalo, this time enrolling in the PhD program in philosophy.

Buffalo attracted national attention as a node in the student anti-war movement. In August 1968, nine young men destroyed their draft notices and sought refuge in a local church. On August 19, police stormed the church and arrested the group that became known as "the Buffalo Nine." Federici was back on campus in time for their highly publicized trial in February 1969. That same month, a new underground newspaper appeared in the city called the *Town Crier*, with the mission of "telling the news that is suppressed," setting itself up in opposition to Buffalo's two "Establishment newspapers," the *Buffalo Evening News* and the *Courier Express*. Its editors all contributed $5 to get the newspaper started. One of its founding editorial board members was Buffalo Nine member Ray Malak, and another was Bob Cohen, an organizer with Students for a Democratic Society (SDS). The board also included as its Labor editor Tim Greenlee – a Black war veteran who reported stories about racism and the struggles of working-class Black Buffalo. In the first issue, Federici wrote about the 1968 massacre of Mexican student protesters in Tlatelolco Plaza in Mexico City. By the newspaper's second issue, she had become its International News editor.

The *Town Crier* editorial collective rankled at Buffalo's national reputation as a cultural backwater, and instead saw Buffalo's working-class community as a source of political creativity. They reported on graffiti, Black food cooperatives, student anti-war demonstrators, and labor unions. They published stories about atrocities against civilians in Vietnam and the plight of Palestinians living in occupied territory.[17] The effect was to locate the clashes that were happening in Buffalo over the military-industrial complex within a larger global struggle against oppression, imperialism, and violence.

Federici credits her roommate Ruth Geller with introducing her to feminism. Geller was an American Studies PhD student who was studying revolutionary Mexican novels, and she and Federici quickly became friends. In Buffalo, they rented the apartment of a couple who had gone to Cuba with the Venceremos Brigade – a collaboration between the SDS and the Cuban government, in which American volunteers traveled to work in Cuba. Geller later caricatured the male left at Buffalo in those years in her novel *Seed of a Woman*. The novel, both hilarious and poignant, has two particularly scathing caricatures of New Left men on campus. Paul is a serious PhD student, frustrated that his wife is not sufficiently revolutionary, and his righteous idealism becomes a tool to bully and control her. His comrade, David, is a young, philandering professor who sexually exploits and deceives multiple women in the name of rejecting bourgeois norms and whose work on revolutionary Third World struggle is based on research done by his female graduate students.

Geller's novel also fictionalizes the consciousness-raising meetings that she began holding at the apartment she shared with Federici. She described the awkwardness of an initial meeting, as women fumbled around to figure out what to talk about. But as the evening went on, the conversations slowly meandered toward more profound topics. "Humorous grumblings about diets opened into deep dissatisfactions with their bodies; light complaints about boyfriends opened into feelings of insecurity and worthlessness."[18] Women shared long-held secrets about pregnancies and babies given up for adoption; experiences of rape and fantasies of revenge.

Federici attended meetings like these, but initially she remained aloof. While she had first-hand experience of the sexism of men on the left, she wondered: how would this personal exploration stand up to the great forces of capitalism and imperialism and the military-industrial complex? Can changing your consciousness really change the world?

In 1970, she married a comrade whom she had met through *Telos* and moved with him to Brooklyn.[19] She reached New York right on time for the crisis. Materially, the city's infrastructure was deteriorating. The real-estate market in the 1970s was such that, rather than maintain their buildings and collect rents, many landlords evicted tenants and left their buildings vacant, with plans to tear them down and build new ones, avoiding rent-control protections that only applied to older buildings. A vibrant squatter movement formed in response, in which participants took over emptied run-down spaces and transformed them into housing, or space for art or music or politics. Such was the case, for example, with the West Side Women's Center, which a group of feminists claimed and fashioned into a space where squatters could move in, exchange clothing and food, and discuss women's issues.[20] The cost of living was low, public services still plentiful, and with industries and white middle-class people fleeing the city for the suburbs of Westchester and New Jersey, there was space. For people with creative ambitions, there was space for staging their vision – put on a show, call a meeting, plan a revolution, publish a magazine.

Federici arrived a few years into the Women's Liberation Movement. Feminist bookstores such as Labyris in Greenwich Village and Womanbooks on 92nd offered space for women to gather, share information, hold meetings and throw parties. The increasing ubiquity of Xerox copy shops throughout the city facilitated the flourishing of self-published literature. She encountered the ideas of feminists who imagined a world of female autonomy from men, free from the oppressive demands of male egos, feminine gender roles and biological reproduction, and read texts such as Solanas' SCUM Manifesto and the newsletters of Lesbian Separatist groups, such as the Furies and the Radical Lesbians. A friend of hers was a member of the WITCHes – Women's International Terrorist

Conspiracy from Hell, who showed up at the New York Bridal Show in Madison Square Garden in witch costumes singing, to the tune of "Here Comes the Bride," "Here come the slaves / off to their graves!" – before releasing mice into the stadium. She joined a Marxist-Feminist study group, but was gradually becoming impatient with academic conversations about feminism. She was eager to act.

Federici felt more at home politically in the Women's Bail Fund, a coalition of women from the Black Panthers, Young Lords, and Youth Against War and Fascism. It started with a protest outside New York House of Detention, where Angela Davis was incarcerated in 1970, charged with conspiracy to commit murder after guns she had purchased were used in an armed takeover of a courtroom in an attempt to free prisoners. (Davis was later acquitted.) A crowd of women gathered outside chanting: "The rich set the bail and the poor go to jail!" Yelling through the windows, the protesters took down the names of incarcerated women so they could raise money to bail them out. They bailed out their first incarcerated woman in December 1970, and within a little over a year had bailed out 150 more. Their vision was about more than bailing individual women out of prison, though: they wanted to delegitimize the prison system itself. Their red campaign buttons read "All prisoners are political prisoners," and they argued that the criminalization of prostitution and the drug trade was nothing more than the criminalization of the poor and oppressed.[21] This was a kind of feminism that made sense to Silvia Federici: it sought to challenge structures of power and liberate everyone, rather than create pathways to liberate some women to join the ranks of the powerful.

Living in Brooklyn, Federici continued her academic work, though her attention was increasingly elsewhere. She taught as an adjunct, worked intermittently on her dissertation, and wrote and edited for *Telos*. She changed her dissertation topic to the work of Hungarian Marxist cultural critic György Lukács, and worked with Piccone on a special issue of *Telos* on the subject. The burning question that runs through her writing as a graduate student is the relationship between art and social change. In a dense theoretical essay, addressed to fellow philosophers, she assessed Lukács' engagement with the same issue. She ended her essay on a note of disagreement with Lukács: art, she insisted, "can encourage us to action, but never substitute for it."[22]

Through *Telos*, she became friends with Mario Montano, a political militant who had come from the student movement in Rome and now taught sociology at Clark University in Worcester. One weekend, she traveled to Boston to visit him and work with him on an article for the journal *Radical America* titled "Theses on the Mass Worker." Over a series of twenty-one "theses," they applied the rebellious spirit of Italian *operaismo* as a challenge to the American Labor movement. The problem, as they saw it, was this: With the rise of mass assembly-line production in factories across the country, American workers were more productive than ever before. They had demanded, and won, higher wages in exchange for their increased productivity. But this was not liberation: this was simply a greater share of the spoils of capitalism. Rather than challenging their exploitation, workers were becoming more invested in the very system that exploited them. Meanwhile, more and more aspects of human life were distorted in order to serve the assembly line. Public education was increasingly geared toward cultivating disciplined workers, rather than independent minds. Social services like public transportation and housing prioritized shuttling people to and from work on time, rather than on fostering community and connection. Capitalism did not serve the needs of the people; instead, American society molded human bodies and minds in order to serve the needs of capitalism. "From the plant to the university," they wrote, "society becomes an immense assembly line." In order to get free, they concluded, workers needed another mindset; an autonomous stance from which to articulate their own desires and demands.[23]

It was Montano who introduced Federici to the ideas of Mariarosa Dalla Costa. As Federici was getting ready to return to New

York, her friend gave her a copy of "Women and the Subversion of the Community." If, as in the article they had just written together, society was molding itself to the rhythms of the capitalist workplace, with society itself becoming an extension of the factory assembly line, Dalla Costa showed how that assembly line stretched into the home, where women produced, nurtured, and maintained current and future generations of workers for their place in the production cycle. The factories stayed in motion because of women's unpaid work. The invisibility of that work was not a coincidence: capitalism needed it to be invisible, naturalized as "love" and as "femininity." The first step toward a revolution was to see that work, name it, and make it visible.

Revolution, then, need not be an epic clash between bosses and waged workers. The terrain of struggle against capitalism included encounters in the bedroom and at the dinner table, tensions over the grocery bills and over childcare. To recognize that capitalism depended on women's unpaid work was not just to see women's oppression but to recognize that women had a vital source of untapped power that could be organized. In Dalla Costa's words: "This is where our struggle begins."

That summer, Federici returned to Italy – first to Parma to visit her family, and then to Padua, where she met Mariarosa Dalla Costa and Selma James and helped to draft the statement of the International Feminist Collective. In the months that followed, Federici and Dalla Costa began exchanging letters. Federici sent Dalla Costa some of the feminist literature she was most excited about, including a pamphlet by the Radicalesbians group arguing that it was only in the company of other women that women could find their authentic selves and seek liberation.[24] "What do you think?" she asked. Federici thought they were onto something: "Or at least it seems that way to me, especially after two months of life with three men with whom I have to fight to get them to sweep or wash the dishes . . ."[25]

Federici wrote to Dalla Costa: "It is difficult for me to find women to work with. I work with a group of women, but for such a long time we have been in the phase of theoretical and practical clarification. It's not useless, but little activity and above all, little clarity."[26] Dalla Costa, in turn, lamented her difficulty in finding women with the skills to put out a newspaper of their own: because their male comrades on the left had "deskilled them," never letting them do that high-level work before, they now had to start from scratch.[27] They commiserated about the difficulties of working with domineering men on the left – Toni Negri from Potere Operaio in Dalla Costa's case, and Paul Piccone in Federici's; both male mentors who refused to take feminism seriously. (Federici wrote to Dalla Costa that, when she suggested to Piccone that they invite her and Selma James for the *Telos* annual meeting, he told her that he "didn't want to hear any bullshit about women."[28]) In another letter, Federici shared that Piccone was going to let her do a special issue of *Telos* devoted to women, and Dalla Costa responded that she ardently hoped something would come of that.[29] But, soon, they weren't seeking the permission of gatekeepers like Piccone and Negri.

Back in New York, in the days that followed the summer meeting in Padua that launched the International Feminist Collective, Federici quit *Telos*. She parted ways with most of her other feminist study groups. She started to assemble a group of women that would become the New York Wages for Housework Committee.

6.

The New York Committee

Federici came back to Brooklyn at the end of the summer of 1972 ready to bring Wages for Housework to New York City. At first, she struggled to figure out how to translate her intellectual excitement into action. Most of all, she struggled to figure out how to get others to join her.

Her material circumstances were precarious. Now separated from her husband, she took on roommates to make rent. She pieced together a livelihood traveling from adjunct job to adjunct job teaching philosophy around the boroughs of New York City, occasionally earning a bit of money translating political pamphlets from the Italian left into English. In letters to Dalla Costa, Federici voiced her frustrations with life in New York. "The quality of everyday life here is shit," she wrote. "I am strongly tempted to return to Italy. What do you think of that?"[1] But even as she wrote these words, she was putting down roots in Brooklyn.

She was still, in theory, working on her philosophy dissertation, but her attention was elsewhere. She attended her regular political meetings and talked to anyone who would listen about Wages for Housework. Male comrades, for the most part, were dismissive. Some argued that housework was not "productive," and was already accounted for in Marx's concept of social reproduction as part of male workers' wages. At first, Federici, James, and Dalla Costa invested a lot of time and ink trying to engage with their detractors – after all, they didn't see Wages for Housework as a movement for women only but as a movement for the entire working class. They sent materials to be published in journals like *Radical America* and *Socialist Review*, and then, when rebuffed, wrote back arguing with their rejection letters and misrepresentations of their work.[2] But they soon decided there were better uses of their time.

Feminists were also skeptical. "Building a group turned out to be more laborious than we imagined," Federici later recalled. "Enthusiasms experienced in the midst of public presentations waned when our priorities had to be concretized . . . what stands out in my memory is that it was difficult for many women to see the meaning of WFH other than as a productivity deal."[3] In discussions and long letters mimeographed and sent to comrades across the international network, the core members of the campaign went back and forth: was the wage supposed to compensate and uplift housework, was it part of a push to refuse and abolish housework altogether; or was it a tactic for the larger goal of overthrowing capitalism? Some early members of the network objected to the fistful of dollars in their logo, saying it was too "economistic."[4] Federici was clear in her response: you could not confront capitalism without dealing with money.[5] And yet, at the same time, getting money was not the point. When people asked her how much the wage should be, Federici and other members of the campaign had no answer for them. Many were genuinely confused.

As a feminist perspective, Wages for Housework asked a lot from people. It required them to participate in a struggle that had no clear immediate objective – if the money was necessary but also not the point, how would you know when you had won? Intellectually, people were fascinated, but, as a political movement, many found it simultaneously too material and too abstract.

On one level, Federici embraced the demand for Wages for Housework as practical: a way of destroying the capitalist system by making it uneconomical, and, eventually, impossible to sustain.[6] There are vested interests in calling women's efforts "love" instead of work. States and employers save billions by relying on the labor women provide for free. If women refused the unpaid work, or demanded compensation, the system could not sustain itself. This was the ambition. At the same time, for Federici, it wasn't just the end goal but also the struggle itself that was transformational. By demanding wages for housework, refusing to work for free, refusing housework as a "biological destiny,"[7] women could contemplate other ways of living. In this vision of Wages for Housework, the struggle against capitalism is inseparable from the internal striving to free the self; to reconnect with authentic emotions, to reclaim the body, and to make meaningful relationships with other people. She ends her manifesto "Wages Against Housework" on a question: "why are these our only alternatives and what kind of struggle will move us beyond them?"

The first person to join with Federici to form what would become the New York Wages for Housework Committee was Nicole Cox, a Swiss feminist living in Brooklyn. Soon afterward, she was joined by others, including Jane Hirschmann and Hedda Matza – both of them radical New York-born Jews working as social workers and community organizers.

On a cool and misty Mother's Day in 1974 they went public for the first time, taking a stack of flyers to Brooklyn's Prospect Park, titled: "May Day or Mother's Day?" "All women are unwaged workers," the flyers proclaimed. "We work from morning to night but at the end of the week we have no money to show for it . . . This is what is glorified on Mother's Day, our unwaged work . . . We want wages for housework." Rather than a Hallmark holiday romanticizing the selflessness of mothers, women should instead claim their place on May Day: the day when international workers of the world celebrated their strength, and protested their exploitation, as organized workers. "Women unite," they proclaimed. "We have nothing to lose but millions of sinks, millions of mops, millions of diapers, millions . . . "[8] They handed their flyers to caregivers pushing babies in strollers, stooping to walk hand in hand with a toddler, walking home from the laundromat or grocery store, and asked them what they thought. Then as now, and everywhere, when asked about their work, the women had a lot to say: they told the young activists about their long workdays, their lack of money and recognition. They asked what Wages for Housework was all about. Thus began the first of many conversations initiated on the street, on playgrounds, in laundromats, and in welfare offices over the next several years.

In an attempt to bring clarity and unity, Federici and Hirschmann convened a conference of the international campaign in October 1974. Suzie Fleming arrived from the UK, dragging a suitcase full of feminist books. Selma James came, as did others from across Italy, the UK, Canada, and various groups that were forming in Boston, Cleveland, Philadelphia, and New Orleans. Together, over the course of several days, they collaborated on "Theses on Housework," a series of twenty-eight points, divided into three categories: Wages for Housework as an analysis of capitalism, Wages for Housework as a strategy, and "organizational questions." The gathering lasted several days. By the end of it, the committed were separated from the merely curious, and while many of the women in attendance left the group, those who stayed behind remained in the campaign afterward.

Members of the newly constituted New York Wages for Housework Committee primarily included "women who have a long experience in neighborhood politics, including rent strikes and welfare organizing."[9] In the New York Committee, Federici's ambitious and imaginative thinking about the possibilities of a post-capitalist world came together with the more grounded knowledge and activism of women who worked in the community, and knew something about what housework looked like in working-class Brooklyn.

The core members of the New York Wages for Housework Committee were white women, recent college graduates who had been active in student politics of the 1960s. They included Hedda Matza, Nicole Cox, Barbara Silverman, Joan Ennis, Pat Sweeny, Jane Hirschmann, Sharon Freedberg, and Diana Richardson. Many of them were social workers who worked in the public hospitals and clinics of New York City. They were part of a movement of practitioners who were critical of the very idea of social work. They wanted to do more than provide services to the poor; they wanted to change the systems that exploited them.

Hedda Matza was a community organizer with the Maimonides Neighborhood Service Center, a satellite of the Community Mental Health Center of Maimonides Medical Center in southwest Brooklyn, in a neighborhood predominately populated by Hasidic Jews and Puerto Ricans. It was one of several storefronts created in the wake of the Federal Community Mental Health Acts of 1963 and 1966, which aimed to deinstitutionalize mental illness and allow people to get care within their communities. The ethos driving the storefront's activities was community control of health services. They hired community members as mental health outreach workers. These experiments in mental healthcare were controversial in the medical community, attributing mental health to social causes,[10] which implied collective action, rather than individual diagnosis and treatment. But for young idealistic social workers like Hedda, the aim was to destigmatize mental health, to break down the hierarchy between social worker and patient, and to take a more holistic approach to "mental health" that recognized how it was connected to systemic oppression. In the storefront where she worked, at any given time, while some individuals might be meeting for private counseling, in the other rooms groups would convene to talk about the practical everyday struggles of being poor: how to deal with rat infestations, how to confront absentee landlords. Mothers would meet to share their distress about children who were not doing well at school and discuss what could be done: should they demand support from the schools, as was received by children in wealthier neighborhoods; or should they try to do the work themselves, for free? A journalist who visited the center encountered women in a welfare rights group convening to strategize about a possible rent strike. As Hedda Matza explained to me years later, Wages for Housework didn't seem like a radical departure from the work she was already doing. The women she encountered on a daily basis were working all the time, in their homes and in their communities, without being paid. The demand seemed like common sense.[11]

Jane Hirschmann also worked as a social worker at Maimonides, and the matter of unpaid women's work spurred her to question the relationship between the social worker and the patients she was hired to counsel. What if these "patients" were not victims of circumstance but rebels against their unjust poverty and exploitation? What if the much-pitied "unwed mother" was not deprived of a bourgeois marriage but didn't want it in the first place? What if "unfit mothers" that social workers were supposed to rehabilitate were refuseniks, rejecting the unpaid work shunted on mothers as the public support systems collapsed? "They come to us as patients," Hirschmann reflected, "and we offer them therapy and a speedy return to the position against which they rebelled . . . unwaged work at home, or 'upgrading' by joining the low waged work force."[12] What if, rather than rehabilitation, social workers like her offered them solidarity instead?

When she and several co-workers, including fellow committee members Matza and Silverman, demanded company time to convene a Sex Discrimination Committee, their progressive male bosses likely expected them to demand that more of the top leadership positions in the hospital go to women. As it was, the leadership and administration were all men. Instead, they threw in their lot with the lower-paid workers and the patients. Whether it's the secretary who is expected to act like the office housewife, who does a million tasks outside her official job description, or the welfare mother expected to patch up a broken society with her extra housework, or the highly educated psychiatrist, who, at the end of a full day of work, goes home at night to put in a second shift caring for her husband and children: though their circumstances and privileges differed, at the root of their struggles was the expectation of their free labor. Jane, together with her Wages for Housework sisters at the Maimonides Center, formed a committee and held meetings on company time, for all of these women to discuss and make visible in the workplace unpaid and underpaid women's work.

These experiments were short-lived, as storefront social work clinics, part of the vast public hospital system, would soon be eliminated by a wave of budget cuts that decimated New York's social services. In the meanwhile, the New York Committee searched for more spaces to organize. The women they wanted to reach did not have time to spend in the evening at a consciousness-raising meeting, or at a protest, or hanging out at a feminist bookstore. Instead, the New York Committee tried to organize in "places where housework has to some degree already been socialized, like the supermarkets and laundromats. Other places where women come together are unemployment and welfare offices. Women stand there for hours, getting more and more angry . . ."[13] Housework isolated women from each other; they had to find spaces to bring them together.

On a chilly, cloudless November Saturday in 1975, the New York Wages for Housework Committee held a street party to inaugurate the opening of a storefront on a brownstone-lined street in Brooklyn. They hung multicolored bunting and banners across Park Slope's Fifth Avenue, one in English and one in Spanish, emblazoned with the words "We demand wages for housework from the government." Jane Hirschmann had procured a massive, car-sized balloon, emblazoned with the words "Wages for Housework" in red letters, and somehow transported it all the way from Manhattan. They set up a microphone and makeshift platform, and passersby from the neighborhood, many of them women with their children, gathered to hear them speak.

One member of the New York Committee spoke to the audience about her own experience. On the cusp of turning thirty, she was deciding whether or not to have children. It felt to her like an impossible choice: having a child in a society that did not recognize that work or provide adequate support for it was agreeing to one's own exploitation. Yet she wanted to have a child, and to refuse motherhood as an act of protest felt like punishing herself. She told the people who gathered: "I want wages for housework so that all women can decide if we will have children, how many and in what circumstances."[14]

Federici also spoke: "we are suspicious when we hear the press and the politicians celebrating motherhood and our capacity to love and care . . . we know they glorify our work because they expect us to do it for nothing, and they must convince us that there is nothing more we could desire in the world. But in the meantime employers and the state save millions of dollars not having to provide for the services that we do for free. Let's make it clear then. If we were not at home doing housework, none of their factories, mines, schools and hospitals, could run, none of their profits could flow. With our work, we make it possible for other people to go to work; we slave, so our husbands and children can slave. No wonder they say the family is the pillar of society . . ."[15]

There were games for children and feminist books and pamphlets for sale, and there was music: Boo Watson, a lesbian feminist organizer from the Toronto Wages for Housework campaign and co-founder of Wages Due Lesbians, came down to New York and performed a song she had composed. She starts in a snappy, talking-blues style spoken word over acoustic guitar:

> Well, if women were paid for all we do,
> I'll tell you one thing that's true as true,
> We wouldn't be free, but I'm telling you,
> There'd be a lot of wages due!

The storefront was small, consisting of two rooms. The group pooled their meager resources, each member contributing one day of their wages each month, and added to that the little money they made from selling campaign potholders and buttons and pamphlets to pay rent on the space. They held open hours Wednesdays and Saturdays, from 11 to 4, during which time the community were invited to come in and talk about their struggles as unpaid and underpaid houseworkers, and the Wages for Housework campaign.

The storefront gave them a space to meet. It put them physically in the community, facing onto the street. Anyone walking by could see their politics in the front window, where they hung posters, including "Notice to all governments," a text written by Judy Quinlan proclaiming:

The women of the world are serving notice. We clean your homes and factories, We raise the next generation of workers for you. Whatever else we may do, we are the housewives of the world . . . We are serving notice to you that we intend to be paid for the work we do.

We want wages for every dirty toilet, every painful childbirth, every indecent assault, every cup of coffee and every smile. And if we don't get what we want, then we will simply refuse to work any longer.

Next to the text was a picture, drawn by Nicole Cox, which had the outline of a woman and the image of a city and factory with smokestacks and workers depicted within the outline of her body. A passerby would have also seen a poster of the Statue of Liberty, rendered as a woman holding a broom in one hand and a wad of cash in the other, piles of dishes at her feet and children clinging to her robes. Years later, Federici laughed as she recalled one of their plans to make a gigantic apron and to dress the actual Statue of Liberty with it. "But when we went to take the measurements, we realized we would have needed about a kilometer of cloth!"[16] With these images, they could project their politics into the street, to be a continuous presence in the community.[17] That was the intention, anyway. Jane Hirschmann recalls that some people saw "Wages for Housework" in the window and mistakenly came into the storefront seeking a housekeeper.[18]

The Wages for Housework New York Committee opened their storefront scarcely two weeks after the now-famous New York *Daily News* headline that announced: "Ford to City: Drop Dead." New York City had run out of money, and the federal government was not going to help them stay solvent. In the following months, the city slashed public services. They cut welfare rolls, both increasing eligibility requirements and lowering the amount given to recipients. They closed down public hospitals. They shut down public schools and laid off staff and teachers, resulting in larger class sizes, of up to fifty and sometimes sixty students, and shorter school days. Shorter school days meant more demand for childcare for younger children, but they cut public subsidies for childcare as well. They laid off police officers and firefighters. Subway fares were increased. The City University of New York (CUNY) system – a historic public institution, producer of Nobel laureates from the city's working classes – was unable to pay faculty salaries or maintain its facilities, and began shutting down branch campuses throughout the five boroughs. By summer 1976, CUNY announced the end of free tuition for city residents, putting college once again out of the reach of many New Yorkers. Over the next six years, the city would slash its public expenditures by 20 percent.[19] Perhaps most palpably, the city laid off thousands of sanitation workers, leading to wildcat strikes followed by massive cuts to sanitation services. The city could not clean its streets or take care of its waste – or, put a different way, it could not afford to do its "housework." Some PR folks from the city government suggested New Yorkers might provide those services themselves, on a volunteer basis. New York residents responded to cuts in the sanitation services by piling their trash in the middle of the street – including in Park Slope, where the Wages for Housework storefront was located. In some neighborhoods, desperate to get rid of the trash, people set the heaps on fire.

In the midst of the crisis, in 1977, the artist Mierle Laderman Ukeles inaugurated a year-long work of performance art in which she would visit and personally shake hands with each of the 8,500 sanitation workers employed by the City of New York. Having recently become a mother, she felt that her drop in status, from being a well-respected artist to doing work that was unvalued and invisible, was of a piece with the contempt people had for sanitation workers. She sought solidarity with them as a fellow self-proclaimed "maintenance worker" responsible for the unglamorous, necessary work of repair and maintenance and care. Every day, she went out to meet with these men who dealt with New York City's waste. One day on her rounds, a sanitation worker said to her: "Do you know why they hate us?"

"Why?" she asked.

"They think we're their mother."[20]

The New York Wages for Housework Committee formed in the context of the fiscal crisis. In their early pamphlets, they highlighted how the challenges of inflation were borne most severely by women who ran household budgets. By late 1975, they were confronting the underlying political logic of austerity directly. The 1970s fiscal crisis became a turning point not only for New York City but for global capitalism. Debates over the budget were debates about what a city could be, whom it served, to whom the government was accountable. New Yorkers took to the streets to defend their public schools and universities, their libraries and subways and hospitals and fire departments, but, in the end, it was to investors and financial elites that the city would remain accountable. As historian Kim Phillips-Fein shows, austerity was a political choice presented as a mere accounting problem, and it inaugurated New York's transformation into a vastly unequal metropolis, a center of finance capitalism where apartments are bought as investment properties for the global elites and left empty, while tens of thousands of New York residents are homeless.[21]

Even as it was unfolding, Silvia Federici saw New York's fiscal crisis as the harbinger of something bigger, transcending the city itself, and it had everything to do with women. The benefits that were on the chopping block – welfare for mothers, subsidized daycare, college tuition for mothers, healthcare, public education – might be thought of as forms of support for unpaid women's work; in other words, wages for housework. The city was banking on the fact that the work would still get done: mothers would still look after their children, the sick would be tended to, broken down apartments maintained and repaired. But it would be done for free, by women who were stretched increasingly thin. Women's time and work were simply a resource to be extracted at will, to make up for society's collective failures. Austerity, Federici argued, was not belt-tightening, or a simple accounting decision: it was the exploitation of women's unpaid work. "We don't believe New York City is poor," she told a journalist in 1976. "We know we're poor. We've been defaulting in our lives week after week."[22]

The New York Committee focused much of their attention on housing. Neglected, abandoned buildings had become safety hazards, with regular reports in the news about floors caving in and bricks falling from rooftops, and landlords setting fire to their own properties in hopes of collecting insurance money. New York's policy of rent control, which protected tenants by keeping the cost of rent down, only applied to buildings constructed before 1947; if a building was destroyed and a new building was built in its place, the landlord was free to charge higher rents. Many families faced eviction. Women were disproportionately affected by threats to housing. They had trouble accessing housing on their own terms long before the fiscal crisis because of the invisibility and unwaged status of their labor. Even a woman who took care of an entire extended family was not entitled to a roof over her head: if she had no waged job or income, she would be considered a risk to a landlord. To get an apartment, it wasn't enough for a woman to be doing vital work, essential to the City of New York: she had to be the dependant of a man who had a paycheck. The New York Wages for Housework Committee questioned this accepted logic. Housing, they argued, has everything to do with women's unpaid housework. As they wrote in a pamphlet on the topic:

> Where we live determines how much we have to walk to shop, to do the laundry or to take the kids to school. Whether or not we are near a park or a playground decides whether we can let the kids go out without worrying they may be run over by a car, or we are stuck with them (and they with us) all day in an apartment. A run down apartment is more work for us.

Absentee landlords were offloading work onto women, who had to do the cleaning, battle cockroaches and rats, figure out waste management when garbage pickup was not reliable, repair broken light fixtures and stairs and refrigerators, carry groceries and baby strollers up five flights of stairs if an elevator was broken. Making neglected, dilapidated buildings livable took an immense amount of work. New York City's housing crisis was more than unpleasant: it was more work for women.

They printed their accusations in pamphlets and flyers distributed around the neighborhood. They blamed:

> The landlords . . . who don't give us heat, warm water, or repair the elevator during the day, because they wait until "the workers" come home. The city, who, with the excuse of the crisis, tries to cut

rent controls and throws us in the streets, while giving tax breaks to the landlords. The courts, who pass anti-rent strike laws and send the police to break our struggles. The government, who has grown rich from our work but gives billions to real estate speculators while denying us a decent place to live.

The New York Committee framed rent strikes, squatting, and struggles for rent control and neighborhood playgrounds as components of wages for housework. In demanding housing, they were not demanding benevolence or generosity but accountability. At a time of great transition in the New York real-estate market, they argued against the emerging cultural logic: housing was not a luxury, or a private commodity, or an investment, but a workplace that was part of the economy of New York City. The apartments were spaces in which the entire workforce of the City of New York were maintained and nourished. And what other worker had to pay rent on their own workplace?

The New York Wages for Housework Committee at the 1977 International Women's Day March in New York City.

The New York Committee saw themselves as building on the struggles of others, rather than inventing a movement from scratch, and they looked for places in the city where their perspective was already being advanced in order to build coalitions. They found it most clearly in the struggles of welfare mothers. The city was cutting off welfare benefits, and politicians justified their actions using stereotypes of welfare mothers as lazy and unproductive. The welfare rights movement of the 1960s had demanded welfare not as poverty alleviation but as payment for the work of mothering. Welfare mothers, by demanding payment for their work and refusing the low-paid jobs offered to them as further exploitation, were radically redefining work. This also challenged mainstream liberal feminism, which portrayed work outside the home for wages as a (perhaps *the*) key site of women's liberation. While politicians depicted them as, at best, pitiable women in need of charity and, at worst, as dysfunctional and undeserving, the women of Wages for Housework saw the Welfare Rights Movement as visionaries. Federici and others in the committee saw them as "the first wages for housework movement," and they wanted to join that struggle.

For them, the welfare system was a microcosm of the whole capitalist system and its gendered assumptions. They argued: "Every woman is a welfare woman."[23] They meant: welfare women worked but were told that they were not working, just like all women, and that any money given to them was charity, rather than fair compensation. Welfare women had government agents snooping into their sex lives to make sure they had no men in their lives, because if they did, they were expected to be the financial dependants of those men and would lose their benefits. In other words, the state tried to force them into heterosexual nuclear families and a position of vulnerability and dependence on men, just like it did to all women. They wanted to take the organizing and analysis of the Welfare Rights Movement and make it universal. "We wanted them to call it wages for housework," Federici said.

In April 1976, they convened a conference which aimed to mobilize women in New York City against the cuts in welfare, and to define welfare as wages for housework. Their storefront was too small to accommodate more than a few people, so instead they held it in the wood-paneled common room of a Unitarian church down the street. They set up a few dozen folding chairs and hung posters on the walls, some with slogans specifically addressing the struggle for welfare, such as "Our Kitchens are Factories: No Food Stamp Cuts," and "No Sterilization of Welfare Recipients," as well as more general campaign slogans, such as "Every Mother is a Working Mother!" and "No Charity, a Paycheck!" The racially diverse audience that packed the room included people of all ages: white-haired ladies in headscarves and hats holding shopping bags, young women in jeans smoking cigarettes, children and toddlers perched on their mothers' laps. Among the conveners were Wilmette Brown and Margaret Prescod: two Black women who had been involved in organizing welfare mothers at Queens College and who had recently formed their own group, Black Women for Wages for Housework. Members of the New York Committee spoke from the stage and circulated around the room, joining the audience members in fervent discussion. Women turned their folding chairs to face each other and talk. At the front of the room was a microphone where women stood up to share their stories: a suburban woman who was middle class when she was married but became poor when she divorced while her ex-husband retained his socioeconomic position; a student who became disabled and could no longer work; a grandmother who still had no money despite working and caring for grandchildren far past the age of retirement; a lesbian mother who, like welfare mothers under state surveillance, feared being deemed an unfit mother and losing custody of her kids. The key was the connection across women: to illuminate what they shared under capitalism, to gain power from their shared struggle.

The Wages for Housework campaign tried to build a movement by changing how people think about capitalism, starting from their own lives. In New York, as well as in Chicago, Boston, Philadelphia, New Orleans, San Francisco, Los Angeles, Cleveland – across the country, Wages for Housework members spoke on daytime talk radio and public access television, at YMCAs and in church base-ments and retirement home rec rooms. "I was always on the radio and on TV," recalled Beth Green. "On talk radio, talk television. I was insulted by Regis Philbin, which was, like, getting insulted by the best of them! And every time I got on, the phone lit up, because the time was right."[24]

They were joining a public conversation that was already well underway. Often cited in these discussions was a study commissioned in 1965 by Chase Manhattan Bank, called "What's a Wife Worth?"[25] It was intended as an advertising ploy, rather than a serious piece of social commentary, and it was presented as a window display (another window display in the series, titled "Night on the Town," compared the cost of a night out in various cities of the world). The director of the campaign reasoned: department stores used provocative window displays to attract foot traffic; why not a bank? To create the display, the advertising team assembled a group of economists and accountants to calculate the market value of the work performed by a housewife. The statisticians calculated that a housewife's duties would cost more than $8,285 per year if she received the market rate for those services – or roughly $81,535 as of this writing in 2023.[26] Articles and editorials appeared all over the country debating the issue, in mainstream pub-lications like the *New York Times*, *Boston Globe*, and *Wall Street Journal*, as well as women's magazines, such as *McCall's*, *Glamour*, and *Woman's Day*, and even in Christian publications, such as *U.S. Catholic*.[27]

Programs that seemed to overlap with Wages for Housework were on the agenda in the US Congress as well. As divorce rates climbed in the 1970s, politicians had to address a system in which women's social security benefits were earned and disbursed through their "breadwinner" spouse: what happened to these women after divorce? Conservatives and liberals alike agreed that older women who had raised children, like their own mothers, should not spend their old age in destitution.[28] Bella Abzug, the formidable congress-woman from New York City, proposed a bill to create social security accounts for homemakers based on the value of their housework to the US economy. Others proposed that divorced women get access to a proportion of husbands' earnings calculated based on the number of years they were married. Was it about addressing poverty, giving charity to the vulnerable, or was it about recognizing the role of unwaged women in the economy? And if you recognized working in the home as having economic value, how could that be reconciled with a public discourse that portrayed single mothers and those on welfare as "parasites"? In the end, it was the virtue of marriage, rather than the economic value of housework, that would be upheld in the laws governing social security benefits.

As the more mainstream feminist movement fought for legal rights for women, the women of Wages for Housework kept their focus on economic power. When rape within marriage was finally recognized as a crime in various American states throughout the 1970s, Federici was unimpressed. "How many women will ask a prosecutor to put their husbands in jail if this means that he will lose his job, and she will find herself stranded with at best the prospect of spending a few days in a shelter and, after that, either endless lines at a welfare centre or juggling between kids and a job, which usually pays little more than minimum wage?" The legal recognition of rape within marriage gives women the *right* to not be raped; but only money would give them the power to actually leave a violent relationship.[29] They were similarly critical of the emphasis on the legal right to abortion, for, important as it was, it was narrow: what about women who were pressured into sterilization, or living in poverty, and who could not afford the children they wanted to raise?[30] Perhaps the most controversial stance of the committee was their criticism of the Equal Rights Amendment (ERA), the centerpiece of the mainstream Women's Movement in those years, which proposed to prohibit discrimination on the basis of sex in the workplace. "Let's face it, work is shit," Silvia Federici told a journalist. "Work is liberation for nobody. And part of the problem with the women's movement is that they haven't touched the question of housework as simply free labor." For most women in Wages for Housework, advocates of the ERA missed the mark, upholding the workplace as the singular site of women's liberation, when most of the work women performed was not counted. They asked: for whom was work a source of liberation? To members of the New York Wages for Housework Committee, it seemed that the mainstream feminist movement ignored poor women and especially welfare mothers, rather than making common cause with them.

In small ways, Wages for Housework made its way into public discourse. In April 1976, an image from Silvia Federici's kitchen in her Brooklyn apartment, mustard yellow walls and bare lightbulbs overhead, appeared in a special issue of *Life Magazine*, titled "Remarkable American Women," celebrating two centuries of women in America, from 1776 to 1976.[31] The photograph was taken by Neal Slavin, renowned photographer of group portraits, and it presented the thirteen women from the New York Wages for Housework Committee, seven of them standing shoulder to shoulder around the kitchen table and six on chairs behind them. Bookending the image, on one side, Joan Ennis stands tall with her shoulders back and chest out, holding a broom, and, on the other side, Barbara Silverman has one foot on a chair and the other raised up on the table, arm in the air with a wad of dollar bills clenched in her fist, jaw set and eyes looking into the distance, mimicking the Statue of Liberty in their poster. The kitchen table is cluttered with piles of dishes and pots and pans and kettles, and dish towels emblazoned with the Wages for Housework logo are hanging from it.

In the front row and center is Silvia Federici, a placid, thoughtful look on her face. The sidebar reads: "The group contends that since housework benefits the state, the government should compensate them for it. 'But it's premature for us to work out the details until we've built a mass movement,' says Federici of her crusade." The quotation was likely taken out of context, and yet, to an earnest and curious observer, it might have seemed frustratingly vague. The women in the photograph were educated women in their twenties and early thirties. They were clearly not housewives; at least not in the conventional sense: to an outside observer, they seemed to be striking a pose. These were not women who wanted to do housework and be paid for it. What did these women want?

Surrounded by the archival ephemera of the New York Wages

for Housework Committee – the photographs and artwork and pamphlets and speeches and, most of all, Silvia's writings – I find no instruction manual toward liberation, no singular vision of what "winning" would look like, or what it would actually have meant for the City of New York to do what they were asking: reject austerity and pay women what they were owed for their work, rather than paying off investors. There are, however, glimpses and impressions of the possibilities they imagined. In campaign materials, they envision mothers coming together to set up the kind of community daycares they wanted for their children, and the government paying for it. Elderly women are rewarded for decades of housework with beautiful apartments of their own, in the best locations, and enough of an income to allow them not just to survive but to socialize and participate fully in the life of the city. Public housing works are designed according to the desires of the communities who live and labor in them, rather than by those seeking to extract profit from real estate. Less work in general; more time for living meaningful lives. Calling work what is work, in order to rediscover what is love.

The archives tell us little about what New York women outside the committee thought about Wages for Housework. But there is some undated archival video footage that shows Barbara Silverman interviewing a woman identified only as "Sarah", a welfare recipient, and mother of six children. The two women sit on a couch, angled toward each other.[32]

"You wanna know what it's like to get on welfare? Well, I'm gonna tell you what it's like to get on welfare. It's one big fat hassle." In a thick Brooklyn accent, Sarah describes the indignities of being on public assistance: the endless paperwork, and ever-changing requirements. One day, after waiting in line for hours, you may be told that you cannot collect your payment because you need your rent receipts. So you come back another day, with the receipts, only to be told that the requirements are different, and now you need a letter from your husband. You go to the office, and you have no idea if you will be out by dinner time, or if you'll have to come back the next day. Even applying for, and then collecting, welfare seems a part-time job in itself. Often, when the checks don't come on time, or don't last until the next month, you have to borrow from friends to keep body and soul together.

After a run-down of all her work, all day, every day, including weekends and without vacation time or sick days (the last time she had a day off, Sarah explains, was the day her youngest daughter was born years ago), Silverman asks her: "How would wages for housework affect your life?" Sarah responds simply: she might buy herself a pair of shoes, or go to the movies, or go bowling.

The interviewers, both Silverman and another woman who is behind the camera, seem disappointed with the answer. They have something else in mind. They keep rephrasing the question, but Sarah's answers remain stubbornly focused on the practical. Silverman tries a different approach: "Do you think it would give you the opportunity, if you wanted, to leave your husband, because you'd be more economically independent?" It gets a little awkward, as she keeps pushing and Sarah tries to avoid that line of questioning. Eventually, Sarah says: "I'd have to cross that bridge when I came to it."

Then Silverman tries again. "Sarah, can you imagine some women going out on strike to get a wage for housework?"

Finally, a connection is made. Sarah's face relaxes into a warm, dreamy smile. She leans back into the couch. "I think that would be sooooome dynamite situation," she says, and grins. "Really! It really would be something. We would tie up the whole world, let's face it."

For a moment, Sarah looks delighted, lost in her imagination. But the moment quickly passes. Silverman asks her what she thinks about the possibility of a women's general strike, like one that women had staged recently in Iceland. Sarah replies: "I dunno, a woman's strike is a good thing if you're going to get something out of it. If you're not going to get anything out of it, why bother? Just for recognition alone? I don't think so."

How do you go from that moment of naming your exploitation, and imagining another world, to a series of concrete acts that might call it into being? This was, and, perhaps, still is, the central tension of Wages for Housework.

7

Wilmette Brown

Wilmette Brown speaking at the 1977 International Women's Day March in New York City.

On a chilly day at the Ellis Island Ferry Terminal in Battery Park, Lower Manhattan, two women bundle up against the wind. One of them is Silvia Federici, fresh-faced in big round glasses and a coat and scarf. The other woman is Wilmette Brown, a taller Black woman in a red beret, long hoop earrings, and a plaid checkered peacoat. They stand side by side at the waterfront, the Statue of Liberty visible in the background, speaking before a film crew hired by the National Commission on the Observance of International Women's Year in 1976.

Silvia's black hair whips across her face as she reads from a prepared statement. "Money, the question of money, is very key to all the problems we women have. Because having money is really the possibility of having some choices in our lives." When it is her turn to speak, Wilmette Brown gazes at a space just off camera as though thinking aloud, her hands clasped behind her back, rocking from foot to foot as she speaks. "The last line of the poem engraved on the Statue of Liberty is 'I lift my lamp beside the golden door,'" she says. "That's supposed to symbolize sharing the wealth with immigrants from all over the world. That has never been true for women. The unpaid work that women in the Third World have done for generations, for centuries, is stored here in New York."[1]

By the time Wilmette Brown joined the Wages for Housework campaign, in 1975, she was already a skilled organizer with experience in the civil rights movement, anti-war activism, the Black Power movement, and anti-colonial liberation in southern Africa. Over the next several years, Brown would radically expand the scope of Wages for Housework. She took the campaign decisively out of the kitchen, out of the heterosexual nuclear family, and directed her gaze into some of the darker spaces of global capitalism – into cancer wards and urban ghettos with toxic soils, into scenes of police violence and harassment on street corners and at the lesbian bars where she hung out, and into the war zones where women cared for ravaged bodies and land. The housewife, married to the archetypal male factory worker, was not the central protagonist. Brown took on James and Dalla Costa's analysis of how capitalism extracts profit from housework, and turned it over to reveal another side: much of the unpaid work necessary to sustain and protect human life is *created* by the harms of capitalism. Housework, for Wilmette Brown, is more than free labor for capitalism. Housework is repairing the damage. It is healing work.

Today, Wilmette Brown is not as well known as some of the other founders of Wages for Housework, but as soon as I began my research it became immediately clear that her influence was decisive and singular. In archival audio recordings, I soon learned to recognize Wilmette Brown's New Jersey accent and her clear, crisp diction – pronouncing "call" as "cawl" and enunciating each syllable of the word *reality*. One journalist describes "her sober speech, her steady gaze and unstoppable stream of facts and figures."[2] She comes across as someone who has no time to waste. In the late 1970s and 1980s, she introduces herself at various political meetings of feminists, lesbians, and Black activists, in the old-fashioned way of leftists announcing their political tendency: "Wilmette Brown, Black Women for Wages for Housework."

Wilmette Brown was born in 1946 in Newark at a time when it was becoming increasingly Black and segregated. "Newark is . . . my hometown," she wrote, "my point of reference for comprehending the changes the USA goes through."[3] A thirty-minute bus ride from Manhattan on the Passaic River, Newark was one of the world's busiest ports, located in the crosswinds of heavy industrial activity. Brown grew up in the Central Ward, which, by the 1950s, was 85 percent Black. The first two decades of her life coincided with white flight to the suburbs and the impoverishment of the city center. The Central Ward of her childhood was built up with dilapidated housing stock, with the vast majority of urban residents renting from landlords, rather than owning. As those with means deserted the inner city for the suburbs, the shrinking tax base depleted city services. The underfunded public-school system had a high drop-out rate, especially among Black students, and though the population of the city was mostly Black, the political system was controlled by white men, in the grip of political machines. Adding further tension to the strained city, Newark had proportionally the largest police force of any major city in the country, with the heaviest policing in the Central Ward.[4]

Brown's family was Black and worldly, with a sense of history and a diasporic awareness. Her mother was from Liberia, and spoke with an accent that marked her difference in her American community. Brown was the granddaughter of prominent Liberian bishop Theophilus Momolu Fikah Gardiner, the first indigenous African bishop in the Anglican Church, and, according to Brown, the first Black bishop to preach in St Paul's Cathedral in London. "We had a lot of Black pride, of knowing where we came from in Africa," she told journalist Winsome Hines. "But we also had a very realistic picture of the level of corruption in a country like Liberia: of one set of Black people exploiting another. My mother gave us a sense that because Black people were in government didn't mean that all the problems were solved."[5] Her father had migrated north to Newark from Iron City, Georgia. He was one of 20,000 Black New Jerseyans to serve in World War II and had been stationed abroad in Europe. Back in Newark after the war, he became a schoolteacher, and usually worked an additional night job to support his family. When Brown was only four years old, her older brother was killed in the Korean War. "I could see how it affected my mother," she recalled years later. "She had raised her son to die in one of the US' pointless wars. She was devastated by that."[6]

She watched the Montgomery bus boycotts on television with her family, and, at the age of twelve, became involved in the local chapter of the NAACP Youth Council, going door-to-door in Newark registering Black people to vote.[7] A brilliant student, she went on to college at Wellesley, the prestigious predominantly white women's college on the outskirts of Boston, returning to Newark during the summer of 1963 to join the Congress of Racial Equality (CORE) under the direction of the Black community leader Robert Curwin. CORE's 1963 summer program in Newark included participants aged eighteen to twenty-five. They demonstrated against racist labor practices, picketing all-white construction worker crews, and coordinating mass phone-ins to Newark Bell telephone to jam the phone lines in protest of their practice of hiring only white phone operators. They coordinated rent strikes and protested poor-quality housing and the neglect of slumlords. They staged sit-ins at City Hall in protest against the refusal of the sanitation department to collect trash from poor Black neighborhoods.[8] For six weeks, CORE youth members were deployed to work under field-secretary Norman Hill.

As the program description explained, "Not only will this northern contingent work on breaking down discrimination in housing and employment, but it will also attack the conditions within the ghettos which destroy the will and motivation to participate in an integrated and democratic society."[9] At the end of a summer of civil disobedience and organizing in Newark, Brown went as part of the delegation on the bus to the 1963 March on Washington.

"What was most remarkable for me," she wrote,

> was the journey down from Newark: on the highway busloads of people from all over passed each other, waved, yelled greetings. We did not know each other but we knew we were all going in the same direction. When we reached Washington and marched to the Lincoln Memorial, the common vibration of so many different kinds of people – each with their particular placards, refinements and specifications on the common theme of freedom – was dazzling and wonderful. I knew I was part of a mass movement determined to win.[10]

In July 1967, the same streets where she had grown up and canvassed and organized erupted into violence after white police officers beat up a Black cab driver, John Smith. News of the abuse spread over cab radios, and residents of the massive housing project blocks that faced the fourth police precinct looked out their windows and watched police officers drag Smith to the station. Over the following days, crowds gathered, some residents broke windows, police officers shot bullets into crowds and at the windows of Black-owned businesses. The National Guard was called in and set up 137 road-blocks throughout the city.[11] In the end, twenty-three people were killed in the Newark uprisings, twenty-one of them Black. It was the culmination of many of the tensions that Wilmette Brown had grown up with, and became a pivotal moment in American race politics, resulting in the famous Kerner Commission report that revealed the depth of racial inequality in American life. But Wilmette Brown was not in Newark at the time of the riots. By that time, she had left the East Coast, transferring from Wellesley to the University of California in Berkeley.

"I went to Berkeley because in '64 that was the place to go to continue organizing," she told Sarah Schulman and Sophia Mirviss in 1980, in an interview for the underground lesbian newspaper *WomaNews*.[12] At Berkeley, Wilmette Brown majored in Russian and History but was increasingly drawn toward her political work outside the class-room. She arrived the same year as the mass demonstrations of the Free Speech Movement that shut down the campus. Berkeley was a national epicenter of student anti-war activism. Brown was elected to the executive Peace Rights Organizing Committee (PROC), a group that included both students and activists from the community beyond and which protested the war and the university's complicity with the US government and its involvement in the war.[13] They pro-tested the ceremony in which UC Berkeley gave an honorary degree to Arthur Goldberg, US Ambassador to the UN and supporter of the war in Vietnam, and they protested army recruiters on campus. PROC distributed black armbands to students and faculty, so like-minded people could identify each other, and instructed students to disrupt their classes, using the space and time of the class session to insist on talking about the war. If the instructor refused and walked out, students would lead the conversation without them.[14]

"Were you welcome there as a Black woman?" Schulman and Mirviss asked. "I was welcomed on a very token level and in a token way. 'Oh yes, we have a Black' kind of thing. But there was no way for me to be integrated into the white left. What we had to do was found our own organization. I was vice-president of the first Afro-American students organization at Berkeley."[15] When Wilmette Brown arrived at Berkeley, Black students made up less than 1 per-cent of the student body and came from many parts of the United States. She arrived the year after Malcolm X and Stokely Carmichael had spoken on campus, and right as Huey Newton and Bobby Seale had joined up with the Afro-American Studies Association founded by Black UC Berkeley students and had started their own linked organizations at Merritt College in Oakland. Describing this cohort, historian Donna Murch writes: "Berkeley's first real generation of Black students experienced intense social isolation that encouraged them to look to the world beyond campus."[16] At the peripheries of campus life, Brown took part in Black intellectual connections stretching across the Bay Area, from the study groups of upwardly mobile cosmopolitan Black students at Berkeley, to the community actions in Oakland and at Merritt which were the antecedents of the Black Power movement.

Eventually, she drifted away from campus life and joined the Black Panther Party. She lived in South Berkeley, off Telegraph Avenue, down the road from the Chinese restaurant where the Afro-American Association used to gather to hold their meetings and near the apartment where Mary Lewis, a Berkeley PhD student who later joined the Black Panthers, used to host study groups with fellow Black student organizers. There she would have participated in discussions about Black self-determination and autonomy, which was controversial at the time, when liberalism, unity, and race-blindness were the dominant themes in thinking about coalition-building on the left. In study groups, she read Fanon and Malcolm X, which had a deep impact on her. In particular, she was drawn to Fanon's analysis of the connections between health and colonialism, and his call for reparations, rather than charity, for formerly colonized peoples.[17] She returned to the ideas of Fanon and Malcolm X again and again in years to come in her articulation of a global feminism rooted in Black liberation and anti-colonial struggle.

Meanwhile, in 1966, across the bay at San Francisco State, students formed a Black Student Union. Public universities were admitting more Black students than ever before, and this raised a new set of questions for these students and their communities. It was one thing to increase enrollment, but what did that really mean if there was no curriculum that was relevant to their experiences? Many students who were now being admitted found they were then expected to leave their culture and community behind and integrate into a university system designed for white middle-class elites. Were working-class students simply being co-opted into the middle class? Or could the university be democratized, made into a resource for the community, and transformed to reflect the communities and values from which their students were drawn?

Students in the San Francisco State Black Student Union wanted to make the university a tool of justice and freedom not just for themselves but for the entire Black community, in the Bay Area and beyond. Many of them worked around the clock, moving seamlessly from campus life to community work and activism. Dhameera Ahmed recalls waking at 5 a.m. to work serving children breakfast with the Black Panther Free Breakfast Program before going to campus for her own classes. "School was for the theory," she said. "And the community was for practice to see if the theory worked."[18]

The Black Student Union did not wait for the university to recognize their demands but instead launched their own Experimental College to pioneer a Black Studies curriculum. Aubrey LaBrie, a graduate student, taught the first Black Studies course in 1966 with the course title Black Nationalism. They recruited a number of Black intellectual luminaries to teach in their department. Sonia Sanchez, LeRoi Jones (later Amiri Baraka), and Nathan Hare – a sociologist who had recently been fired from Howard University for his anti-war activism – were among their teachers. From the Experimental College, the Black Student Union launched the student strike in 1968, demanding that the university fund a Black Studies Department. The strike lasted from November 1968 to March 1969.[19] Wilmette Brown joined the students at San Francisco State in what would become a pathbreaking movement for Ethnic Studies.

As she recalled later, her reasons for doing so were both political and personal. She was a lesbian and was out in some circles but struggled to reconcile her identity with her political commitments. This was especially true of her life with the Black Panthers, which advanced a mode of Black liberation that, in her experience, centered Black masculinity and heterosexuality.[20] Brown recalled feeling pressure from the men in the movement to take on a feminized role, to have children to "build the Black nation."[21] "I was not out as a lesbian in the Panthers," she said. "I was living a double life of doing my political work and, when I could steal the time, go out to lesbian bars in San Francisco. I say 'steal the time' because the Panthers were a paramilitary organization so we all had ranks and if someone told you to be in a certain place at a certain time, you had to be there."[22] Participating in the struggle at San Francisco State was both an extension of her activism and a way of creating some distance from the strict gender discipline of the Panthers, while staying firm in her commitment to the project of Black liberation.

After five months, the strikers succeeded in compelling the university to establish a school of Ethnic Studies, including a Department of Black Studies. Eleven faculty positions were created, and Wilmette Brown was chosen by students to be hired in the first cohort of Black Studies faculty. Having participated in the strike, she shared their radical vision of the role of the university. "The main function of a teacher is as catalyst, discussion leader, organizer and participant," she said. "The classic way to break down authoritarianism is through student participation, self-determination in practice."[23] In the fall of 1969, after the end of the strike, she began teaching a class on Black Nationalism, which had been introduced by LaBrie in the Experimental College.[24]

After the strike was over, students and faculty who had participated in the movement struggled to pursue the principles of self-determination and community involvement that had first motivated the creation of the Black Studies program. Students sometimes found themselves at odds with faculty when they tried to assert control over the curriculum. They also resented that university president S. I. Hayakawa refused to hire Nathan Hare, whom they had selected to lead their department. Then, a year later, Hayakawa fired all the Black Studies faculty who had been involved in the strike, including Brown. One of them, Patricia Thornton, who had been dean of Third World Studies, expressed her dismay: "We expected them to dismantle the department," she told a reporter. "We just expected it to be more subtle."[25] For Wilmette Brown, the point was not just the Black Studies curriculum but the principle of a university program controlled by, and accountable to, the community. By that criterion, in Brown's view, the student strikers had been defeated. "That was really the battle we had at San Francisco State. Were we going to actually be incorporated as Black Studies into part of the system, or were we going to actually be about putting ourselves out of a job? Making the liberation process so strong that you no longer needed a Black Studies program to discuss it?"[26] As she saw it, the program had been coopted, and, with it, the principles of student participation and community control were lost.[27]

Though the influence of the strike at San Francisco State reverberated far and wide on campuses across the United States, the faculty members who had been chosen by students to lead the historic and hard-fought Black Studies department moved on to other endeavors. Two of them – Patricia Thornton and Wilmette Brown – looked to continue their work in Africa, in Zambia. As Brown later explained, "I felt living in Africa was another way to see how Black people were going about liberating themselves."[28]

Brown had heard that, in the newly independent African nation of Zambia, they were hiring expatriate teachers to help with the program of national development, so she applied and accepted a position teaching high school. She arrived in Zambia with a keen awareness of a continent ravaged by the accumulation of histories of imperialism, slavery, and extractive capitalism. "They are not our roads," she wrote in 1972 in a poem called "Bushpaths":

> *That trample through the maize field*
> *And cramp the lion in her kingdom*
> *That steal across whole villages*
> *And parcel out the continent*
> *Into national thoroughfares*
> *To deliver the goods*
> *To Europe.*[29]

Brown was part of a larger wave of Black American civil rights activists who traveled to Africa in the 1960s and 1970s. "Since my mother is African, it was particularly for me 'going home,'" she later wrote. "But going 'back to Africa' was a crucial part of the civil rights movement: at once affirming a heritage which the white Establishment had trained Black people in the US to despise, and testing the limits of Black self-determination in an independent African state."[30] A number Black Panther Party members had traveled to Africa to create new lives in exile. Many went to Dar es Salaam, Tanzania, to witness for themselves and participate in Julius Nyerere's program of *Ujamaa*, or African socialism. Others went to Accra, Ghana, attracted by Kwame Nkrumah's vision of pan-Africanism, and others to Algiers and Nairobi and Lagos. Brown was one of three from her cohort of African-American faculty at San Francisco State University – the other two were Patricia Thornton, who, during her time in Southern Africa, took on the name Chinosole, and Jimmy Garrett – who made their way to Zambia.

Zambia was part of a global story about postcolonial Black sovereignty. Like Tanzania to the east, Zambia pursued a socialist path, funded in large part by the country's mineral wealth. Kenneth Kaunda, president and leader of the political party that led Zambia to independence from British colonial rule, financed social programs by partially nationalizing the mines, directing the wealth from copper mines toward the development of the country. Zambians were promised that the money from copper would be used for free education and healthcare, and for "milk and buns" for school children. The ambitious Tanzam railway, a collaboration with Tanzania funded by the Chinese, allowed newly sovereign African nations to bypass the ports of apartheid South Africa and instead ship out of Dar es Salaam.[31] Kaunda made it known that African-Americans were welcome in his country as part of the effort to build a modern African nation in the wake of colonial underdevelopment.[32] "Afro-Americans in the States could do a lot for Zambia by filling our manpower gap," he said before an audience of students and faculty at Cornell University in August 1970. James Brown, Arthur Ashe, and Duke Ellington were among those who visited Zambia during Wilmette Brown's years there.

Part of what placed Zambia in the 1970s in the story of Black liberation was its location in Southern Africa, surrounded by countries still fighting white minority rule. To the south in Rhodesia, ZANU and ZAPU were waging guerrilla warfare against Ian Smith's white supremacist minority regime. To the west and east, parties in Angola and Mozambique fought against Portuguese colonial rule. And in South Africa, Apartheid was the law of the land, Nelson Mandela in prison on Robben Island, and the ANC was banned. Zambia's capital of Lusaka became a hub for freedom fighters in exile from South Africa, Angola, Namibia, Mozambique, and Zimbabwe.[33]

Brown spent three years teaching high-school English, learning about the political struggles of the movements exiled in Lusaka, and writing poetry. In Africa, she searched for a kind of belonging that eluded her in the Black Panthers. But she didn't find it in Zambia. "During the time that I lived in Africa," she wrote, "it was very painful not to be able to connect in a certain way with African women on the continent because I could not get beyond the appearance of their subordination and dependency on men. I could not get beyond the appearance of their enslavement to motherhood and to rearing huge families of children."[34] Nor, despite her deep commitment to anti-colonial struggle, did she find personal fulfillment with the African liberation movements, which adhered to strict gendered ideologies, similar in some ways to the Black Panther Party she had left. Years later, Brown recalled that she had been "hoping that the African movements would be in a better place in terms of women." However,

Fundamentally, it wasn't. All during this time, I was going through a period of, on one hand, I had left the Panthers because I wasn't prepared to give up being a lesbian, but on the other it was very difficult to maintain because I was cut off from the power of the Black movement . . . It was a crock but you didn't want to be divided off from other black women . . . I kept thinking, "Well gee, maybe I just ought to give up. Is lesbianism just some trip I'm on or perversion on white influence?" I thought it was white corruption. At the same

143

time I found the same crap over the division of labor that I found in the States. Who did the typing as opposed to the content of the communiques coming out of the bush.[35]

She reflected further:

> The turning point for me came when brothers in the liberation movements said that after independence the women who had taken up arms as well as taken on the job of giving political leadership – all the while continuing to do the physical and emotional house-work, the washing-up, and taking care and putting the pieces back together for everybody, last and least of all for each other – would be going back to "normal." "Normal" was what I had been fighting against. In 1974 I returned to the US convinced that the best route to Black liberation – which had been called civil rights – was starting from my own experience as a woman.[36]

Brown was also increasingly frustrated by the position of African women, caught between multiple forms of reproductive coercion. The high school where she taught was funded by the World Bank, which, she later was dismayed to learn, stipulated that in order to be eligible for such schools and other forms of aid, African countries had to agree to population-control measures. Yet at the same time that women experienced policies meant to curtail their fertility, they faced cultural pressures in the opposite direction. "I used to hear about the African women who were having to fight with their husbands in order to get birth control pills and, you know, were actually like running away, and carrying on a big struggle to get the right to abortion."[37]

In spring 1974, after three and a half years in Zambia, Wilmette Brown came back to the United States. She moved to Brooklyn just after the early years of New York's feminist movement, and right in time for the city's fiscal crisis. She published some poetry reflecting on her experiences in Zambia in *Black World* and the lesbian feminist journal *Conditions*. She enrolled in an MA program in Anthropology at the New School for Social Research at a time when the department was offering new, cutting-edge courses on feminist economics. As usual, her academic work was inseparable from her activism outside the classroom.

One of the places where feminism intersected with the fiscal crisis was in the City University of New York (CUNY). While the city devised ways to slash the budgets, feminist faculty members were organizing to seize the university for women, claiming space on campus and setting up women's studies centers, lobbying to form Women's Studies departments, and breaking down the barriers between the university campus and the surrounding City of New York. Once again, Wilmette Brown found herself in a struggle for community control of the university. She got a job working with Brooklyn College for Project Chance, a program started by a group of socialist feminist faculty members, including Tucker Pamella Farley, which aimed to open the city college to include poor, working-class, and immigrant women, especially welfare mothers, from the surrounding community.[38] The program was part of a larger project to rethink the family and labor and the university. Farley and her collaborators asked critical questions: How does the university reproduce class? How does the professionalization and accreditation offered by universities affect women in particular, both in terms of the curricula on offer, and in terms of structural factors like availability of childcare and employment opportunities to women with college degrees? Instructors in the program recalled women enrolled in the program bringing their mothers and grandmothers and sisters to class with them. In the classroom, women talked about their experiences seeking an education, for example, being beaten by abusive partners for coming to class, or dropping out multiple times because of their carework responsibilities.[39] Wilmette Brown worked alongside Puerto Rican activist Digna Sanchez, developing a curriculum for women in the community, echoing some of the same principles of the struggle for Black Studies in San Francisco State: making university accessible and relevant to the community.[40]

Soon afterward, she became a member of the faculty at Queens College, in the SEEK Program. SEEK stands for Search for Education, Elevation, and Knowledge, and it was spearheaded in 1966 by civil rights leaders from New York as a program to make the city university system accessible to the city's residents, especially those historically excluded, including Black, Puerto Rican students, and all who had been underserved in their high schools. SEEK's teaching faculty included an extraordinary community of literary and intellectual luminaries, including poets Audre Lorde and Adrienne Rich and Joan Nestle, playwright Toni Cade Bambara, the Guyanese activist Andaiye, and the political organizer Margaret Prescod. Wilmette Brown started at the SEEK faculty at Queens College as a lecturer of Political Science.[41]

She joined a Black women's consciousness-raising group, together with Prescod, Lorde, and Andaiye. But for someone with her political experience, consciousness-raising was unsatisfying. She had faced down the police with the Black Panther Program. She had helped seize control of a public university. She had seen, first-hand, the rapacious effects of imperialism, extractive capitalism, and the military-industrial complex in Southern Africa. "I was fed up with consciousness raising," she recalled. "I already felt pretty conscious. It was a form of organization, but it wasn't one that dealt with how to organize. How do you confront the government? How do you confront men? How do you get higher wages?"[42] Still, there was one text she came across in her reading group that moved her: *The Power of Women and the Subversion of the Community*. Its analysis of the role of housework in global capitalism helped her to connect what she had struggled to reconcile in her own life and activism. She explained:

> It brought things home for me because I knew that my fight as a lesbian was a fight against doing the work that women were supposed to do . . . There is no separation between my fight as a lesbian or the fight of a prostitute woman or a woman who is on welfare or the question of sexuality as opposed to bread and butter issues.[43]

This shed light on her connection with welfare mothers and African mothers she had known in Southern Africa. She used it to make sense of the coercive sterilization of women of color around the world, which she now understood as an effort to control Black women's reproductive capacity and labor, and the fight against it as part of a broader struggle of all women to reclaim their bodies and labor from capitalism.[44]

Brown and Presod were all in for Wages for Housework. "I remember the day that Margaret and Wilmette came running down the street with a pamphlet by Selma in their hands," recalled their friend Andaiye.[45] Brown and Prescod gathered with their group in the newly formed campus Women's Center to discuss Wages for Housework and how it related to their political aims as Black women. They began attending the meetings of the New York Wages for Housework Committee, and soon were doing organizing of their own on the Queens College campus. They got in touch with Selma James and Mariarosa Dalla Costa and joined the international Wages for Housework campaign, and started their own group, Black Women for Wages for Housework.

In spring of 1976, Brown planned a trip to Europe, which began in Italy for the May Day demonstration in Naples. She took a flight to Brussels and, from there, made her way by train to Milan and then Padua. Dalla Costa was to meet her at the station early in the morning.

Mariarosa Dalla Costa's archives contain several mementos of Wilmette Brown's visit to Italy. There is video footage of the train ride down to Naples, with Lotta Femminista women singing and playing the guitar in the aisles. The atmosphere seems joyful and boisterous as the camera pans up and down the carriage, pausing briefly to capture a more quiet moment: Brown and Dalla Costa seated across from one another, leaning over a table deep in focus on a document as the landscape hurtles by outside the window.[46] There is a photograph of the two of them standing in a field, both looking gravely over their shoulders at the camera, an unnamed man with long hair lounging under a tree in the background.[47] There is a picture of Brown sitting in the grass at the May Day demonstration in Naples, wearing her usual jeans and plain T-shirt, and chunky-heeled boots, long earrings dangling by her neck. She is surrounded by young women and many have rolled up their pants and taken off their shoes, leaning against each other, some smoking, some in mid-conversation. There are pictures of her marching through the streets of Naples under the Salario al Lavoro Domestico banner as women bang on pots and pans with wooden spoons, holding megaphones to their mouths, chanting slogans and singing songs. Above them, elderly women and children are leaning out of windows and over balconies, waving the red flags of the PCI. That night, on stage, SLD groups from around Italy performed their songs to huge crowds of women dancing, singing, clapping, holding candles to light up the dark city square. In all of the photographs and videos, Wilmette Brown seems to be the only Black person present.

At a certain point in the trip, she got out her tape collection, which she had brought with her, and used it to structure a public talk connecting histories of racism and the Black liberation movement with the tenets of *operaismo* and Wages for Housework. It was a somewhat awkward experiment. She would speak for a few seconds, and then an interpreter would translate her words into Italian. Somewhere in the room, someone fumbled with the tapes and a tape player to coordinate Brown's playlist with her words. She played the John Coltrane song "Alabama," and told the story of the 1963 Baptist Church bombing, in Birmingham, and in the same year, of the March on Washington for Jobs and Freedom that she herself had been a part of. She played Bill Withers and the Isley Brothers and Nina Simone, commenting on how each selection fitted into the broader struggle for Black freedom in America. She gave the most attention to the Labelle album *Nightbirds*. "In the song 'Nightbird,'" she told the audience, "we can see that the moment of struggle of Black women which began with Nina Simone in the 60s with the hope to be able to fly is in fact realized in the autonomous organization of Black women." She continued, going through several more songs on the album. "In the song 'You Turn Me On,' you can see also the struggle of all women to find our own modes of sexuality and sexual expression and to realize ourselves as revolutionary subjects in all aspects of our life uniting the personal and the political."[48] In her discussion of each of the songs, which played in the background as she spoke, she worked to explicitly connect the lyrics to the Wages for Housework movement.

In the recording, Brown comes across as stilted but earnest. It's as though you can see her mind working, trying to connect her experience as a Black woman to the Italian context of *operaismo*, seeking a common struggle.

From Italy she went to Germany, and then to Paris. She addressed a conference convened by a collective of prostitutes. "I am Mary Brant," said a speaker, who is likely Brown herself, taking on the pseudonym Selma James had used in her original 1953 pamphlet "A Woman's Place." "I live in New York, and I work with a group of Black women who are fighting for Wages for Housework . . . I am here this evening to give my support to you in the struggle of women prostitutes in France, because this fight is also the fight of Black women in the United States . . . I salute you, and I am sure that our international struggle will win."[49] The speech cited almost verbatim much of the talk she had given in Padua, drawing on music as a way of illuminating themes of race and sex work in America. From there, she traveled to the UK, where her comrades in the Power of Women Collective had organized a speaking tour for her. Then she returned to New York to carry on with her work.

In July, Wilmette Brown prepared a speech for the occasion of an international Wages for Housework gathering in Toronto, convened by a group of lesbians who had recently joined the campaign. She used the occasion to reflect on her life up to that point. Wages for Housework revealed housework, housewives, and the nuclear family as integral to the entire global economic order; where did a

Black lesbian fit into this capitalist order of things? And where, then, did she fit into the struggle for freedom?

"The Black lesbian," Brown wrote, "is a super freak. Because not only is she a freak in relation to other women – because she is refusing heterosexual work – she is a freak from Blackness as well. Because Blackness under capitalism is defined sexually."[50] She gave a bit of historical context: under the American system of plantation slavery, she explained, Black women were treated as animals – as "breeders" – denied the possibility of femininity or marriage or motherhood on their own terms. In the aftermath of slavery, heterosexual marriage was held out as an antidote to the violence and instability of slavery. Generations later, marriage still offered the illusion of economic stability so often denied to Black women in reality, in the form of access to a Black man's wage and the social approval that comes from being in a nuclear family. In Brown's experience, the Black Power movement allowed Black women to "define some of our own interests, to begin to recover and to discover our dignity and our sense of self." However, "the price we had to pay was subordination . . . to the power of Black men, under the guise of Black liberation." Heterosexuality and subordination to men, she wrote, was a price she was not willing to pay.

Brown recalled how her inability, or refusal, to fit into culturally available versions of womanhood had caused her pain and isolation in her early adult life, but now she saw in those experiences a source of power and creativity and revolutionary potential. To identify as a Black lesbian was to reject capitalist discipline on Black women's bodies, and to reject economic dependence on men. The struggle of Black lesbians for economic autonomy is, by definition, a struggle against capitalism.

According to Brown, in order to access this radical potential, Black lesbians needed to be autonomous from Black men. But, as she told the audience of mostly white women, their needs could not simply be folded into a notion of universal sisterhood, as so many white feminists presumed. They also needed autonomy from white women who, while oppressed by patriarchal capitalism, enjoyed protections by virtue of their whiteness. They had access to white men's wages, and the cultural capital of respectable femininity. Their children were deemed deserving of protection, while Black women's children were subjected to racism and violence. These protections made white women's situation fundamentally different from that of Black women, and it made their freedom struggle different too. "It is Black women who work as maids for white women and not the other way around," she wrote. "We are the whores. We are the illegitimate mothers."[51]

Finally, she concluded, Black lesbian women needed autonomy from Black heterosexual women. Forced to bear children for the slave economy, pressured into respectable marriage for the sake of racial uplift, denied access to safe contraceptives, forced through economic scarcity into prostitution: so much of racism against Black women, Brown argued, had taken the form of "severe heterosexual discipline." Brown posed the question: "What is my connection as a Black lesbian woman – with the refusals that I have made – with Black women who have children, who are married to men?"[52]

Having begun to identify what was unique about her position as a Black lesbian, she could then uncover precisely what she shared in common with others. It all came back to the various forms of unpaid labor that capitalism demanded of women. Now, she said, she could understand her connection with the Southern African women caring for large extended families, and with welfare mothers who were dependent on the state and pathologized for their independence from men. She also saw connections with prostitutes, criminalized for laying bare what was supposed to be hidden: women's sexual subordination to men by virtue of their economic dependence. "The Wages for Housework perspective," she wrote, "has made it possible for me for the first time in my life to be able to connect with other Black women in whatever situation, because we are all struggling against housework, against heterosexual discipline, heterosexual work discipline, and for money – to be independent."[53]

8.

Margaret Prescod

Margaret Prescod (center) shaking hands with Johnnie Tillmon and Beulah Sanders at the 1977 National Women's Conference in Houston.

A photograph taken on the floor of the 1977 National Women's Conference in Houston frames a crowd of about a dozen and a half people, almost all of them Black women. At the center of the photograph is Margaret Prescod, co-founder of Black Women for Wages for Housework, her hair pulled back into a bun at the crown of her head, bag slung over her shoulder, wearing an apron, signifying that she was part of the Wages for Housework campaign. She is grinning and reaching her arm out to shake the hands of two other women. One of them is Johnnie Tillmon and the other is Beulah Sanders, the pioneering Black woman who led the National Welfare Rights

Organization in the 1960s. In the background, women hold up signs, including one that reads "Black Women Speak Out: No Cuts, Just Bucks," one of the slogans of Black Women for Wages for Housework. Other signs read "Welfare is a Wage," and "Every Mother is a Working Mother." In the background, over Prescod's shoulder, Wilmette Brown smiles broadly, holding up a sign that says: "Wages for Housework for All Women from the Government."[1]

This historic conference to honor the International Women's Decade marks a critical moment in the history of American feminism. The centerpiece of the conference was the nationwide struggle to ratify the Equal Rights Amendment. Iconic photographs of the event show Gloria Steinem, Coretta Scott King, Betty Friedan, and Shirley Chisholm speaking from the stage in front of a massive blue banner emblazoned with the word WOMAN. In perhaps the most well-known image from the conference, New York Congresswoman Bella Abzug, wearing her signature wide-brimmed hat, marches arm in arm with a multi-racial coalition of women in their pastel blue convention T-shirts that said "Women on the Move," holding aloft a torch that had been carried to Houston all the way from Seneca Falls, New York, symbolically linking the conference to the 1848 Seneca Falls convention that launched the suffragist movement. The ritual passing of the torch tells a story of continuity and progress from one feminist generation to the next: first voting rights, next equality in the workplace. Meanwhile, across town, a counter-convention led by conservative Phyllis Schlafly made the opposite argument: stop the ERA and defend the nuclear family and "traditional" gender roles. The ERA subsequently failed to gain the support needed to ratify it. The story of the struggle for the ERA is often told as a story about two opposed positions: women as equals in the workplace vs. women in the home as housewives. Democrats vs. Republicans.

The photograph of Prescod with the leaders of the welfare rights movement suggests an alternative feminist genealogy. Prescod, present at the conference as a delegate from the State of New York, came with a clear objective: to change the Plan of Action issued by the conference so that the right to welfare be defended, welfare payments be increased, and welfare recognized as a wage. A proposal by the Carter administration was already underway to reform welfare, adding onerous work requirements as a condition of eligibility. One of the key principles of this proposal was "to ensure that work will always be more profitable than welfare." In other words, welfare was defined as the opposite of work. Prescod saw things differently. She knew that raising children is hard work and that women on welfare are among society's hardest workers. In a newsletter printed up by Prescod and Brown and handed out at the convention, they wrote, "We don't need more work. We need more *money* to work less."[2]

Together, Black Women for Wages for Housework and welfare rights activists lobbied the conference delegates to recognize that women's unwaged work was a feminist issue. They faced stiff opposition, including from some whose priorities were in national party politics, and who tried to strip away any language critical of the Carter administration.[3] Yet after several days of lobbying, bolstered by support from delegates from several Southern states, the National Plan of Action ratified by the conference included a plank labeled Women, Welfare, and Poverty, which stated: "We support increased federal funding for income transfer programs. And just as with other workers, homemakers receiving payments should be afforded the dignity of having that payment called a wage, not welfare."

The conference's call to recognize and compensate women's unpaid work has not captured the imagination in the way the failed battle to ratify the ERA has in public memory. In the years that followed the conference, the mainstream feminist movement did not embrace welfare as a core priority, focusing more on legal rights than on economic justice. Carter's reforms were only the beginning of what was to come. Over the next two decades, welfare would be eviscerated, replaced with onerous workfare programs, bolstered in public discourse with the racist stereotype of the welfare queen. The demand encapsulated in the Women, Welfare, and Poverty plank of the Plan of Action, the result of lobbying and organizing by Black, working-class, and poor women, was perhaps the most visionary proposal to come out of the conference. Their aims were far more ambitious than legal equality with men. In their vision, recognizing poor women's unwaged work as having economic value was a first step in overturning every hierarchy entrenched over centuries of racial capitalism. This feminist path not yet taken is a product of the radically egalitarian imagination of Margaret Prescod.

In an event celebrating the fiftieth anniversary of Wage for Housework, Prescod reflected on what first drew her to the campaign.

> Part of what led me to Wages for Housework and to grasp it, not in an intellectual sense but in a very practical sense, was really my experience of the village. Watching the way the women worked there, whether it was Nana from across the street, who was really a full-time housewife, and who worked tirelessly caring for the nine or ten children she had, or other women who worked in the home and also worked in the fields. Few women worked in town, but all of those women, whatever they did, their first job was in the home, cooking the food and taking care of the children. It was an enormous amount of work and, of course, they got absolutely nothing for it. So, when I ran into Wages for Housework, and saw the button that says Wages for Housework, I thought of my mother, I thought of Nana. I thought of all those women from my village.[4]

When Prescod describes her childhood in Barbados, a common motif is the mail received from abroad. In Christ Church, the southernmost parish of Barbados, everybody knew someone who had relatives living and working abroad in New York, London, or other cities in the United States, Canada, and the UK. Prescod's grandmother lived and worked in New York as a domestic and in factories, leaving her daughter at home to be cared for by other relatives. Many of those who went abroad worked as housecleaners, nannies, health aides, or factory workers, and, especially if they were women, they would send home packages to those who remained behind. The parcels held a kind of fascination for the children, who looked forward to the boats coming into Bridgetown with the deliveries from abroad: handmade dresses, shoes, canned food, and other treats. Prescod recalled the anticipation they would feel at the possibility of a $20 bill tucked into the envelope brought by the mail carrier; a gift that, for some families, could mean the difference between a child continuing another semester at school, or having to drop out; a new pair of shoes for the season, or going barefoot. Prescod describes the mixed feelings evoked by the remittances: the exotic frilly dresses also made the wearer stand out among the other children; brand new shiny shoes that were too big had to be uncomfortably stuffed with crumpled paper to keep them from falling off.[5] The gossip about whose relative in America had a new television, and whether it was black and white or color, brought both excitement and a sense of a widening gap between those who still lived in Barbados and those who had left.[6]

Prescod grew up during the final years of British colonial rule in Barbados. She describes a childhood of relative poverty, imbued with the warmth of a close-knit community. She and her siblings roamed and played in the open fields near their house. Her parents, Elsa and Stanley, were schoolteachers who instilled in their children a sense of communal obligation and care for each other. Prescod recalls her and her sister being hungry at dinner time, begging to be allowed to eat, but her mother insisting that they first bring a plate to their elderly neighbor who lived alone before they could eat their share.[7] She remembers her father taking it upon himself to run around the community during Hurricane Janet of 1955, warning everyone to prepare for the storm.[8]

Eventually, the Prescods managed to leave Barbados, having made the heartbreaking decision to sell their family's small house to raise the funds to go abroad. "I remember my father putting up the 'For Sale' sign outside the house, a typical little Barbados wooden house. He and my mother had struggled for years to build that house and to pay for that house. And I remember the morning he painted the sign and was ready to put that sign up. He just sat in a chair, long drops of water coming out of his eyes, coming down his face. I felt all of that."[9] A photograph featured in the local newspaper *Barbados Advocate* shows Elsa Prescod with her three children, Margaret, Peter, and Rosie, in 1961, dressed up, ready to leave the island to move their family and seek new opportunities in New York City. In the photo, the girls wear pretty knee-length cotton dresses with puffed sleeves, white ankle socks, and bonnets in their hair. Their brother Peter wears a suit and tie.[10]

Years later, after she had traveled the world, participated in various political organizing drives, worked with mothers, and become a mother herself, her childhood in Barbados took on additional layers of meaning for Prescod. In a panel discussion I attended in January 2021, she was asked to reflect on her first political act. "I actually think I did it when I was four years old," she said. She told us how she had fled her family home in protest when her grandmother, visiting from Brooklyn, had proposed that she return with her, leaving her parents and siblings behind. "I refused and ran out of the house," she said. "There was no way I was going to leave my mother, father, sister, brother, no matter how much of a big house they said I would live in, or how many pretty, pretty dresses I would have. I preferred to live close to relative poverty than the riches of the United States and to be torn apart from my family."[11] What at the time she experienced as a personal family drama, years later she came to understand as deeply political; an economic reality that was wrong in a way she could feel in her entire being, even before she had the words to articulate the reasons why. Now, with the hindsight of decades of political organizing with poor mothers who are often torn apart from their children by either labor migration or the state child-welfare system, she understands her act of refusal as a rejection of a brutal global economic system that tears families apart.

She also learned that the beloved family house that her father had wept for was called a "chattel house," a style of house that sat on cement blocks, rather than being anchored into the ground, easily assembled and disassembled: movable, like the formerly enslaved people who inhabited them but could not own the land upon which they sat. The open field not far from their old house where she and her sister would run around and play turned out to be part of the island's cruel history as well: in the 1970s, archeologists discovered that it was the site of the largest slave burial ground in the Americas, where slaves who worked at nearby sugar plantations were interred. But despite the poverty of her childhood village, Prescod discovered, Barbados had, at one time, been the richest colony in the British empire. It was there that plantation owners innovated a system for producing sugar that would soon become the template for the most brutal and profitable forms of plantation slavery. As a laboratory of the plantation system and a leading global producer of sugar – the key commodity of Europe's consumer revolution, fueling the daily rhythms of the industrial proletariat – Barbados was far from a village backwater: it sat at the very heart of racial capitalism. The family names of the great sugar barons whose wealth was acquired on the backs of enslaved men and women in Barbados still adorn the buildings of the most prestigious university campuses in the US and UK.[12]

Her ancestors had produced the wealth that would build sumptuous mansions and universities in England and the USA, and yet her community survived by sending its people to work in low-wage jobs abroad. "Looking around us," she wrote, "we knew that our lives in the village were about work, were about years, centuries of hard work. Every year, day in and day out, it's the same thing. And it was clear that the wealth that we were creating was not there – we had to go and get it."[13]

In 1961, the Prescods joined the wave of migration from the West Indies to New York. But it was not the land of opportunity and wealth they had been led to expect. The mailed parcels that arrived in Barbados told a story about the wealth available abroad, but it hid evidence of the personal toll these journeys took on those who made them. Life was hard for immigrants. Prescod had left a village that was like an extended family, where everyone looked after each other's children. Unlike the collective ethos of care modeled by her mother, in her Brooklyn neighborhood families were isolated in their brownstone apartments. Many West Indian women would ride the subway across the boroughs to clean or work as nannies in the houses of wealthier families, for wages so low that few were able to bring their own children from the islands to live with them in the United States.

At first, Prescod said, "I considered myself a kind of non-political party girl on the circuit of New York City transitioning from a village girl to a city girl."[14] At the same time, her family nurtured her political instincts. Her grandmother had been married to a Garveyite – a follower of the ideals of pan-Africanist visionary Marcus Garvey – and other members of the extended family had become Garveyites as well.[15] As packages went back and forth between New York and Barbados, so did ideas about Black freedom. Prescod and her sister went to live in Brooklyn with their aunt, Mildred Scott, who was active with the Congress of Racial Equality (CORE). Almost immediately after arriving, Prescod found herself on a picket line with her at SUNY Downstate Medical Center, where CORE shut down a worksite for a new facility in protest of racist hiring practices, demanding that Black and Puerto Ricans be hired.[16] "We would take a little paper bag lunch and we would stand there and block the cement trucks," Prescod recalled. "And that's how we would spend our summers."[17]

After finishing high school, Prescod went to Long Island University, and following in her mother's path became an elementary-school teacher. Her first job was in the Ocean Hill–Brownsville neighborhood of Brooklyn, Selma James' old neighborhood, which, by the 1960s, had become a predominantly Black community and a key site in struggles for civil rights. She joined the African-American Teachers Association – an organization that had originally been formed in 1964 as a subsidiary of the United Federation of Teachers (UFT), in protest of the union's slow and lukewarm response to racial integration of the schools. Many Black teachers were frustrated by what they saw as the union's indifference toward addressing racism and helping Black students access the resources that the state was obligated to provide. Black parents and teachers protested the poor treatment of Black students in schools, and former students recall the condescension and contempt they experienced from some of their white teachers.[18] The reality in Ocean Hill–Brownsville was that most teachers did not live in the same neighborhoods as their students and did not know their lives outside the school day and year. Some teachers resented the demands of the community as an attack on their authority as professionals and on their power as unionized workers. The African-American Teachers Association demanded an anti-racist curriculum that would include lessons on Black culture and history. They also demanded that an effort be made to hire more Black teachers, and that white teachers involve Black parents in decisions about the education of their children.

With a Ford Foundation grant, in the 1967–68 school year, Ocean Hill–Brownsville was one of several New York districts that experimented with community control of schools, allowing school boards selected by community members to participate in day-to-day decisions about how to run the schools. In Black neighborhoods, teachers introduced Black History into the curriculum. Schools serving a predominantly Puerto Rican population introduced bilingual education. But New York's experiment in community control of schools was short-lived. It ended in a dispute when the community board in Ocean Hill–Brownsville fired thirteen teachers. The UFT responded with a strike that shut down the schools for six weeks. In the end, the district was placed again under state control.[19]

Prescod started teaching in Ocean Hill–Brownsville right after the community-control experiment ended. It was a formative experience for her. During her lunch break, rather than sit with her fellow teachers, most of whom were white, she would sit with the school aides, who were mostly lower-paid women of color.[20] She got to know her students and their families. "It was there that I got to work with, and was trained by, welfare mothers," Prescod recalled. "Welfare mothers were central to that struggle, although they have not been credited. We raised all kinds of hell. They taught me what their children needed."[21] Prescod saw that many of the same mothers, who were depicted in the media as lazy, as unfit parents, as living on "handouts," were leaders in their community, advocating for their children, and all children in the community. Far from idle, Black mothers were doing necessary and unpaid work to fill in the gaps of a system that was failing their kids, and to repair the damage of systemic racism. Raising and educating children in a racist system depended on Black women's unpaid work.

After the struggle over community control at Ocean Hill–Brownsville, some members of the African-American Teachers Association concluded that the public schools could not be reformed enough to meet the needs of the community and left the public-school system to form their own institutions to do that work. Prescod went in a different direction and started working at the City University of New York in Queens, where she met Wilmette Brown.

The collaboration that would become Black Women for Wages for Housework grew out of an extraordinary community of activists, intellectuals, and feminists affiliated with the SEEK program at CUNY, Queens. Margaret Prescod was hired as one of their instructors to work in remedial education for students who had come from underserved high schools. Prescod and Wilmette Brown formed a Black women's reading group, which also included poet Audre Lorde and fellow SEEK instructor Andaiye, a literature teacher and activist from Guyana.[22] They gathered in the newly formed campus Women's Center to discuss Wages for Housework and how it related to their political organizing as Black women. From early on, they knew that they wanted to start their own Wages for Housework group. Wilmette Brown and Margaret Prescod helped organize the New York Wages for Housework Committee Welfare Conference in April 1976, and they led much of the discussion that went on at the conference, drawing on Prescod's experience working with welfare mothers and connecting their struggles with the international Wages for Housework campaign. By the end of the conference, Prescod and Brown officially launched

Black Women for Wages for Housework. They started holding weekly meetings.

Soon afterwards, they issued a Birth Announcement, complete with an image of a stork carrying a bundle in its beak. "We are pleased to announce our presence as an autonomous group of Black Women for Wages for Housework," it began. "Our group is a rainbow of Black women; some of us are married, some are single; some of us have children, some don't; some of us are straight, some are lesbian; some of us have second jobs, some are on welfare; some of us are older, some younger. ALL OF US WANT WAGES FOR HOUSEWORK."[23]

Though at first they joined with the New York Committee, Brown and Prescod both later said that they discovered genuine collaboration to be impossible. "When I first got involved in Wages for Housework," Brown recalled, "there were a number of social workers, white social workers. Some of those social workers found that they weren't really ready to organize with Black women who had less money than they did and who were lower in that hierarchy."[24] Prescod and Brown had years of experience with grassroots organizing in Black communities. Prescod reflected that there was no way she could join a majority-white organization, in which the ideas of Black women would be used but their leadership not recognized, without some way of protecting their autonomy. In recent years, she has written that she personally experienced racism from members of the New York and Italian branches of the campaign.[25] Both Brown and Prescod felt they had more in common with Selma James, who had a long experience in anti-racist activism with Black organizers, and they looked to her for support.

For Black Women for Wages for Housework, autonomy was much more than a defensive gesture; it was a positive, productive, creative act. They took care to distinguish "autonomy" from "separatism," a term much debated among feminists at the time. Some feminist groups argued that, to free themselves, women needed to be separate from men; or that lesbians needed to organize separately from straight women. Autonomy, by contrast, was about seeking a space from which to identify one's unique experience – whether as lesbians or Black women – and to have that space defended and respected as a place of safety, creativity, and political theorizing, yet to do so while acting in awareness of, and accountability to, the collective aims of a larger movement. The thinking was: everyone loses when oppressed people are splintered and divided from each other. Various groups, whether Black women, lesbian women, disabled women, all shared a common enemy in capitalism and its cannibalization of women's unwaged work. As an organizing practice, autonomy created space for the specificity of different struggles, to allow people to speak from their own experiences, in their own words, yet to participate in a broader struggle – for, without the broader struggle, a minority movement had little chance of winning. And winning was always the point.

Black Women for Wages for Housework was inspired by a group of lesbians in Toronto who, a few months earlier, had joined Wages for Housework as an autonomous group called Wages Due Lesbians. Boo Watson and Francie Wyland were driving around Ontario in their feminist bookmobile, fashioned out of an old school bus, when they came across one of the Wages for Housework pamphlets in their inventory. As lesbians, they were particularly interested in how it pertained to their struggles over child custody. In Canada, as in the US and UK, lesbians were discriminated against in child-custody laws, which pressured many to remain in heterosexual marriages for fear of being deemed "unfit mothers" and losing their kids. They saw a striking resemblance to the struggles of welfare mothers, who lived with the constant surveillance of their sex lives by the state to qualify for their benefits. In Wages for Housework, they saw an argument for financial autonomy and freedom from compulsory heterosexuality. Wages Due Lesbians theorized unwaged work from the perspective of lesbians, contributing their strength and insight to a collective struggle without being subsumed within it.[26] This became the organizing model for Wages for Housework, including Black Women for Wages for Housework. As Wilmette Brown put it, "Our autonomy is not a splitting of our power but really an extension of our power. Because the more we are able to articulate each and every one of our needs and to organize on the basis of those needs, the stronger we become."[27]

In fall 1976, at the height of New York City's fiscal crisis, months after the city announced that it would start charging tuition in its public universities, a story broke in city newspapers claiming that CUNY students, particularly those who were mothers, were defrauding the government by collecting two kinds of benefits – welfare and student benefits. Though student grants and loans were often paid directly to the university and not to the students themselves, the Tuition Assistance Program (TAP) was categorized as "discretionary income" and therefore counted against students' eligibility to collect welfare. In early November 1976, working-class mothers across the city received letters from the executive director of the New York City Agency for Child Development, telling them that they were no longer eligible for publicly funded daycare because they were receiving assistance for their four-year college degree program. Local media outlets depicted the students as savvy scammers, expert in gaming the system to collect duplicate payments.

Brown and Prescod's first action as Black Women for Wages for Housework was to form the Queens College Action Group, a coalition of students and community members fighting to defend students who collected welfare. They met every Tuesday at 1 p.m. Their slogan got right to the point: "No Cuts, Just Bucks." They held speak-outs, inviting students in the SEEK program to testify about their lives and their work, both inside and outside the classroom. "The first thing I do when I wake up – the first thing I start thinking about is my financial situation, and how I can handle this problem so I can attend school," one woman said. "Fridays I go to unemployment, where I try to hide the fact that I'm in school in hoping to get a higher-paying job when I get my degree."[28] Some students recited hour-by-hour daily logs of their work, describing a day that began early with a full slate of household responsibilities, taking kids to school or elderly relatives to doctor's appointments, a full day of classes on campus, followed by a shift at their paid job, then home for more housework, finally starting their homework after everyone else is asleep. Unlike the typical image of college students living together in dorms, dividing their time between studies and part-time jobs and partying, these students had major responsibilities. Many were in college in hopes of someday being able to earn higher salaries to support their families, and to lessen their onerous work burdens. Many of them had children of their own, and no access to reliable childcare, especially now that the city was cutting subsidized childcare. Prescod affirmed the importance of CUNY's generous open admissions policies, guaranteeing a spot to all New York high-school graduates, and was invested in the remedial education that she provided to students in SEEK but insisted that these were only the first steps in making the university accessible to all. If the entirety of students' lives was considered, and particularly all of the unpaid work they were doing, they would need additional forms of support in order to succeed as college students. As one flyer read, "We are the same women whether we're holding a dish towel, a baby, or a chemistry textbook. And we know wherever we are – campus or community – we are expected as women to work for free."[29]

In an article in the *Phoenix* – a CUNY Queens campus newspaper – Margaret Prescod wrote:

> Many women students are constantly being told by Income Maintenance workers, supervisors, etc., at the welfare offices that they should be out working and not spending their time as students. Two assumptions are being made here: 1. Women on welfare are not working. 2. Being a student is not work. These are attacks not only on women on welfare who are also students, but attacks on *all women* and *all students*. Going to School is Work! The Stipend is not charity, it's a wage![30]

Black Women for Wages for Housework argued that college tuition and welfare were not duplicate but separate payments – or wages – for two kinds of essential work: the work of studying in order to do higher-skilled work, and the work of caring for children.

The number of women directly affected by the specific predicament of the double payments was relatively small, but they stood at the intersection of two much bigger struggles that Prescod and Brown wanted to connect. They asserted that if you are a woman who does housework, you have a stake in the struggle of these students, for the same principles that devalue these mothers' work devalue yours. Similarly, if you are a student, the argument that a scholarship is charity, rather than payment in recognition of socially valuable work, denigrates you, casts you as a debtor rather than someone contributing to society by educating yourself. In recognizing the rights of these women to further their education while also doing the work of social reproduction, Queens College Action Group affirmed the rights of *all* women and *all* students to do so.

What Prescod saw in these attempts to roll back benefits was a system that has contempt for women, and especially poor mothers. As a case in point, welfare recipients who qualified for subsidized daycare for their children could enroll in two-year degree programs but would lose those benefits if they enrolled in four-year programs. Prescod considered this as proof of the real intentions of welfare: to keep women in low-paid jobs as a kind of underclass. She wrote:

> When a woman . . . tries to become economically independent and raise her standard of living, thereby expanding the possibilities for herself and her children, she is harassed by welfare and her children are thrown out of daycare. We can only see this as an attempt to use welfare as something against us, to discourage us from collecting that money in the first place, and at the same time forcing us into the lowest-paying and dirtiest jobs . . . In other words, one is not allowed to move from welfare to physicist but from welfare to lunchroom assistant.[31]

Many men from the SEEK program joined their campaign. In various neighborhoods in Brooklyn and Queens, young Black and Latino men could be seen wearing bright orange buttons with the Black Women for Wages for Housework slogan in red lettering: No Cuts! Just Bucks! "The men who were SEEK students who hadn't forgotten the experience of their mothers being on welfare, and so didn't feel threatened by women demanding money but saw the advantage for them," Prescod recalled. "These men were able to come around the Action Group and say, 'Well, we know there's something in here for us also, what can we do to help?'"[32] They would join them at their meetings and events, acting like bodyguards, waiting outside the CUNY president's office while the women were inside staging a sit-in.

The Queens College Action Group, together with Black Women for Wages for Housework, took their demands to president Saul Cohen's office, and then beyond, to the Board of Education, holding a speak-out in February 1978. About 100 people attended, including faculty, staff, and students.[33] Paula Henderson, a single mother, student, and member of Black Women for Wages for Housework, read a statement on behalf of the group to the Board of Education, ending with these words: "We as women and as a people have worked long and hard; it is upon our wageless work that this city and this county were built. We are not begging; we have earned the right not to be poor. We are entitled to our money!"[34] They lobbied Al Vann, the progressive New York State representative from Central Brooklyn and champion of civil rights and welfare, whom Prescod knew from their days together in the African-American Teachers Association in Ocean Hill–Brownsville. At his invitation, the Queens College Action Group took a bus up to Albany to speak in the assembly in support of his bill, proposing that student grants in four-year degree programs should not count as income, and therefore should not disqualify them from other forms of support, such as welfare. In June 1980, Al Vann's Bill 1564 passed the New York State legislature, stating that educational grants or loans to students would not count against their eligibility for welfare.[35]

The Queens College Women's Action Group, led by Margaret Prescod, lobbied for daycare facilities on campus for students, faculty, and all workers at the university.[36] They demanded that student stipends should be in line with the cost of living. They also demanded a women's center and support for a women's studies program, and the creation of a welfare advocacy center on site, separate from the financial aid office, tasked with helping underserved students access information on welfare rights, housing, and social services. This too challenged the discourse on welfare: whereas public perception was of a system that was overused, the Action Group reframed it – accurately– as a system that was dramatically underused.[37] Claiming the money they were already legally entitled to was a first step toward eventually claiming the rest.

Reading about the Queens College Action Group now, as a professor at a public university beleaguered by the constant threat of budget cuts, I'm humbled by the ambition, idealism, and creativity of Prescod's vision of a university in which care is supported as part of how we educate each other, rather than shunted off campus, out of sight, out of mind, as though the university and the pursuit of knowledge can exist without it.

"For years welfare recipients have been labeled as lazy, dependent, indifferent child-breeders with little ambition or self-respect. But now, there has emerged an organization that views these same women as pioneers in the struggle against the oppression of all families."[38] So wrote journalist Gail F. Baker in the *Chicago Defender* in April 1977, when Wilmette Brown and Margaret Prescod were visiting Chicago. As part of a longer trip across the country, they gave talks at community centers and appeared on local television programs and on call-in radio programs, where listeners – many of them housewives – would call in to talk about Wages for Housework.

That year, Brown and Prescod connected with other groups with similar aims. They found natural allies in Wages Due Lesbians, who, like welfare mothers, defended their work as mothers outside the heterosexual nuclear family and a state apparatus that sought to force them into nuclear families, under threat of having their kids taken away. Wages Due Lesbians and Black Women for Wages for Housework also made connections with the struggles of sex workers. In the most immediate sense, the police harassment of sex workers in public spaces reminded them of how their own gay bars and hangout spaces were patrolled. A statement from Wages for Housework activists in California in 1977 proclaimed: "An Attack on Prostitutes is an Attack on All Women." Stripping away notions of morality and respectability, they saw it as a matter of labor and economics: sex work was work. They argued that the division between paid sex and unpaid sex was arbitrary in a society where women were financially dependent on men, and in which women's bodies were commoditized. "Although the government tries to isolate our struggles," they wrote, "we refuse to be divided. All work is prostitution, and we are all prostitutes. We are forced to sell our bodies – for room and board or for cash, in marriage, on the street, in typing pools or in factories." Wages for Housework, they argued, would free women up to refuse prostitution, and, for that matter, to refuse heterosexual marriage if they so chose.[39]

Black Women for Wages for Housework took the analysis further, in an essay called "Money for Prostitutes is Money for Black Women." Drawing on the collective wisdom of their group, Prescod and Brown wrote:

> The struggles of prostitute women against police harassment on the streets, against beatings, against fines and jails, against being declared "unfit mothers" in the courts and having our children taken away, against being treated like animals and outcasts, against pimps, racketeers and businesses that profit from our misery, and, what is key to all these attacks, against not having any money to call our own, are struggles that we as Black women are forced to make.

Black women shared with prostitutes of all races the experience of police violence and harassment. To be a Black woman in public in a racist society, they argued, is already to be suspected of prostitution, to face harassment. They linked the plight of sex workers with the demand for welfare; a refusal to be penniless; a refusal to work for free. Prostitutes, they said, were used as a whip against other women; used to show just how low someone could sink, how desperate things could get, to keep all women in line. Rather than respond by distancing themselves, denying the accusation and taking pains to differentiate how they were different or more respectable or better than prostitutes, Black Women for Wages for Housework took the opposite approach: to emphasize their sameness, their unity. What prostitutes and mothers who demanded welfare and all who demanded wages for housework shared in common was poverty, the audacity to put a price on their work, refusing to work for free.[40]

They made common cause with sex worker advocacy groups, including US Prostitutes, Prostitutes of New York (PONY), and Call Off Your Old Tired Ethics (COYOTE), "a loose women's organization" founded by Margo St James in San Francisco. St James had become a fierce advocate of sex-worker rights after being arrested for prostitution and then living with the consequences of having it on her police record. She founded COYOTE, opened a sex-worker healthcare center in San Francisco, and coordinated the annual Hookers Ball fundraiser, which drew up to 200,000 people. Flamboyant and irreverent, one year she rode into the ball on a horse. Together, in 1977, Margo St James and Wilmette Brown went on a speaking tour on the theme Hookers and Housewives.[41]

As part of this collaboration, in May 1977, for Mother's Day, Wages for Housework groups across the US staged a series of mock trials in Boston, Los Angeles, and San Francisco. Turning the moralizing language of prostitution on its head, they accused the state and businesses of "pimping." They wrote scripts in which members of the group, playing the roles of judges, defendants, lawyers, and star witnesses, accused police officers, politicians, and businesses of "pimping" off the unpaid work of women. In Los Angeles, on the day of the event, they marched to the protest site banging on pots and pans to announce their arrival. The accused came dressed up like corporate fat cats, with cigars and bowler hats. Over the course of the mock trials, the "prosecution" accused credit-card companies, who honored charges made at massage parlors that relied on the criminalized labor of prostitutes; hotels that gave rooms to men who took prostitutes there; cops who harassed prostitutes while profiting off their illicit trade; church leaders who shamed women while not providing them with other options for their well-being and the care of their children; and customers who didn't stand up to defend the women they paid for sex. A whole cast of characters profited from sex work, but only the prostitute was criminalized. The script read: "The twenty dollars it costs to keep a woman in jail for a day could pay for her education and childcare." Writ large, the mock trial raised a bigger question: what was the state's interest in the criminalization of prostitution?

The Boston trial was held on the Boston Common. Participants posted a sign on the trunk of a tree that read "The Women's Court." Before an assembled crowd of around one hundred people, Wilmette Brown, in the role of prosecuting attorney, read out her lines: "The state tries to divide us from each other. They tell us that prostitutes are 'sluts,' welfare women are lazy bums, lesbians, queers, because these women have refused to work for free. They want to divide us into bad women and good women – the good women work hard for nothing. But women are refusing to be divided. We're all struggling to refuse our unpaid work."[42] All three mock trials ended in the same verdict: prostitution must be decriminalized. At the Los Angeles trial, Prescod's closing line was: "Your honor, that is a good beginning but only a beginning. What we really want is the money and therefore the power to get these pimps off of our backs. We demand wages for housework for every woman so that we can refuse to prostitute ourselves in any way – on the street, in marriage, at the office or in typing pools." The problem with sex work, in other words, was not the sex part but the work part.

Then, in San Francisco, Boston and Los Angeles, a final line was read out by the judge: "I hereby sentence the defendants to an ETERNITY OF UNPAID HOUSEWORK."[43]

★

The year 1977 was incredibly generative for Black Women for Wages for Housework, culminating that November at the National Women's Conference in Houston. When Margaret Prescod and Wilmette Brown and their Wages for Housework sisters showed up at the International Women's Year Conference, wearing their aprons that said "Every Mother is a Working Mother," they announced a struggle that was simultaneously grassroots and global in scope. They brought with them a newsletter they had created called *Safire*, laying out their vision. The term "Safire" was a re-appropriation of the racist Sapphire stereotype, from the 1950s radio and television *Amos 'n' Andy* show, which portrayed the Black character Sapphire Stevens as aggressive, overbearing, and materialistic. With this re-appropriation, they turned the stereotype on its head and presented themselves as part of a global movement of Black women who were righteous, informed, organized, and materialist in their analysis. In *Safire*, Prescod and Brown connected their platform for the Houston conference – that welfare be recognized as a wage – with a broader global vision. They framed welfare payments as "the basis of our power to demand everything else." Black welfare mothers, in their view, "established once and for all that EVERY MOTHER IS A WORKING MOTHER. They won the first wage for housework. In claiming their money, they staked everyone's claim."[44]

What they elaborated in *Safire* was not just a transfer of money to include Black women in middle-class life but an inroad toward a fundamentally different kind of world. They quoted from James Baldwin's *The Fire Next Time*: "Do I really want to be integrated into a burning house?" Prescod and Brown recast Baldwin's line through the perspective of Black domestic workers who serviced white middle-class America as housecleaners, caregivers, and nannies. "To be equal with white Americans was not our idea of paradise," they wrote. "We knew it from living in their homes, doing their housework."

They contrasted Wages for Housework with the Equal Rights Amendment. "Equal compared to what?" they asked. "Equal pay for equal work is the Man's best cover for getting us all to work more, for next to nothing." Equal pay for equal work did nothing to address the way work was itself gendered. It assumed that work was rewarding, something that was not true for poor women, for whom employment usually meant degrading jobs at poverty wages. Prescod and Brown presented Wages for Housework as an alternative path to liberation. Then they widened the aperture to reveal a global movement: welfare mothers protesting for their benefits in the US; mothers in South Africa caring for the wasted bodies of sons and husbands who mined the gold that underwrote the global economy; the Iceland women's strike of 1975, in which women marched in the streets and refused housework for a day. As Prescod wrote:

> Now when the State decides that it's going to move against women on welfare, it can no longer isolate those women and say, "They're just some Black women over there who are lazy, who want to collect some money," because there's a whole international campaign going on with women saying, "No more. We're all doing housework and we're all going to get together and demand our money."[45]

Brown and Prescod brought distinct and complementary political approaches to Black Women for Wages for Housework. In archival audio recordings, Wilmette Brown comes across as bookish and professorial – she was, after all, a professor. She framed Wages for Housework as an extension of the Black freedom movement as embodied by its great revolutionary minds: Frantz Fanon and Malcolm X and Eric Williams and Martin Luther King Jr. She imagined how a global network of women demanding wages for housework and their vision of a world beyond racial capitalism might go down in history like the original pan-Africanist conferences of the first half of the twentieth century.[46] She thought and spoke in grand historic terms.

Prescod's public persona is more down to earth. She is colloquial in her style; she laughs, code-switches, and uses slang, depending on her audience. When speaking in public, she elaborates her anticapitalist politics from the lives and insights of grassroots people.

Where Brown quotes Fanon, Prescod uplifts welfare mothers, children, prostitutes, undocumented immigrants, and even delinquent teenagers as her teachers. She aims her anti-capitalist analysis less at abstract historical systems than at their visible everyday manifestations, in the denial of dignity and worth to people she knows and cares about. Listening to her speeches from over four decades of her career, I am struck by how she rigorously, consistently, and with absolute clarity refuses any political logic of divide and rule in which some lives – sex workers' lives, incarcerated people's lives, drug users' lives, undocumented women's lives, Black women's lives – are deemed to be of less value than others. And when she describes her commitment to Wages for Housework, it is less as a dramatic intellectual conversion than an organic continuation of what she has known and had fought for her entire life.

As I follow the paths of Prescod and Brown through the archives of 1970s feminism, from the time they started Black Women for Wages for Housework, the conversations about "housework" become more and more capacious. Participants in conversations and demonstrations become more queer, more Black and Brown, more poor and working class. Conceptions of housework explode outside the walls of the nuclear family home, so that housework is more than a married woman serving her husband and children: it's also someone who takes it upon herself to feed and check in on her elderly neighbor; it's a mother spending hours of her days fighting to get basic social services for her kid, and, in the absence of those services, trying to provide them herself; it's sex workers, criminalized for trying to get paid for their services, rather than living in virtuous poverty. This radical expansion of "housework" sparked new conversations and solidarities, such as this one, from 1980: Iris De La Cruz, a former sex worker, recovering heroin addict, and spokesperson for Prostitutes of New York (PONY) interviewed Yolanda Jones, a member of Black Women for Wages for Housework on her radio show for WBAI, a local New York public radio station. A few months earlier, when a venue tried to back out of a contract to rent their space to PONY for their annual Hookers Ball fundraiser, Black Women for Wages for Housework had shown up on a picket line to support them. [47] Now, the two women met to talk in more depth about what they had in common.

Iris De La Cruz: "What does Wages for Housework have to do with prostitution?"

Yolanda Jones: "Well, first of all, Iris, let's face it: the whole deal in terms of marriage is a form of prostitution, OK? You give your husband a certain amount of services and in return he gives you a certain amount of cash."

Iris De La Cruz: "I see it. But I don't think the people out there would see the correlation between housewives and prostitutes. I've always been led to believe, at least when I was hustling, that there's a big difference between good girls and bad girls, that hookers are out there for sex and housewives bring up the children. Fact is . . . most hookers and prostitutes have kids."[48]

Over the course of an hour, they contemplated money and work, both paid and unpaid, in their lives and communities. They talked about the harassment by police that women faced when they tried to get paid for their various forms of work. They talked about student debt and all the women they knew who turned tricks to pay their way through college. Iris spoke about finding political allies in gay men, because, she suggested, they understand patriarchy and the pressures of compulsory heterosexuality and housework in ways that straight men never could. A few years after this conversation, Iris De La Cruz tested positive for HIV and became a vocal member of ACT UP, the historic, pathbreaking HIV-AIDS self-advocacy organization that responded to the epidemic of the 1980s. De La Cruz, who wrote a column under the pen name "Iris with the Virus," became an outspoken, irreverent, and compassionate observer of her community as it struggled with death, stigma, and copious amounts of loving, unpaid carework in the face of a bigoted society that had left them to die. She died in 1991 at the age of thirty-seven. I encounter this conversation between Iris De La Cruz and Yolanda Jones as an unintended time capsule, one small window into the kinds of connections and coalitions that become possible when women start to talk about their unpaid work.

Throughout the second half of the 1970s, Prescod was a regular presence in Queens College President Saul Cohen's office, bringing various demands on behalf of students and employees of the CUNY system. She made herself a thorn in his side for years until, in 1979, after a sabbatical in Los Angeles, she decided to stay on the West Coast. In 1980, Prescod and Brown both left New York. Margaret Prescod married Selma James' son, Sam Weinstein and organized with Wages for Housework in Los Angeles. Weinstein got to work as a union organizer with Southern California Gas and Electric. They were married for five years and in that time they had a daughter. A photograph accompanying a newspaper article in the *Los Angeles Times* shows Sam and Margaret walking side by side, their daughter Chanda perched atop her father's shoulders.[49]

Wilmette Brown moved to the UK to join the Crossroads Women's Centre, where she would deepen her political analysis on the intersections between imperialism, racism, environmentalism, and war. From their new respective new homes, Prescod and Brown continued to pursue the global and historic implications of their basic premise: that global capitalism had been built, and continued to develop, on the backs of Black women's unwaged work. Wages for Housework was a form of reparations.

9.

Reclaiming the Earth

In 1980, while in Copenhagen for the UN World Conference on Women, Wilmette Brown suddenly collapsed in pain. After being rushed back to the UK, she was hospitalized, diagnosed with colon cancer, and began to undergo treatment administered by NHS nurses and staff. "Recovering," she wrote, "involved not only the emotional and physical work of learning how to be at home again in my body, but the political work of negotiating the international economic order as it was practiced at my bedside." Day in and day out, as immigrant NHS nurses cared for her, beyond the hospital walls politicians decried immigrants as "freeloaders" and cut funding to the NHS. "This is not 'the triumphant story of one woman's victory over cancer,'" she wrote. "My cancer crisis was less the poetry of facing imminent death than weathering the daily harassment of life in the 80s."[1] Brown described how cancer had led her deep into her own body. At the same time, she understood her illness as the embodiment of global processes of environmental racism, war, and capitalism. Cancer is presented to the patient as an individual, heroic fight for survival, but for Wilmette Brown, together with her Wages for Housework sisters, it raised a bigger political question: how do you confront capitalism across boundaries?

Wages for Housework was perhaps never more alien from the zeitgeist than in the 1980s. In Britain, Margaret Thatcher's government orchestrated the selling-off of public goods, including public transit, housing, and land. They slashed the NHS budget. Council flats were sold to private owners at low prices, initially giving a generation of working-class people an opportunity to own their own homes. Soon, though, housing prices soared as flats formerly rented out at stabilized prices were subleased at inflated prices by the private landlords who now owned them. Women entered the workforce in higher numbers, and the biggest proportion were women with children under the age of five.

In Britain's cities, Black youth faced regular police harassment, and violent repression when they protested. Tactics that had been developed for counter-insurgency measures in Northern Ireland were brought "home" to police various sectors of the British public: striking miners and protesters, gays and lesbians, football "hooligans," and, most frequently, Black youth. Some immigrant Londoners would find swastikas painted on their houses and racial slurs shouted at them in the streets. Throughout the 1980s, the white supremacist National Front terrorized Asian families in a wave of arson attacks.

In response, the Greater London Council declared 1984 a "year of anti-racism." At a community meeting in Bristol, Wilmette Brown expressed her irritation at one of their slogans: "One million Londoners are getting a raw deal because the other 6 million Londoners are letting it happen." It was as though racism was simply a problem of bad neighborliness. What irritated her most was that the slogan divided people, envisioning the defeat of racism through benevolent white people defending victimized Black people, rather than showing people their shared interest in fighting the turn toward conservatism and austerity. For their part, the Wages for Housework campaign came up with their own anti-racist slogan: "Share the Housework, Sweep Out the Nazis." Surviving racism and violence, after all, is another form of unpaid work.

The campaign tried to chart a path through the landscape of austerity and militarization. James and Brown worked closely together at the head of the campaign together with Solveig Francis and Anne Neale, members from the earliest days of the Power of Women Collective. In 1978, they were evicted from their premises. In protest, they took over the Members Room in Camden Town Hall. Francis chained herself to the balcony and unfurled their petition to the chair of Camden housing, on which they had gathered over 1,000 signatures of support from their neighbors, arguing for their vital role in the community and demanding a space for their center. They were forced to relocate to 71 Tonbridge Street, near King's Cross Station, and became the King's Cross Women's Centre, where they remained for eighteen years. Their new center was located in the heart of one of London's red-light districts, and Nina Lopez, an activist mother from Argentina, coordinated the English Collective of Prostitutes, which protested the criminalization of sex work. Cristel Amiss, a mixed-race lesbian and former semi-professional basketball player, started traveling up from Bristol and spending time at the center, lending her carpentry skills to the renovations. She worked together with Wilmette Brown and Sara Callaway, organizing Black Women for Wages for Housework in the UK. Claire Glasman, a woman with cerebral palsy, joined the group and started applying the political perspective of Wages for Housework to her own experience. She argued that living with a disability in an inaccessible society was hard work and advocated for more resources for disabled people and their caregivers.

For women of color, lesbians, sex workers, socialists, disabled people, and immigrants, 1980s London could be a hostile place. From their small rundown storefront on Tonbridge Street, the group faced terrifying attacks by the National Front. They'd arrive at the center to find swastikas and racist slogans painted on their windows. After a particularly harrowing incident involving threats of arson and physical violence, they moved their operations into the Members Room at Camden Town Hall in protest and demanded police protection.[2] They were no fans of the police, Selma James explained years later, but, as long as police existed, they were going to make them do their jobs protecting vulnerable people, rather than beating up Black youths and harassing prostitutes.[3]

Margaret Prescod continued organizing in California, and a small group, assembled by Phoebe Jones and Pat Albright, continued the Wages for Housework campaign in Philadelphia. Others carried on the work across the US and Canada, meeting up periodically to connect and work together. Chanda Prescod-Weinstein, Margaret's daughter, remembers members of the international network coming together in New York, at her grandmother Elsa's house: "The Wages for Housework campaign would occasionally descend on New York to lobby at the United Nations, and I got to go on one of those trips . . . and their home base for those activities was my grandmother's house in Brooklyn. She cooked for them, she let them take over her kitchen, people stayed all over the house."[4]

In the United States, the Reagan administration was dismantling the welfare system and replacing it with "workfare," requiring mothers to be employed. In practice, this meant that mothers of young children were pressed into low-paid, low-status jobs. In 1987, Terry Brown, a welfare mother who identified herself as a member of Black Women for Wages for Housework, was protesting the new proposed work requirements outside San Francisco City Hall when a journalist approached her with an audio recorder and asked her to comment. She told him workfare was a "cheap labor scheme," meant not to alleviate poverty but to coerce poor women to take on society's shittiest, lowest-paid jobs that no one else would do.[5] Workfare was presented as "self-sufficiency" for women; Wages for Housework argued that it was a massive giveaway of women's labor to employers. As Wilmette Brown said:

> Now the left has been demanding jobs. That's been their platform for the twenty years that I've been active in the movement, and before then. And they're not looking at the reality that women are facing of doing two-thirds of the world's work. We want the work we've already done to be counted. And we want the wealth back for it. We're not demanding more shit jobs as any form of liberation.[6]

Austerity politics had been reshaping the international economic order. In the global south, international institutions, including the International Monetary Fund and World Bank, imposed austerity measures in the form of structural adjustment policies, which required poor, formerly colonized countries to slash their public expenditures and prioritize foreign investment in order to qualify for bank loans and development aid.

Wages for Housework had always, in theory, been international, and in the 1980s Selma James, Margaret Prescod, Wilmette Brown, and their fellow organizers got serious about their internationalism. They turned their attention to the global economy; to the flow of women's labor across national borders; to the institutions of international banking; to the United Nations; and to the military-industrial complex.

In the early 1980s, Selma James recruited the Trinidadian trade unionist Clotil Walcott to join the International Wages for Housework campaign. A working-class woman of Afro-Caribbean descent and a single mother of five children, Walcott started out as a union organizer in a poultry-processing plant where most of the employees were women. For decades, she worked at various stations on the assembly line, pulling out windpipes, plucking feathers, cutting the toenails of chickens, and eventually became shop steward. But she found herself continually frustrated by the union, which dismissed the issues faced by women workers. One of the earliest grievances she raised concerned equal pay: despite her skill and experience, she had repeatedly been shunted into lower-paid positions within the factory hierarchy, and, when she did the same jobs as men, she was paid less.[7] She fought on behalf of a woman who miscarried while working on the assembly line but was told that this was a "woman's issue," not a labor grievance. "If this is not a grievance," she shared years later at a Wages for Housework meeting, her voice shaking and rising in pitch in her rage and sorrow, "what it is? What it is, if not a grievance?!" Then, in a voice so soft and quiet it is almost inaudible, she posed a more philosophical question: "So, what is a woman's labor?"[8]

Throughout the 1970s, unable to get traction with the union or the labor board in Trinidad and Tobago, she went directly to the public, typing out reams of letters and pamphlets to distribute on the streets of Arima and Port of Spain. Her reputation as a fierce advocate of women factory workers led domestic workers to approach her for help forming their own union, which led in turn to the founding of the National Union of Domestic Employees (NUDE). In Trinidad and Tobago, as in many countries, domestic workers were not recognized by labor law. Not only did they not have rights of collective bargaining, but they could also not even get access to a union hall to hold their meetings. Their headquarters was Clotil Walcott's house.

In the early 1980s, she was invited to a conference in the Netherlands. "It had a woman there, C. L. R. James' wife," she recalled. "From the time she see me, she sit me down, she said *come and sit here.* And she could dominate all of them."[9] Wages for Housework made sense to Clotil Walcott as an organizer of domestic workers, for it clarifies that the home is a workplace. Now, her house in Arima became a hub of women's labor organizing, the epicenter of NUDE and its fight for domestic workers rights in Trinidad and Tobago and at the International Labor Organization (ILO), and the headquarters for the Trinidad and Tobago branch of the International Wages for Housework campaign. A housekeeper represented by NUDE visiting her home to discuss a labor grievance would find a stack of dish towels with the Wages for Housework logo for sale – a connection between the unpaid work of women and the underpaid, unrecognized, liminal status of domestic work. Comrades remember Walcott's home as a community space, where she welcomed her children and grandchildren and neighbors for shared meals and political meetings alike. She exemplified the idea, expressed by another Wages for Housework member, Andaiye, that "there is no frontier between the home and the street."

Andaiye was a comrade of Prescod and Brown from back in the days of their Queens College activism, when she taught English in the SEEK program. In New York, she had been in a Black women's consciousness-raising group with Prescod and Brown but did not join them in Wages for Housework. Instead, in the late 1970s, she returned to Guyana, where she worked alongside Walter Rodney in the Working People's Alliance (WPA), a leftist opposition party committed to multi-racial democracy, against the authoritarian regime of Forbes Burnham. She reconnected with her old friends Prescod and Brown while on a trip to London in 1982 in her capacity as international secretary of the WPA. Her trip coincided with a church occupation by the English Collective of Prostitutes, protesting the criminalization of sex work. Many of the women involved in the occupation were

Caribbean, many of them mothers, and their stand against police harassment spoke to the larger issues of repression facing immigrant women in the aftermath of imperialism.[10] Andaiye was inspired.

But it was only when she returned to Guyana that she started to come around to the Wages for Housework perspective. As she told anthropologist David Scott in an interview, "I said to a group of working-class Guyanese women that housework produced labor-power every day – and they got it. Immediately. Because what I was talking about was their work."[11] She and several fellow organizers formed Red Thread, a women's self-help group. These were days of scarcity and political turmoil in Guyana, and their goal, at first, was simply to generate income. These women didn't care about lofty political ideals, Andaiye found: first and foremost, they needed money and food. So Red Thread convened a collective of women who embroidered beautiful textiles with images depicting their lives and experiences and sold them for income. It soon became much more. As she recalled later, "Red Thread was this underground formation in which we got pleasure out of changing women's views of their work and the value of their work."[12]

In 1988, Guyana, like most countries in the global south, was forced to take on an IMF-imposed structural adjustment policy. Andaiye made sense of structural adjustment and the economic chaos it wrought through the lens of Wages for Housework:

> When prices rise and incomes plunge, whose job is it to walk from shop to shop and stall to stall in order to find the cheapest items of food, and then to go home and do the extra cooking that is required to make cheap items of food edible? When, as in Guyana, all the systems for the provision of safe water fail – who goes to fetch water daily from downstairs, or the next street, or two miles down the road except women? . . . When, as in Guyana, we become prey to water-borne diseases . . . who has to try to hold the line against the total collapse of the immediate environment of the family, except women? When women fail in this and the disease does strike, who has to run up and down to take family to hospitals which have become ill-equipped

because of government cuts? . . . Structural adjustment . . . assumes correctly that what women will do in the face of the deterioration that it brings is to increase the unpaid work that we do without even thinking about it in an attempt to ensure that our families survive.[13]

Economic austerity, whether in the wealthiest country on earth or the poorest, meant the same thing everywhere: it meant freeloading off the unpaid labor of women.

In 1985, a group including Selma James, Margaret Prescod, Clotil Walcott, Andaiye, and Wilmette Brown traveled to Nairobi on the occasion of the UN Third Conference on the Decade of Women. At the conference, they wore matching campaign T-shirts, in contrast with the sharp pantsuits and briefcases more common among Western attendees. They had saved and fundraised for months in order to be there, and they planned to use their presence to maximum advantage.

The historic gathering had two components: the official UN Conference at the Kenyatta Conference Center, and, down the road, on the campus at the University of Nairobi, a gathering called Forum 85, which invited various feminists from non-governmental organizations to meet and discuss the future of feminism. They had meetings in classrooms all over campus. It included a "Peace Tent," a massive blue and white tent set up by a coalition of feminists from North America and Europe to initiate conversations about feminist alternatives to war. Notable participants included Angela Davis, Betty Friedan, and Egyptian feminist Nawal El Saadawi. Wilmette Brown, cancer-free and recommitted to peace activism, set up a table with "Pay Women, Not the Military" on the banner and led a session on the subject. A South African women's delegation offered "revolutionary greetings" in their banner and demanded the attention of the world to the ongoing struggle against Apartheid. James spoke at a particularly heated session in the Peace Tent dedicated to the question of Israel and Palestine. Starting with her own background as a Jewish woman with family members killed in the Holocaust, she insisted that Zionism was not the same as Judaism, but rather an

The Wages for Housework table outside the Peace Tent at Forum '85, the UN International Conference on Women, in Nairobi.

ideology of "imperialism and racism." The crowd shouted loudly in response, some in support, and others in protest.[14]

But they had not come to debate in the Peace Tent. They were there to get access to the UN Conference, to put their demands into the official record for women all over the world to use in their struggles, now and into the future. Only registered NGOs had consultative status with the UN and were allowed into the conference, and with this in mind, back in London, they had formed an organization called Housewives in Dialogue as a registered charity several years earlier. Officially, their mission was "researching connections between human rights issues and women's unwaged caring work within the family and the wider community." In the days leading up to the conference, they scoured the preliminary report, looking for a place where they could insert themselves into the agenda. They zeroed in on paragraph 120, which called for governments to recognize and quantify the value of women's unwaged work.

Margaret Prescod led the effort. She knew well the challenge of lobbying well-heeled professional feminists to recognize and count the work of marginalized women. Her work at the Nairobi conference scaled up her earlier activism at the 1977 Houston Women's Conference, where, alongside members of the welfare rights movement, she had fought to include language calling welfare a wage. Like the fight in Houston, her task was to get the delegates to see poverty not as an unfortunate circumstance from which women needed rescuing but as systemic exploitation and wealth extraction on a global scale. Counting women's work, they believed, was the first step in demanding a more just global economic order.

It helped that the United Nations had recently published statistics demonstrating that women perform two thirds of the world's work, take home 5 percent of the world's income and own less than 1 percent of the world's assets. These statistics were an opportunity to show the role of unpaid women's work in these staggering inequalities. "Sometimes in the women's movement," James recalled, "there is a very narrow view of what housework is and, worse, who does it. So that you would think that housework is a little cleaning and a little washing and you can get rid of that pretty easily, you can get the man to share it." What these statistics revealed was much more stark than a battle of the sexes to be hashed out within private families: collectively, women's unpaid work simultaneously powered the entire global economy and impoverished women. She continued: "Counting this work and remunerating this work and naming this work and discovering this work was the occasion precisely for us as women to come together across many divides. And we determined that this was precisely the focus then of what we had to do at Nairobi. This was our job."[15]

They set up an informational table just outside the Peace Tent, set up their Wages for Housework banners, and brought their petition demanding that governments should calculate the value of women's work. "We petition every government to count the contribution to the economy of all women's work, so that it is recognized and reflected in every Gross National Product." They explained: "If governments count what we do, we – and they – will know what we are owed."[16] While at their table outside the Peace Tent they collected signatures from feminists from all over the world, inside the conference they used the petition to lobby the delegates to amend paragraph 120. They demanded that the paragraph not only call on governments to count the value of women's work, but specifically that it be calculated as part of GNP: that is, as an indispensable part of national wealth.

As James recounted it to a group of her Wages for Housework sisters some months later: "We lobbied till we were insane. And we were sitting up in the balcony, and they took 116 and 117 and 118 and 119 like this [snaps fingers]. And then when they said 120, the woman from Uganda said, 'I have a little, little amendment.' Something like that. Just a little amendment, she said. And she said, 'I just want to add in the gross national product. And then I have just one other little, little amendment.' And she amended it to talk about women's agricultural work and work in the home. And when she was finished, Jordan got up . . . and said, 'I support that amendment.' And then Sierra Leone got up and said, 'I support that amendment.'"

Paragraph 120, in the final version passed in the UN General Assembly, read as follows:

> The remunerated, and, in particular, the unremunerated contributions of women to all aspects and sectors of development should be recognized, and appropriate efforts should be made to measure and reflect these contributions in national accounts and economic statistics and in the gross national product. Concrete steps should be taken to quantify the unremunerated contribution of women to agriculture, food production, reproduction, and household activities.[17]

Those who convened in Nairobi to lobby for Wages for Housework on a global scale were not naive about the power of one paragraph in a 372-paragraph-long official report to materially improve the lives of women. But, in their view, it was a rare opening to advance their politics on a global stage, to use the conference for their own ends. In the process, they acquired experience confronting those in power. Perhaps most of all, that global vantage point allowed them to find and gain strength from new connections between their struggles and those of others.[18]

Afterward, back at her typewriter in Arima, Clotil Walcott wrote a letter to her new prime minister making two demands: first, that the government of Trinidad and Tobago recognize paragraph 120 of the Nairobi Declaration and devise a way to count women's unwaged work; and second, that the Industrial Relations Act – the act that called for the compulsory recognition of trade unions – replace the phrase "household assistants" with "household workers" in order to grant domestic workers collective bargaining status.[19] For her, these two demands were related: both were about recognizing housework as work. Within a decade, after tireless lobbying of her MPs, the first of those demands had been met. In the parliamentary debates leading to passage of the bill, Clotil Walcott received a special mention as the force behind it. Ten years later, Margaret Prescod led a multi-racial coalition of fifty-six women to lobby the Fourth UN Conference on Women in Beijing. Building on their work in Nairobi the previous decade, they called on nations to calculate the value of women's unwaged work in satellite accounts, alongside official GDP calculations. Once again, they were successful: the directive was taken up in the Beijing Declaration and Platform for Action.

For her part, Walcott expressed skepticism about the effectiveness of declarations calling for the calculation of women's work. For the demand closer to her heart – that domestic workers be recognized under labor law – the struggle would be much harder, carried on for decades after her death by her daughter Ida LeBlanc. But for Andaiye, the more important target of these efforts to count women's work was not governments but women themselves. Back in Guyana, she started getting women to count their own daily unpaid work in time-use diaries. They would either write down their work hours and tasks themselves, or, if they were illiterate, they would dictate this to a Red Thread volunteer who would write it down for them. Andaiye reflected that, in doing so, the women "revealed their work to themselves, and in some cases developed a confidence that this work entitled them to the resources they needed to reduce their burden."[20] It was about transforming consciousness and sparking collective action. After all, to organize a new global working class made of unwaged women, women must first see themselves as workers.

By 1985, Wilmette Brown's doctor had pronounced her cancer free. The years she had spent battling cancer had also been years of reflection and political awakening. She framed the experience through the lens of housework: the housework of cancer.

The housework of cancer: it's instantly recognizable to anyone who has encountered cancer. There's getting to and from the many appointments. The laundry. The meals. For some, there is keeping the implanted venous access port clean and dry. For others, there are bed pans and vomit basins. The regime of pills and infusions. The helping to the toilet. For the cancer patient, Brown wrote, there is "relearning basic bodily functions and developing patience." She was in her late thirties at the time of her diagnosis, and was a healthy, active vegetarian who suddenly found herself thrust into the position of a dependent recipient of care. "In the social and physical weakness and dependence of an illness, I experienced the power relations of childhood, disablement and aging, all at once." She also experienced homophobia, as her extended community, who visited with her in the hospital, were met with raised eyebrows from the staff. The racism was more explicit. She wrote: "Another cancer patient, a white English woman, told me, 'I don't mean you personally but . . .' too many Black immigrants were using the NHS."

Later, while convalescing in Newark, relying on social security benefits, healing from cancer was hard work. Trying to eat well in the wake of a cancer diagnosis, to learn new kinds of food preparation, to replace cooking pots she now knew to be made with carcinogenic materials, was expensive, timely, and inconvenient – impossible for many people. She turned to holistic health for answers but found it frustratingly narrow, geared toward individual cures for a disease that she knew had a social basis. For her, cancer was a class issue. The risks of exposure were disproportionately experienced by poor communities, and care disproportionately hoarded by wealthier communities. Without information about the social basis of cancer, "fighting cancer is ghettoized to a single issue . . . deprived of the power and resources of the working class as a whole."[21]

Years earlier, in 1973, the US Department of Health, Education, and Welfare published a report which mapped cancer rates in the United States, revealing the highest rates in New Jersey, particularly along Route 1, which ran through the state, connecting Philadelphia with New York and earning New Jersey the nickname Cancer Alley USA. One of the main reasons for this was the industrial zone along the Passaic River bordering Newark, where the Diamond Alkali pesticide plant manufactured 75 percent of the herbicide familiarly known as "Agent Orange" used by US military as a defoliant in the Vietnam War. Agent Orange contains dioxin, and exposure to dioxin is known to cause birth defects, brain damage, and cancer.

In 1983, scientists collected a soil sample from a spillage site in Newark and found levels of dioxin comparable to those in the forest areas where Agent Orange had been dumped in Vietnam. The area was declared a Superfund site, hazardous enough to require government cleanup, in 1984,[22] confirming what Brown already suspected. It also gave her a new perspective, linking her anti-war activism with her cancer. It connected the poor, mostly Black communities who got cancer and cared for the sick where the chemicals were produced with the families, also predominantly poor and working class, whose sons fought in the war and later became sick from exposure, and with the women in Vietnam who, long after the war, bore the burdens of caring for those with birth defects and cancer. Brown came to understand the work of surviving cancer and her anti-war activism as one and the same struggle.

In December of 1984, shortly after her home neighborhood was declared a Superfund site, in a place called Bhopal in India, more than forty tons of methyl isocyanate leaked from a pesticide plant of the Union Carbide corporation, immediately killing 3,800 people and leaving devastating longer-term health consequences for the surrounding population. Two years later came the nuclear disaster at Chernobyl.

Wilmette Brown's framing of cancer as a social justice issue cut against the grain of a 1980s common sense that celebrated individualism and uplifted the nuclear family, while denigrating public goods, like the NHS and welfare. Brown's old friend from her days in the SEEK program, Audre Lorde, described a "conspiracy on the part of Cancer Inc.," to insist that women with breast cancer smile, put on a brave face, see themselves as heroes, to cure themselves with positivity; even to see cancer as a gift. To do so, though, was not only to make the outrageous demand that cancer patients take on the burden of reassuring everybody else, making cancer seem less threatening and scary, but it was also to participate in a collective cover-up of a broader injustice – the slow violence of environmental toxicity.[23]

Like Lorde, Brown refused to buy into the heroic individual survivor narrative. "Cancer," she wrote,

> epitomizes the crisis of health in our time. Cancer forces the issue of how responsible the individual can be for personal health when our every environment – from the urban Black ghetto in the metropolis to the tropical rain forest in the Third World – is continually being raped for profit by the military-industrial complex.

What kind of work is cancer? In Wilmette Brown's experience, it was mostly unpaid and underpaid. Most significantly, it is repair work, clean-up work, mitigating the harms of environmental poisoning and violence. Attending to the toxicity of bodies and lands is women's work, an extension of housework: the necessary work of reproducing the human species and of surviving war and capitalism. For Brown, this too is where capitalism lives. Housework, in this view, is more than the work that is necessary for capitalism to function and extract profit. It is also the work thrust on us by capitalism. It is the work of surviving its effects. Instead of brave, individual survivors donning pink ribbons, she envisioned a coalition of

> all women who are on the front line in the battle for health – first of all in our own homes fighting poor food, drugs, rats and roaches, pesticides, dirt and disease; on the front line in hospital wards and

clinic waiting rooms everywhere . . . on the front line outside US military bases, nuclear waste dumps, and power plants – on the front line of health, campaigning for peace around the world.[24]

Through the prism of her own illness, Brown remapped the world and the peace movement.

Wilmette Brown had been a peace activist since at least her days at Berkeley, or earlier, when witnessing her mother's grief at her older brother's death in the Korean War. Now, she recommitted herself to the problem of war from a new perspective: that of women's unpaid work.

Throughout the 1980s, one of the most visible sites in the feminist fight against nuclear weapons was in the UK at a place called Greenham Common, in the southwest of England. In 1979, the US military began placing ground-launched cruise missiles and Pershing II missiles at bases throughout Europe, and Greenham Common was one of those sites. In 1981, a group of women walked 120 miles from Cardiff in protest, camped out at the base, and then stayed for several years. They pitched tents and cooked over communal campfires. They chained themselves to the fences, laid their bodies down in front of military convoys. They hung their gorgeous quilted protest banners from the fences. They took turns keeping watch at the different gates so they could keep track of any vehicles entering or leaving. They used bolt cutters to dismantle portions of the fence and invade the base. One of the most iconic photographs of the protest shows the silhouettes of women dancing at dawn on the missile silos. Another shows a candlelit circle visible from the sky above, as 30,000 women joined hands and encircled the entire base. Their aim was to end nuclear weapons. They called themselves Women for Life on Earth.

Many former Greenham Common protesters recall a supportive and collaborative sisterhood that was diverse in terms of class background but not in terms of race. "I think black women were doing quite a lot of other things with their own time and it was not necessarily a priority," one woman who was part of the Greenham movement suggested. "I think women who face survival issues daily on the streets, you haven't necessarily got the time to face nuclear weapons." She acknowledged in retrospect that there are things they could have done to make the movement more inclusive. "It wasn't targeted at white middle-class women," she recalled. "We handed out handouts to anybody and everybody on the street."[25] Others echoed these sentiments.

For Brown, the problem was less that Black women were hurt by their exclusion than the way that their absence signaled a narrowness of vision that weakened the peace movement. All over the world, women of color bore the burden of nuclear radiation and the military-industrial complex disproportionately. The onus was not on Black people to join, she emphasized: it was on the peace movement to be anti-racist and relevant to Black people.[26] That was the work she set out to do. How could she convince the peace movement that they had things to learn from the experiences of Black women; that opposing war and opposing racism were one and the same struggle? She set out to answer these questions in a pamphlet, *Black Women and the Peace Movement*.

She started with a text that many at Greenham Common knew and loved: Virginia Woolf's 1938 book *Three Guineas*. While Woolf's earlier treatise *A Room of One's Own* famously argued that women needed space and 500 pounds a year in order to be intellectually autonomous, in *Three Guineas* Woolf looked outward at how women's lack of money impacted not only their inner lives, but the wider world. Woolf made the case that women's economic dependence on men rendered them complicit in war, unable to resist war or other forms of injustice. Women's financial autonomy was a matter of personal liberation but also of war and peace. The women at Greenham Common were inspired by, and often quoted in speeches and on banners and manifestos, Woolf's words: "as a woman, I have no country. As a woman I want no country. As a woman my country is the whole world."[27]

Brown saw something else in *Three Guineas*. She encountered passages like these:

what are we to call the profession that consists in bringing nine or ten children into the world, the profession which consists in running a house, nursing an invalid, visiting the poor and the sick, tending here an old father, there an old mother? – there is no name and there is no pay for that profession . . .[28]

Throughout the book, Woolf refers to women's work as the "unpaid professions." The consequence of women not being paid for their work is that they have no political power to prevent the wars which kill their sons. Woolf describes at great length the liberation that would come to men if women had independent income and men were not solely responsible for the material upkeep of families. In reality, instead, "three hundred million or so have to be spent upon the arms-bearers," so that there was no money to pay women for their work, and men had to continue to be the breadwinners and women, their voiceless dependents. She directly identified money used for war-making as money that could instead be in women's hands, used for other things.

"It is one of the high points of my life," wrote Brown, "to find in Virginia Woolf, a white middle-class English woman . . . what I know from my own experience as a Black welfare rights organizer in the United States." Welfare rights organizers like Johnnie Tillmon and Beulah Sanders saw mothers as workers. They too were attentive to the "unpaid professions," and they too saw money as the key to their autonomy. While Virginia Woolf lamented that women could not stop war because of their lack of money, similarly, welfare mothers saw their children recruited by the military, used as cannon fodder in wars of American imperialism, because they were impoverished. And, like Woolf, some saw a direct connection between government spending on war and the lack of money for carework. Brown quoted one welfare mother, Mildred Calvert: "When I see money being wasted – sending men to the moon to play golf, dumping nerve gas in the ocean, burning potatoes, killing off hogs, mutilating them, just getting rid of them – and I see hungry and raggedly children running around, this is the kind of country that we live in, and this is what just burns me up."[29]

Virginia Woolf and Johnnie Tillmon may have been worlds apart, but in Brown's view both made a strong argument for women's economic autonomy through the valorization of housework. Wilmette Brown drew on Woolf to reframe Wages for Housework as a strategy for ending war. She wrote: "The common strategy of Virginia Woolf and Black welfare mothers which speaks to most women at the bottom is: *pay women not the military.*"[30]

Brown published *Black Women and the Peace Movement* with Falling Wall Press in 1984, a small book with a lime green and magenta cover, looking very much like an artifact of the 1980s. She made it her platform when, in 1986, she successfully ran for a seat on the council of the Campaign for Nuclear Disarmament (CND), which had a membership of around 250,000 people. She was the first Black person to hold that position since its founding in 1957. In an essay in the official CND publication *Sanity*, she presented her vision for merging peace work with anti-racism. She drew on Dr Martin Luther King Jr's often ignored anti-war stance, which he linked explicitly with poverty. "I knew that America would never invest the necessary funds or energies in its poor so long as adventures like Vietnam continued to draw men and skills and money like some demonic destructive suction tube," King had said. "So I was increasingly compelled to see the war as an enemy of the poor and to attack it as such."[31] Echoing King, Brown argued that one reason the nuclear threat was relevant to poor people was that money being used for war and nuclear proliferation allowed for the austerity arguments claiming there wasn't enough money for welfare and social services. She pressed further. A press release put out by Black Women for Wages for Housework made the following case:

Black people are centrally involved in the anti-nuclear movement – whether struggling against nuclear testing in the Pacific, nuclear waste dumping in Mexico, uranium mining in Namibia, government lying about the dangers of nuclear power and radiation in inner cities or nuclear waste traps traveling through the middle of Black communities in Camden and Brent [in London]. Racism is rampant in the peace movement, but in working against it Black people can gather support from other forces which are challenging the nuclear state.[32]

Wilmette Brown wanted to connect Black communities organizing for liberation with the peace movement against nuclear war. Unpaid women's work was the bridge.

In London and Bristol, the Wages for Housework campaign had a distinctive take on the nuclear threat: they called it "refusing nuclear housework." They recognized that it was women and those they care for who will most suffer the consequences of nuclear radiation. This includes women who live in towns through which trains carry radioactive materials; women who will feed children food that might be grown in toxic soils, or those who have to care for adult workers who are made sick from years working in toxic workplaces. When, in the late 1980s, a proposal was floated to build a nuclear power station in Somerset, several women from the campaign, including Wilmette Brown and Suzie Fleming, submitted a detailed report about why they opposed it.

They drew on paragraph 120 from the UN Conference on Women at Nairobi, and urged the commission to count women's unpaid work as part of the total economic cost of the plant. They gave a detailed account of what that work would entail, including caring for the sick and taking precautionary measures to protect against the threat of radiation. They cited leukemia clusters along train lines that carry radioactive material as part of normal operating procedures, not to mention the work that would come in the event of an accident. The cost didn't stop there, they wrote:

> When women are drained in the effort required to cope with the effects of nuclear production, the entire society is deprived of women's energies in other spheres of human development. In opposing nuclear power in general, the building of Hinkley "C" in particular, we are defending and protecting our investment: on the one hand, the people and communities whom our labor has produced

and whose lives are therefore inseparable from our own; and on the other, our labor-time, which happens to be our lives and which is not recoverable.

They argued in economic terms: though presented as an efficient and affordable expenditure, the plant would be prohibitively expensive if you factored in women's time and unpaid work as having value.[33]

The power station was not built, for unrelated reasons. (It would be, decades later.) But this extensive document, which the women clearly poured their time and hearts into, shows the kind of world that Wages for Housework envisioned: one in which women's labor was taken seriously as a cost, rather than accepted as collateral damage, or as something that could be taken for granted, extracted for free.

Wilmette Brown came to Greenham Common, bundled up against the cold, speaking to crowds of women who assembled at Yellow Gate, standing in front of a banner reading "Pay Women, Not the Military." Her name appears in many of the memoirs and oral histories of the time. Some recount that the Wages for Housework faction of the camp, led by Brown, sowed discord in the community of peaceful, non-hierarchical protesters at Greenham Common. One article accused Brown and her Wages for Housework allies of "attempting to impose their brand of materialist feminism on Greenham, a project which was contrary to the theoretical openness and political autonomy which characterized the movement."[34] Detractors called Wilmette Brown charismatic and "cult-like," and claimed that she used accusations of racism as a cudgel to silence and discredit her opponents. Sasha Roseneil reported that, even years later, when she was writing her book about Greenham, many people who had been there would not go on record talking about Wilmette Brown for fear of being harassed or publicly trashed as "racist" by members of the Wages for Housework campaign.

But others who were at Greenham argued that Brown was doing the necessary, painful work of confronting racism, which most white women there were simply unwilling, or unable, to do. Yasmin Alam, one among a small number of women of color at Greenham, wrote: "During the whole time of my participation, there was little unity on any issue save one – the irrelevance of fighting racism in the struggle for peace. I, the only Black woman, was endlessly patronized, put down, and stamped on by the rest of the group who were all white, rather middle-class but, in their opinion, peaceful women-loving women."[35] Sarah Hipperson, a Glaswegian nun, midwife, and committed peace activist who lived at Greenham for over a decade, told an interviewer in 2000: "Part of [Brown's] excellent connection was that white middle-class women could be part of a struggle but had an opt-out clause that Black people didn't have . . . They could cut their hair, have a bath, change their clothes, and go back into the system. That was not available to Black people."[36] Hipperson found this perspective revelatory and much needed.

Yet Brown's defenders were relatively few. Articles appeared in leftist magazines ranging from CND's *Sanity* to *Marxism Today* to the *New Statesman* attacking her. After one term on the CND leadership council, she was not re-elected to the position. Meanwhile, by 1988, most missiles that had been at Greenham were destroyed. The US Air Force finally left Greenham Common in 1992, and the peace camp dispersed.

Wilmette Brown took Wages for Housework decisively out of the heterosexual nuclear family, and directed her gaze into some of the darker spaces of global capitalism – into cancer wards and urban ghettos with toxic soils and scenes of police violence. She looked into the bar hangouts of lesbians and sex workers, and into the war zones in the aftermath of American imperialism where poor women cared for ravaged bodies and land. The housewife, married to the archetypal male factory worker, was still part of her vision of revolution but was no longer the center. Brown took on James and Dalla Costa's analysis of the indispensability of housework in capitalism, and turned it over to reveal another side: much of the unpaid carework necessary to sustain and protect human life is *created* by the harms of capitalism. Housework, for Wilmette Brown, is more than the reproduction of the capitalist workforce. Housework is repairing the damage. It is healing work.

It is also a vision for a radically different world. Brown and Prescod often described Wages for Housework as a strategy of reparations: a continuation of the Black freedom struggle to repair the harms of slavery and racial capitalism. As Brown wrote, Black welfare mothers "demanded wages for housework as a way of taking back what is ours: as a right; as damages; as back pay for all the unpaid and unwaged work of plantation and domestic slavery; as reparations."[37] In speeches, she sometimes quoted Fanon, who wrote in *The Wretched of the Earth*: "when we hear the head of a European state declare with his hand on his heart that he must come to the aid of the poor underdeveloped peoples, we do not tremble with gratitude. Quite the contrary; we say to ourselves: 'It's a just reparation which will be paid to us.'"[38]

Like reparations, Wages for Housework was about more than settling debts. It is what philosopher Olúfẹ́mi Táíwò calls a "constructivist" view of reparations, redistributing the world's wealth for the purpose of creating a better, more just world in the future. As he explains, the world as we know it was made by slavery, empire, and white supremacy; it will take something equally ambitious to remake it along different lines, and this is what reparations aim for.[39] Reparations are more than a reversal of wrongdoing; they are, to quote political scientist Adom Getachew, a "world-making project."[40] This is the lens through which I understand the Wages for Housework demand "Pay women, not the military." Wilmette Brown called for diverting wealth and power and resources away from entities that cause harm to the vulnerable, and redirecting them toward those who do the work of healing and repair. Hers was a utopian vision, calling into being a different relationship with the planet and all its inhabitants: one based on care and healing and life, rather than extraction and depletion. In Brown's words, it was "a way of reclaiming the earth."[41]

10.

Afterlives

By the end of the 1970s, the Italian Wages for Housework campaign had dissolved. For Mariarosa Dalla Costa, it ended in fatigue. "The rhythm of so much activism was so intense and totalizing that there was no room left for anything else in our lives," she told a group of former comrades at a gathering in Rome in 2002. "By the end of that decade we were worn out. All our reproductive margins had been erased. After so many struggles and so much time spent organizing, we couldn't detect even the outline of a transformation of our society."[1]

For young women in the campaign, the question of motherhood was especially difficult. Dalla Costa herself concluded that having children would have compromised her anti-capitalist political strategy, which had, at its core, the refusal of work. "We could extend our refusal to marriage and even to cohabitation with men . . ." she wrote. "However, we could never have had children and then refused to take care of them."[2] Others in the movement wanted to have children and found that the demands of motherhood were incompatible with the demands of political militancy.

Still others drifted away from the campaign because they needed jobs to support themselves. Dalla Costa had been able to combine her activism with her paid work as a professor, but not everyone had this option. The Italian Wages for Housework campaign had been a movement of young women, most of them students with free time and few obligations: a situation that facilitated their activism but which could not last forever. In her letters, Dalla Costa often described her sadness as members of her close-knit group left Padua and full-time organizing because they needed to get full-time jobs to support themselves. Others still found themselves burdened with carework, as the daughters of elderly parents in a society that designated elder care to younger female relatives. And so, the very condition Lotta Femminista was fighting – women's lack of money and time – was what made it impossible to carry on their struggle.

Mariarosa Dalla Costa parted ways with Selma James in 1978, around the same time that the New York Committee dissolved. In a 2019 anthology of her writings, she attributes their split to "profound disagreements on political and organizational issues."[3] She invites those interested in knowing the full story to follow up in her archives. I did. What I learned is that, from the start, there was warmth and admiration and a deep commitment to their common purpose, but there were also always tensions that regularly surfaced. In letters, James often criticized Dalla Costa for being overly academic in tone and for being too focused on Italy. Dalla Costa accused James of being controlling and overbearing. "I am really disturbed by the entire attitude that you have assumed with me: sincerely, I feel an obsessive attitude from you in judging my speaking, my expressing in every form," she wrote in one letter as early as 1973,[4] and this dynamic would thread through their correspondence for the next several years.

A particular point of tension was the book they published combining both of their writings. In the first editions, in both English and Italian, Dalla Costa was credited as the author of "Women and the Subversion of the Community." But in the second English edition in 1975, James, who was the liaison with Falling Wall Press, credited herself as co-author of the essay. Dalla Costa later reported that she had not consented to the change and was not comfortable with it but had said nothing, for the sake of preserving their political collaboration. Then, in April 1978, as the third English edition was coming out, Dalla Costa spoke her mind. In a letter, she told James that she found the changing of the signature on her essay without permission "completely abusive."[5] For her, more than the signature on the essay, her disagreement with James was about political practice. Dalla Costa wanted Wages for Housework to spread; for their work to be translated, taken up in new and unexpected ways, and to spark creative rebellions among people outside of their organization. She described how James' style of leadership, which she saw as controlling and hierarchical, hindered the kind of rebellion that she wanted to inspire. She concluded her letter by declaring an end to their personal communications. That is the last correspondence between Selma James and Mariarosa Dalla Costa that appears in Dalla Costa's archives.

Lotta Femminista carried on for a while, but then the Italian government took a series of repressive measures that undercut the movement. These started in 1978, when the leftist Red Brigades kidnapped and assassinated former Christian Democratic prime minister Aldo Moro, and the conservative government seized the moment, issuing carte blanche to state agents to arrest and intimidate political activists and intellectuals in the name of "anti-terrorism." Dalla Costa watched as her colleagues at the University of Padua had their offices ransacked, often before being carted off to jail. In the Political Science department, she and her friend Ferruccio Gambino were among the only three who were not arrested. Those imprisoned included her former mentor Toni Negri, along with Alisa Del Re, Oreste Scalzone, Sandro Serafini – people with whom Dalla Costa had been close, and whose names appear often in her archives. When she received a notification from the judiciary informing her that she was being investigated for "participation in armed bands," she feared that she would soon face the same fate.[6]

In her reflections years later, Dalla Costa identified another reason for the demise of Lotta Femminista. In the dark days following the political repression of the late 1970s and the dissolution of the feminist movement, she began to ask herself: why was political work so hard? Why were the years she had spent fighting for a better world so grueling, physically taxing; rooted in suffering but not joy or love? For her, Wages for Housework had been largely about the thing they were *against*. They were against capitalism; against the extraction of value from women; against housework; against work in general; against financial dependence on men and the nuclear family. But what were they *for*? "What was missing," she wrote, "was something capable of moving me in a positive way; of inspiring a strong imagination."[7]

Dalla Costa turned her attention to land and food: topics that had been close to her heart since her childhood in Treviso and her young days protesting the environmental devastation of the land and waterways around Porto Marghera. She visited peasant groups supporting the Zapatistas in Chiapas, Mexico, and survivors of the bombing of Hiroshima, and took inspiration from a movement of fishermen in India committed to protecting the seas. She wrote about the spread of international grocery chains in Italy and its deleterious effects on local food systems, the adulteration of olive oil through imports, the replacement of hundreds of varieties of corn in the hills of the Veneto in her childhood with bland monocrop corn. She remembered: "In Treviso particularly, there was a greatly appreciated variety, Biancoperla corn, which made a soft, sticky polenta, particularly good for soaking up sauce."[8] At the time of her writing, she reported four varieties of corn available in Italy, and 90 percent of it came through two multinational companies. What good is a wage, she asks, "if everything we can buy is toxic?"[9] This, she came to understand, was the site of her true struggle against capitalism:

> I found the door that opened into the flower and vegetable garden: I realized the importance of the question of land. The door was thrown open for me by the new actors I was looking for, the protagonists of indigenous rebellions, the farmers, the fishermen, the people fighting against dams or deforestation . . . They were all treating the land as a central issue. They were all fighting against its privatization and exploitation and against the destruction of its reproductive powers . . . These were the people I was looking for . . . because they let me have a glimpse of a different world.[10]

Near the end of writing this book, I came across a book of poems Mariarosa Dalla Costa wrote in 1963 and 1964 called *Una Mattinata*, published in Padua a few years before she threw herself into *operaismo* and then Lotta Femminista and Wages for Housework.[11] She was about twenty years old at the time. The book was not in her archives: I happened on it by chance, through an interlibrary loan. I searched it for clues to Wages for Housework and her feminism and militancy, but I found no trace of anything like that. Instead, I came away with images of the abundant terrain of her Italian childhood. The forested road through Monfenera, in Treviso. Hydrangeas growing so large children can hide in them. Picking pumpkins in a garden drenched with dew behind a heavy gate, the feel of the leaves covered in little prickly hairs, and going back to the house to cook and eat them with cousins. For Dalla Costa, maybe it is the land and the work of those who sustain life in all its forms that is the through line.

Within months of the *Life Magazine* profile of the New York Wages for Housework Committee, the group had dissolved. After several years of devoting themselves to the cause with little apparent success, some members of the committee moved on to other pursuits. Several lost their jobs in the financial crisis and had to scramble to make ends meet. Federici describes how changes in New York City in the late 1970s made it harder to organize. The New York Wages for Housework Committee had thrived in the New York City of squatters and unemployment benefits and cheap rents and spaces for community meetings. "The spaces we had had to do political work were being eliminated," she recalled.[12] It's amazing to me now, as someone who has lived in a later version of New York, in which every square inch seems to be monetized, to think of a New York in which a radical idea – a provocation; a way of seeing the world and imagining another one – could take up real estate in the city. The New York Wages for Housework Committee had no wealthy donors, no political party affiliation, no profit-making activities. Their members were not rich. Among the things eliminated by austerity politics were these spaces and possibilities of political creativity and critique.

For members of the New York Committee focused on the local campaign, this is how the story ended. But other members who were involved in the international network, both in New York and across North American groups, cited internal tensions that led to a split in the movement, culminating in the confrontation and expulsion of the

New York branch at a Toronto meeting in 1977.[13] Silvia Federici, Maria-rosa Dalla Costa, and other former members of the campaign in Los Angeles and Toronto have said that the split was due to irreconcilable differences with Selma James over matters of political organizing.[14]

The years following the dissolution of the New York Wages for Housework Committee were busy for Federici. In 1979, when the right rose to power in Italy and cracked down in a wave of violence and repression on the left, she rallied support among American academics and feminists in defense of Dalla Costa and her other comrades with the global Campaign Against Repression in Italy. In 1980, she finished her dissertation, "The Development of Lukács' Realism," and got a job teaching philosophy at Franconia College, a small experimental college in New Hampshire, but the position was short-lived. By the time she arrived, the college was spiraling into bankruptcy to the point that they could no longer afford to pay their maintenance staff, and students and faculty were tasked with the cleaning and basic upkeep of campus. Soon, Franconia closed its doors and Federici found herself once again searching for a job.

Though her work in the Wages for Housework campaign was over, she was far from done with the matter of unwaged women's work. Together with Leopoldina Fortunati from Lotta Femmini-sta, who went on to become a prominent Marxist feminist theorist in Italy, she began working on a new book which was to be called *Il grande Calibano* – a revisionist history of capitalism centering on the creation of the gendered division of labor. It was a subject they had been discussing for years. In letters exchanged in the course of organizing Wages for Housework, they sometimes exchanged notes and reflected on deeper historical questions, such as: how did production become separate from reproduction in the first place? How had work outside the home become waged and marked "masculine" while work inside the home became unwaged and marked "feminine?" They took the name of their book from Shakespeare's *The Tempest*, in which Caliban is depicted as a "savage," untamable, rebellious inhabitant of an island, whom the European visitor Prospero can only render compliant using magic. For Federici and Fortunati, he represents both an anti-colonial figure and the world proletariat: a rebel body rising up to resist the incursion of imperialism and capitalism. *Il grande Calibano* was published in Italy in 1984. In New York, Federici also continued to collaborate with some of her former Wages for Housework sisters on a feminist zine called *Tap Dance*, which continued the work of the New York Committee in exploring women's unpaid work in the city through the fiscal crisis and into the Reagan presidency. But soon, that effort petered out as financial constraints pressed her collaborators into devoting more energy to paid work.

After several years of temporary positions, in 1984, Federici accepted a job at the University of Port Harcourt in southeastern Nigeria. Located at the heart of the oil-producing Niger River Delta, the university had been built up less than a decade earlier, during the peak of the oil boom. As the price of oil skyrocketed, the country had borrowed heavily to pay for development projects, but by 1982 the price of oil had fallen, interest rates risen, and the debts had become unmanageable. By the time Federici arrived, Nigeria was in economic crisis. The IMF had begun pressuring the country to implement austerity measures and accept structural adjustment policies as a condition of loans, and Federici witnessed a passionate debate in the Nigerian public about whether to accept. In the newspapers, political cartoons lambasted the IMF as neocolonial hucksters, and headlines had titles such as "IMF=Death." (Nigeria eventually began to implement structural adjustment policies in 1986.) At the same time, she observed the ecological devastation of Niger River Delta, one of earth's natural wonders, which had sustained complex and diverse food systems for centuries, and was now poisoned by the effects of the petroleum industry.

General Muhammadu Buhari had recently come to power in a military coup. Federici arrived to witness his trademark policy "Operation Indiscipline," a campaign of intense police repression in the name of restoring order. People were arrested for minor transgressions, such as littering, or failing to queue in the proper way, or failing to recite the national anthem at public events, or being found in violation of the national dress code. Hawkers had their small shacks demolished in the name of urban "beautification." University students went on strike, including at Port Harcourt, and, when in session, professors often struggled to find even basic supplies, such as paper and pens. Books were in short supply, and faculty members would cycle around town to find copy shops where they could photocopy reading materials to share among students. Yet in the midst of repression and scarcity, Federici loved teaching at the university. She found the students brilliant and eager to learn.

Federici was especially fascinated by the porous boundary between campus and the surrounding community. She saw women near the edge of campus farming unused land and learned they had been displaced from the land on which the university now stood. It reminded her of the process begun centuries ago with the enclosure of the commons that accompanied the transition from feudalism to capitalism in Europe. This time, land was being privatized, and people displaced, in the name of austerity and development and "structural adjustment." It was no longer a matter of history: she was witnessing it in real time, right in front of her.

After three years, in 1987, she returned to the United States and took a job at Hofstra University in Long Island, but her experiences in Nigeria stayed with her. Having watched women displaced as the state and private companies enclosed land and resources, her thoughts turned again to Wages for Housework. She wanted to understand the violent repression and dispossession of women that takes place in order to render them unwaged workers in the first place. She revisited the book she had written with Fortunati and started working on a new book, this time in English, called *Caliban and the Witch*.

Il grande Calibano had focused on the unruly and rebellious figure of Caliban. In *Caliban and the Witch*, Federici shifts her gaze to his mother Sycorax: a witch, pregnant and banished to an island where she gives birth to her son. What led to her banishment? Marx locates the origins of capitalism in "primitive accumulation," the dispossession of people from land and the means of production. *Caliban and the Witch* reveals a much more violent and gendered part of that process: the witch hunts of the late Middle Ages, in which women accused of witchcraft were burned and tortured in the public square. Conventionally viewed as an irrational holdover from a superstitious premodern time, Federici argues instead that the witch hunts were a decisive moment in the creation of the capitalist world order. For capitalism to come into existence, women had to be rendered available as free labor, to reproduce the working classes as housewives and carers. While women were by no means "free" before capitalism, they nevertheless had complex social roles and economic autonomy, acting as midwives, healers, and abortionists; they had expert knowledge of the natural world and agriculture. Such women had to be eliminated, if women were to be rendered the docile helpmeets of men, pressed into unpaid reproductive labor. *Caliban and the Witch* tells the story of how disparate constituencies – scientists, clergy, and even proletariat men – came together in the witch hunts to suppress women, dispossess them of knowledge, and render them into "commons," a resource to be universally exploited to support the capitalist order and its most basic social unit, the nuclear family.

The book was published in 2004, and the following year Federici retired. Almost immediately after, her mother's health deteriorated, and she returned to Italy to join her sister in caring for her. She stayed with her mother in Parma for three years.[15] Her mother required around-the-clock care. The work was physically and emotionally exhausting. Federici also found it deeply meaningful. "My mother was my last romantic love," she told me. The experience also added new dimensions to her thinking about the labor of social reproduction. She later described the years she spent devoting herself to her mother's care as the completion of a cycle: from a childhood spent in refusal of housework, and a fear of being subsumed by it, to a deep respect for reproductive labor as work that might spur radical alternative possible worlds, allowing us to "resist our dehumanization" and "reconstruct the world as a space of nurturing, creativity, and care."[16] While in Parma, she was impressed by the work of a women's cooperative who came regularly to help Federici and her sister with their mother's care, and it inspired her to think in new ways about the commons, and how we might share the work of care as a positive act of world-making. In 2008, her mother died at the age of ninety-seven.

While Federici reoriented her life around the daily work of caring for her mother, *Caliban and the Witch* traveled the world, passed from hand to hand, copied and pirated, and discussed by women's groups and in various activists' circles. Translations appeared in German, Spanish, French, Italian, Portuguese, Turkish, Japanese, Slovenian, Korean, Catalan, Farsi, Chinese, Greek, Romanian, Russian, and Serbian. On a recent visit with her in 2024, she showed me the most recent edition: a lushly illustrated graphic adaptation of *Caliban and the Witch* by the artist Danitza Luna from Mujeres Creando, a Bolivian anarchist-feminist collective devoted to anti-poverty work.

Caliban and the Witch brought Federici's feminism to a global audience, connecting her with readers from all over the world. In recent years, activists have also revisited her writings from the 1970s and used them in new ways. For example, in 2013, artist Laurel Ptak launched a campaign called "Wages for Facebook," meant to disrupt and interrogate the way that tech industries extract profit from our emotions and social connections. Her manifesto playfully redeploys the opening cadence of Silvia Federici's "Wages Against Housework": "They say it's friendship. We say it's unwaged work. With every like, chat, tag, or poke, our subjectivity turns them a profit. They call it sharing. We call it stealing. We've been bound by their terms of service far too long – it's time for our terms." In describing her intentions, Ptak posed a question that could easily have been applied to the politics of housework in the 1970s: "How do you politicize people about a condition of exploitation that society doesn't really want you or allow you to see very easily?"[17] Federici's most recent work, in collaboration with her longtime partner George Caffentzis, is devoted to movements to reclaim "the commons," land, resources, spaces that are shared in common, and alienated by no one for the extraction of profit, where people can imagine and create lives and communities autonomous from the directives of capital.[18]

These days, Federici spends much of her time traveling to lend her efforts and counsel and solidarity to various feminist groups around the world. In her archives, I found an artifact of one such trip: a map of Villa 21–24, a neighborhood in Buenos Aires, labeled by hand. In 2018, she was invited to the city by a group of women from Ni Una Menos, a mass grassroots feminist movement started in Argentina in 2015 to protest violence against women. She joined them at Villa 21–24, a "villa miseria," an informal settlement without state services, where, in the face of neglect, community members take on the work of care: taking kids to school, coordinating garbage collection, checking in on the sick, providing healthcare. There, a women's group had come together to read and discuss *Caliban and the Witch*. On her visit, Federici met with women's groups and marched through the streets with them, some wearing T-shirts printed with photos of women who had been killed.[19] The organizers presented her with a map of their neighborhood that they had created for the occasion: on one side of the document was a list of terms from *Caliban and the Witch*, and, on the other, a map of the neighborhood marking various sites where they were applying those concepts: the public health center where the fight for abortion was ongoing, the communal kitchens where cooking took place, and the routes along which they escorted groups of children to school safely.[20]

Meanwhile, murals began appearing all over the city, some of the most beautiful by the artist Ailén Possamay, depicting women in the act of performing everyday labors: bending over to mop a floor, tending to a child's diaper, cooking a meal over a stove, washing laundry in a bucket of water. Painted next to the images of laboring women are Federici's words: *Eso que llaman amor, es trabajo no pago* – What they call love, we call unwaged work.

In 1995, twenty years after she joined the campaign, Wilmette Brown left it. She continued to live and work in the area around Greenham Common. In 1998, Brown, Ambikananda Saraswati, and Beth Junor represented the Greenham Peace Camp for the West Berkshire District Council and Greenham Common Community Trust Ltd in the presentation of a proposal for a memorial at Greenham.[21] Through interlibrary loan, I located some translations and exegeses of Hindu texts published in the early 2000s by a woman named Swami Ambikananda, who was at Greenham Common, and edited by Manisha Wilmette Brown. Brown, I learned, was a practicing Hindu, a devotee of yoga, and together with Ambikananda had founded an organization dedicated to the traditional practice of yoga. Over the years, Manisha Wilmette Brown had spent time studying the links between yoga and broader health issues, including diabetes and, more recently, long COVID. Was Manisha Wilmette Brown THE Wilmette Brown? I sent an email to ask.

We exchanged friendly messages back and forth. She always took a long time to respond to me, but, when she did, her tone was always kind. She asked after my children and our health, congratulated me when my state, Wisconsin, voted for Joe Biden in the 2020 election, helping to end the Trump presidency. I raised the possibility of meeting or speaking, and she expressed her willingness, but, each time I tried to make a concrete plan, she went silent. Then, in January 2021, I was invited to a virtual event at which she was speaking, sponsored by an organization called Tattva, a think-tank that uses concepts from Hindu spirituality to confront contemporary challenges. The event was on Zoom, scheduled for 10 a.m. in the UK, but I was in the United States, six hours earlier, in the throes of morning sickness from my second pregnancy. I set my alarm for 4 a.m., made myself some tea, and bundled in my bathrobe against the Wisconsin winter to listen.

She was seated in a room with hardwood floors and white walls, wearing a crisp white tunic, a deep maroon scarf draped over her shoulders and two coin-sized gold discs dangling from her ears. She wore large glasses. Her shoulders were relaxed. She looked vital, healthy, beautiful. She still had the same New Jersey accent, but she spoke more slowly than in audio recordings I've heard of her from the 1980s. The speaker who introduced her listed her accomplishments as a member of the student movement for Black Studies at San Francisco State, and as an activist in the peace movement of the 1980s, but neither she nor Brown mentioned Wages for Housework.

The theme of the talk was "Integration," about immigration in the United Kingdom, and she had been invited to speak alongside right-wing commentator David Goodhart, known for stating that Britain was becoming too diverse and calling for border restrictions. But he didn't show up to the event, so instead of a debate Manisha Wilmette Brown (Manishaji, as some in the online audience called her) had the floor for the full hour. The question put to her was: do immigrants in the UK need to "integrate" into British culture?

She described her own journey, as a Black woman becoming a practicing Hindu: "As a person from an African-American Christian background, going to a Hindu temple for the first time, I could see different people were puzzling, you know, like: what's this? What's she doing here?" Over the following years, as she learned the chants and the rituals, that initial shock transformed into a relationship of depth and reciprocity. She spoke about many themes I recognize from her earlier work. She expressed admiration for Rosamund Kissi-Debrah, a Ghanaian immigrant woman whose nine-year-old daughter died from an asthma attack caused by the concentrated pollution in her South London neighborhood. Her fight to make her daughter's case known to the world and to demand action had made life better and safer for everyone in Britain. Integration, Brown said, cannot be about the expectation of keeping one's mouth shut or "assimilating." She spoke of the necessity of people of different races coming together not for the sake of multiculturalism, but because they have a common purpose. That theme, I recognize from her earlier discussion about racism in Britain. People can only act in solidarity with others when they are fighting for their own liberation, not when they are purporting to act on behalf of others. In her talk, Manisha Wilmette Brown turned that point over to reveal the flip side: when immigrants in Britain fight for their own lives, they better everyone's.

Over the course of the hour, she returned to other themes I've heard her speak about since the 1970s: health disparities, environmental racism, hunger, and lack of access to healthy food; reparations for slavery and imperialism. She disparaged the "murderous fantasy" of monolithic national cultures free of the historical legacies of empire and racism that had made their country rich.

After the session, I emailed her my thanks for the invitation and proposed a follow-up conversation, but I never heard back.

In the 1980s, Margaret Prescod was busy, traveling around the world on behalf of the Wages for Housework campaign, lobbying the United Nations, organizing with women against welfare cuts and new workfare requirements being imposed in the United States; all while raising her young daughter. Soon after Prescod's move to the West Coast, another pressing matter demanded her attention. In the mid-1980s, a wave of serial murders was sweeping the West Coast, with a particularly high concentration of homicides in South Los Angeles. The victims were almost all young Black women. At first, the police suppressed the story. When they finally announced the eleven murders, Prescod mobilized Black Women for Wages for Housework to hold a vigil at the central police station. "Eleven women were already dead before the Los Angeles Police Department even mentioned to anybody that there was a serial killer operating in Los Angeles," she recalled. "We knew damn well that if it was happening at UCLA or if it was happening at Beverly Hills somewhere, after the first one or two, everybody would have known about it. It would have been on Dan Rather every night. How come eleven Black women are dead in South Central Los Angeles and nobody knows about it?"[22]

Prescod confronted the officers, demanding to know why these murders were being ignored. When police and media were pressed into acknowledging what was going on, they fixated on the one aspect of the women's identities that they believed justified their neglect: the fact that many of the women earned income from sex work. As Prescod recounted, "the first thing they said to us, they turned around to me and asked me if I was a prostitute. Then they asked the Black women who were with me: were they prostitutes? And the guy who came to talk to us couldn't understand that if we weren't prostitutes, why were we concerned? I mean, they were only hookers getting killed, after all. That's where they were coming from."[23]

Prescod, who had been organizing with sex workers for years already, set up the Black Coalition Fighting Back Serial Murders and began showing up regularly to protest at the LAPD headquarters. She went directly to the people, hitting the streets holding a stack of flyers, warning people in the community about the "South Side Slayer," getting the drawings of suspects out there so the community could protect itself. The coalition was made up of people from the community, including family members of the victims, such as Patricia Williams, whose beloved niece Verna Patricia Williams was found strangled on a playground by several young children. "We called her Patsy," Williams told a reporter.[24] Members of the coalition walked the city streets distributing flyers, raising awareness about the dangers, and humanizing the victims, whom the media and police seemed to deem unworthy of their attention. A journalist described Prescod as stylish, poised, and determined, making her case to anyone who would listen: tough-looking young men on the street, addicts, neighborhood people, proprietors of shops in the wealthiest neighborhoods. "Handbill out, eyes meeting theirs, 'Hi, how're you doin' today?' followed quickly by, 'Have you heard about the South Side slayer?' "[25]

It was hard to find allies. Prescod recalls with pain and frustration the attitudes of the police: as far as they were concerned, these were "cheap homicides."[26] Media accounts from the time reveal a dismissive and insulting attitude from the police toward the women who were fighting to save the lives of Black women. Prescod remembers that they also didn't find allies in many of the city's prominent Black political organizations, which distanced themselves from the victims rather than be associated with the stigma of sex work. Perhaps most disappointing was the lack of widespread support from other feminist groups who were at that very moment protesting rape and violence against women. Many mainstream feminists at the time protested pornography and prostitution as sources of women's denigration, and called for the criminalization of the industries and a stronger police presence in public spaces to protect women. For Black women, criminalization and policing were a *source* of their harassment and violence, not a solution to it.[27] Many women knew from experience that a call to the police could result in their murder, or incarceration, or that of their children. They also knew from experience that efforts to police illicit economic activity would lead to indiscriminate targeting of Black men. Black Women for Wages for Housework had long called for the decriminalization of prostitution and for all women to make common cause with sex workers on the basis of their shared exploitation. What they wanted was for the police to investigate the murders, to treat these women's lives as worthy of protection. Over and over again, Prescod criticized the media and the police department for referring to the women as "prostitutes," and not as mothers, sisters, human beings. "Even if they are prostitutes and drug addicts, every life is of value," she said. "We don't accept a hierarchy of human life."[28]

Whenever I've seen Margaret Prescod's work mentioned in histories of feminism, it is usually about either Wages for Housework or the Coalition Fighting Back Serial Murders, as two different political projects. In 1987, she traveled to Bristol for a Wages for Housework meeting, and in a speech before her movement sisters she made the connection clear:

> Our work is kept hidden. You know, the work of living in poverty, the work of just surviving, the work of suffering at the hands of racism. The work of organizing. The work of providing leadership that is then made invisible. The work of holding communities together that are being devastated by Reagan' social policies, by Thatcher's social policies, and by Reagan's war. The work of fighting for healthcare, of fighting for our children's lives, of watching our children beat up and killed by the police. The work that keeps the empire going. That work that is hidden, that isn't counted, that isn't recognized. That how dare they tell us that we're scroungers or we're beggars and that our life is worth nothing when we have helped to create practically everything that exists on this planet.[29]

For over two decades, Prescod and her coalition did the unpaid work of keeping a community safe in the face of violence and racist neglect from the state: work that a wealthier, whiter community would have been able to rely on the police to do. Over a hundred women were killed in Los Angeles before Lonnie Franklin Jr, who was responsible for at least ten of the murders, was finally arrested in 2010, and convicted in 2016. At the press conference announcing the arrest, Prescod stood on stage with the LAPD Chief Charlie Beck. In video footage posted to YouTube, as he held forth before a room of reporters and community members, you can hear a member of the press ask to hear from Prescod. Margaret Prescod edged her shoulder in closer to the podium, and then, in a quick gesture, grabbed the mic from the police chief as he shot a raised eyebrow at the uniformed colleague who stood next to him. She turned her body, at times facing the men on stage, at times pivoting to face the audience and media. "If we have our man," she said, facing Beck, "I want to congratulate you." But she urged them to not stop; that there were other cases out there not accounted for, with victims and families still wanting answers. "Finally," she said, "I want to say to the press and any officials. Please stop referring to these women as prostitutes. They were women, they were mothers, they were loved by their families and their communities." Cheers and applause erupted in the room.[30]

In London, the Wages for Housework campaign continued into the 1990s, though a number of women left it, many of them on bad terms. "I want to put on tape that I'm not in touch with these people anymore because I don't want to be," said Suzie Fleming, once a campaign stalwart, in an oral history recorded by her daughter Rachel in 2019 for the Feminist Archive South collection in Bristol. She explained, "The Wages for Housework campaign became an extremely unpleasant organization. People were bullied. Demeaned."[31] I encountered many similar accounts in my own research. An article in the *Guardian* by Madeleine Bunting in 1992 presents testimonies from other former Wages for Housework members who made similar claims of bullying and intimidation, being pressured to subordinate their personal needs to the vision as articulated by the leaders of the movement.[32] One of them maintained her commitment to the principles of Wages for Housework, but suggested that perhaps the campaign had "turned in on itself" in response to the hostile climate of Thatcherism. Members of the campaign, including James, were quoted defending the campaign and denying the accusations. In the following weeks, a flurry of letters appeared in the newspaper in response, some corroborating the accounts and some from members of the campaign defending themselves and denying the accusations.

In 1995, the London Crossroads Women's Centre was once again displaced by gentrification, this time relocating from Camden to Kentish Town, where it has remained ever since. It was there that I first met Selma James in person in June 2021. It was a sweltering hot day, and I had walked from an Airbnb a few miles away with my partner and infant son, who was still breastfeeding. The three of us traveled around London together, Stephen pushing our baby around in the stroller while I did my research, meeting up for breaks every few hours so I could breastfeed. My older son spent his days with my mother.

The center doesn't look like much from the outside – I walked by it several times before I could locate it – but when I finally found the right door, it opened into a light-filled space, buzzing with people and activity. During the days that I was there, women from the community flowed in and out – asylum seekers came to discuss their legal cases; mothers came for consultations on breastfeeding and homeopathic medicine. Some were organizing protests against a recent wave of deportations directed by the Home Secretary. One woman from the asylum-seekers group was in the kitchen chopping kale and plantains – it was her turn to prepare the communal lunch that members of the center shared each day. As I waited for Selma James and her partner Nina Lopez to arrive, I perused the walls, on which they represented their history through newspaper clippings and photographs featuring present and former members of the group, as well as women who had inspired them, among them Eleanor Rathbone and Johnnie Tillmon.

James and Lopez were preceded by their two collies, Litowa (named after a socialist village in Nyerere's Tanzania) and Comrade

Nye (named after Nye Bevan, founder of the NHS), who came bounding in. James, thin and spry in shorts, sandals, and socks, her white hair worn in a twist at the back of her head, strolled around the center, greeting each person warmly. She and Lopez made silly faces to make my baby laugh. Then the three of us ascended in the lift to her tiny office and we sat across from each other. James turned to address me: "I have to tell you, I don't have a very high opinion of academics." She leaned forward and placed her hand on my forearm. "It's nothing personal."

Members of the Global Women's Strike, headquartered at the Crossroads Women's Centre, consider themselves the present-day stewards of the Wages for Housework campaign. Some of them have been with the campaign since the 1970s, while others have joined in more recent years. Today, rather than demanding wages for housework, they are campaigning for Care Income Now, for everyone who labors in the care of human beings and the earth, wherever they live, whatever their gender. Their network extends across Europe and the United States and in Asia, Africa, Latin America and the Caribbean, fighting the capitalist exploitation of unpaid work in all its different guises. From their center in London, and a sister center in Philadelphia, they have worked with sex workers seeking decriminalization, and asylum seekers defending their rights. Their community includes disabled mothers and mothers of disabled children fighting for resources in the face of state neglect, and victims of rape and domestic violence seeking the financial resources to live autonomously from abusive men.

Members of the network have a deep sense of their history. They track their genealogy through Selma James, to whom they are devoted and of whom they are very protective. On my multiple visits to the centers in London and Philadelphia, everyone is warm and welcoming and generous. Some have the habit of weaving quotations from James' writing and speeches seamlessly into our conversations about even the most mundane of topics.

For decades, their work has cut against the grain of mainstream feminism. Every once in a while, the informed consumer of political news might come across Selma James speaking on television, or on the radio program *Democracy Now!*, or showing up at Occupy Wall Street, or advocating for Haiti, or co-writing a book with imprisoned political activist Mumia Abu-Jamal. But when the COVID-19 pandemic hit and the economy shut down, their seemingly out-of-fashion, Marxist-feminist politics suddenly seemed very relevant. Within weeks of lockdown, Selma James, Margaret Prescod, and Nina Lopez were on Zoom leading teach-ins. It was in this context that they updated their demand to speak to the current moment: Wages for Housework became Care Income Now.

In the United States, Global Women's Strike rallied behind the 2021 Child Tax Credit (CTC): a monthly payment to parents and guardians of children started during the pandemic and which quickly became one of the most effective anti-poverty programs in American history. Childhood poverty rates were slashed, malnutrition went down, people paid off their debts, mental health improved; by nearly every conceivable measure of well-being, this was an incredibly successful program. In Philadelphia, the Crossroads Women's Center worked tirelessly helping women apply for benefits. They marched together with the Poor People's Campaign demanding that the government keep the benefit going after the pandemic subsided. At the same time, they advocated for a shift in the underlying logic. As Margaret Prescod and Phoebe Jones wrote in an op-ed for *Ms. Magazine*: "The pandemic brought caregiving and the necessity of its financial recognition to the attention of many – or so we thought. The CTC does not officially acknowledge mothers as workers . . . It does, however, acknowledge children's poverty. It is up to us to connect the dots to acknowledge that children are poor because their mothers are poor."[33] It was a familiar theme for the campaign, building on the arguments Prescod had made at Houston in 1977, and that the UK Wages for Housework campaign had made in defense of the Family Allowance campaign in the early 1970s. They fought tooth and nail to keep the Child Tax Credit, supported women who were making a claim for it, and simultaneously made a case for changing the rhetoric, from one of charity to one of a wage for women's work. Seeing how they responded in real time to the Child Tax Credit – which I also received – helped me understand the old question about the role of money in Wages for Housework. Was it about a cash payment, or about changing the system? For them, the answer is obvious: both.

The Child Tax Credit was allowed to expire at the end of 2021. The justification offered by the men in power making the decision: it would disincentivize women from working and reward idleness. When I read a version of this argument in an op-ed by a Harvard economist in *The New York Times*, I shook with rage. Soon after it expired, childhood poverty rates doubled; infant mortality increased; malnutrition increased.

In June 2023, I traveled to Philadelphia for an international gathering of Global Women's Strike at the Crossroads Women's Center, which is coordinated by Phoebe Jones. A member of the Wages for Housework campaign since she was a college student at Oberlin in 1970s, Jones had founded the center, modeling it on its namesake in London. It was a big, warehouse-like space, the sign from the hardware store that used to occupy it was still hanging on the wall. The poured-concrete floors were sanded and painted the color of red clay, the brick walls were freshly whitewashed, displaying banners from various campaigns of the past and present: Lesbians for Wages for Housework! Queer Strike! Take Away Our Poverty, Not Our Children! No Cuts, Just Bucks! The center is located in Germantown, a historic neighborhood north of downtown, where some blocks are still lined with the grand mansions from colonial days, many of them now dilapidated. These days, the neighborhood is predominantly Black and low-income, reflecting the racist practice of blockbusting and white flight in the post-World War II decades. Many of the people who visited the center while I was there had come because they needed practical help solving problems: getting support for their kids and grandkids, applying for their benefits, protecting their grandchildren from the foster-care system. A sign in front of the center states its intention: End Women's Poverty.

On this occasion, a number of visitors had come from out of town. A few days earlier, the city was filled with smoke that had drifted south from a forest fire in Canada, and many of the speakers were red-eyed and hoarse from the polluted air. The conference was a modest-sized affair. At any given time there were around thirty to forty people in the room, and between twenty and thirty joining the event remotely through Zoom. Among them were members of the original Wages for Housework campaign. In the audience were also former members of the Student Nonviolent Coordinating Committee, the Black Panthers, and the Welfare Rights Movement, as well as members of local community groups that were fighting against child separation. There were researchers from the Center for Guaranteed Income Research at the University of Pennsylvania. At the heart of the event was Selma James, with weakening eyesight at the age of ninety-two but as powerful, sharp, and charismatic as ever. Throughout the conference, she sat near the front, listening intently, and occasionally taking the microphone to offer her perspective.

For three days, I attended panels and workshops about matters connected to the Care Income Now campaign. Representatives from a sex workers self-advocacy group spoke. A panel on child separation included anti-deportation activists fighting against ICE (Immigration and Customs Enforcement), an indigenous women's organization, a network of formerly incarcerated women fighting to end the incarceration of mothers, and poor mothers threatened with losing their kids to the child protective services. We heard from disabled mothers, whose disabilities were misinterpreted by the state as incompetence, fighting for the resources to care for themselves and their children, rather than lose children to the care system. Pranom Somwong had come all the way from Thailand to talk about the work she is doing with women's groups resisting mining and displacement from their land. Swati Renduchintala, from India, spoke to us through Zoom about her work with women's agricultural self-help collectives in Andhra Pradesh, organizing to keep their land and to be paid for their vital work protecting the environment. We heard from Leddy Mozombite, founder of the first union of paid and unpaid domestic workers in Peru. Gwen Moore, congresswoman from my home state of Wisconsin, had pre-recorded a talk about her proposed bill, called the Workers Relief and Credit Reform Act, which would treat caregivers and students as workers and compensate them with a tax credit.

At times, the broad sweep of ideas being discussed felt overwhelming. Over the course of a few hours, we contemplated a government stipend for breastfeeding mothers, reparations for Haiti, solidarity with Palestinians, justice for incarcerated mothers, an income for those who protect the soil from depletion. I wondered: could any single movement really bring these struggles together? Then, in the final session of the weekend, we were directed back to the demand: Care Income Now. When a member of the audience asked about how poorer countries would afford it, Margaret Prescod took the floor and spoke about care income as a form of reparations, redistributing money from wealthier countries to those they had impoverished.

In the final session, Nina Lopez gave a historical account of the demand, recounting how a group of feminists seeking wages for housework in the 1970s had grown into a movement seeking a universal income for all carers around the world. "We were never against caring," she said. "We were against housework. Caring is a relationship: we don't want to abolish it. We want support for it." If at different times in the campaign there had been debate about the role of money, here, in this group, there was no ambiguity on this point. "We have always been about the cash," said Lopez. Selma James added: "Once we have it, it is very hard for them to take it away. It feels so *good* in your pocket!"

Epilogue

I started working on this book shortly after giving birth to my first child and am finishing it as my second child nears his third birthday. In other words, I have spent what are likely my most intensive years of housework immersed in the radical feminist tradition of Wages for Housework. It has made my everyday labors – ranging from the sublime, to the disgusting, to the mind-numbingly boring – into a source of contemplation and connection. At first, I found the subject "housework" somewhat embarrassing. Perhaps I had internalized the premise that, for a person to be taken seriously, the basic facts of their social reproduction must be hidden, and, by extension, the further I am from the quotidian work of reproduction, the more interesting, skilled, and accomplished I appear. I felt more at ease in political conversations about "care," "radical care," "carework," and "ethics of care." But in the end, I've come around to the old-fashioned ring of "housework." I like how it reveals a chain of connection with generations of women who came before me, and how it indexes change over time. I find the materiality of "housework" useful as a way of thinking of myself in relation to those who labor in other places, showing what we share as well as showing in embodied form the deep structural forces that make our struggles different. "Housework" strips away the aura of virtue from these labors and makes it plain: whether personally fulfilling, or a total drag, some work simply must be done.

In recent years, Wages for Housework has resurfaced in public discourse like an unearthed treasure, presented as a relic from a different era that could help save our own. When schools and daycare shut down during the COVID-19 pandemic, and more people were working from their homes, women's unpaid labor of social reproduction became impossible to not see. Someone, I forget who, pithily tweeted something like: "I keep seeing memes about WFH [working from home] and hoping it means 'wages for housework.'" The comical futility of sitting with a child on my lap while in a committee meeting evaluating grant proposals on Zoom reminded me of Selma James' words: 'You can't make Ford cars and change nappies at the same time.'" An op-ed for Mother's Day 2020 in *The New York Times* titled "Forget Pancakes. Pay Mothers" invoked Wages for Housework in a demand for economic support for the work of mothering, and I thought of the New York Wages for Housework Committee in Prospect Park in 1974, when they confronted passersby with their flyers "May Day or Mother's Day?" And when we all waxed lyrical about essential workers, clapping out our windows each evening for healthcare workers while their work conditions deteriorated and while certain areas of the business sector exponentially increased their profits, I thought about Bernadette Maharaj and the London Wages for Housework Committee and their insight about nursing: that the more a job resembles housework, the lower its status and pay.

When Wages for Housework is invoked in these contemporary conversations, it is often stripped of the frictions, the critical edge, and the world-making ambition. I felt particularly irritated when, during the pandemic, Wages for Housework was discussed in reference to overworked middle-class mothers like me lamenting that our careers were taking a hit, with long-term economic and professional consequences. This isn't unimportant or incorrect, but it's a very narrow and selective interpretation of Wages for Housework, which was hostile to the idea of "the career woman" as the central feminist protagonist: if the movement has had a hero, she is a poor Black welfare mother resisting the demand that she work a second job outside the home. In other circles, I see it invoked as a way of imbuing housework with skill or status, conflating it with its more virtuous cousin, "care." But in the campaign, housework was not something to uplift as virtuous but something mundane and necessary to the economy and to human life: a site of economic exploitation, an Achilles heel in the capitalist system, and a place from which we could organize to overthrow it. In revisiting and reclaiming Wages for Housework for our moment, I want to resist the urge to smooth over its sharp edges, blunt its anti-capitalist critique, and gloss over the depth of what it asks of us.

Yesterday I packed a lunchbox, squeezed toothpaste onto a little sparkly green plastic toothbrush, and bundled my firstborn child off to school to participate in that American ritual of the lockdown drill, in which students practice what they would do in the event of a mass shooter. I cannot comprehend a society that allows for the possibility of my child being murdered at school, but as a worker I can grasp the work that is shunted onto me and onto all of us caregivers and teachers and aides as we figure out how to sustain life and contain the damage – the unpaid work forced upon us "which we never invented" (to quote Dalla Costa) – of surviving a gun-saturated militarized society. I read about Flint, Michigan, where the water supply has been poisoned by lead pipes and ongoing legacies of environmental racism. Here too, thinking of children's brains damaged because of the failures of adults overwhelms me with useless rage and sadness, but I have learned a habit of mind to focus on the housework: of sustaining households without safe running water, and caring for those vulnerable to the lingering and lifelong health effects of lead poisoning, and, though I can't know their suffering, it feels possible for me to join their struggle as unpaid workers, because I am an unpaid worker too. As wildfires descended on the Midwest last summer, and summer camps and daycares had to either close or keep children occupied indoors for days because the air was unsafe to breathe, my younger son rubbed his eyes red and snot poured out of his nose, making it hard for him (and therefore me) to sleep. My son is robust, and we are protected from the worst effects, yet, as I held him upright against my chest late into the night so the snot could drain from his sinuses and allow him some sleep, I wondered if his little body was an early warning of what is to come, and if this was a glimpse of what the unpaid work of climate change will look like for his generation. If our grandmothers mopped the floors and washed the linens and peeled potatoes and changed nappies so our grandfathers could make Ford cars, perhaps our housework will involve filtering the air, healing damaged bodies, making our environments livable as the earth heats. I often think these days of the work of the late Andaiye, who led her comrades in Guyana to keep account of their daily unpaid labors in time-use diaries. This attention to daily unpaid labor acquired additional layers of meaning in the aftermath of Guyana's devastating floods of 2005, when women took on the burdens of caring for the sick and displaced and traumatized, and keeping communities fed and sheltered and safe when entire neighborhoods and urban infrastructural systems were destroyed. Andaiye observed how their knowledge of their work, and their confidence in its importance, emboldened poor and working-class women to demand the resources to support it. What would it mean to demand what we need in the face of this survival work that is imposed upon us by climate change? And what would it mean to refuse this work; which is to say, to refuse the conditions that impose this work upon us?

What would it look like to act on these politics? Does it mean demanding the Child Tax Credit be extended? Is it the community work of building a school lunch program, paying the workers and farmers generously, and teaching our children to respect and participate in that work, to understand themselves as part of the flow of generations? A guaranteed income for mothers? Is it campaigning for a twenty-hour workweek? Is it blowing up a pipeline?

Theorist Fredric Jameson remarked, "It is easier to imagine an end to the world than an end to capitalism."[1] Above all else, what Selma James, Mariarosa Dalla Costa, Silvia Federici, Manisha Wilmette Brown, Margaret Prescod, and all of their Wages for Housework sisters have given me are new habits of imagination: a daily, quotidian practice of desiring and imagining a world beyond capitalism. We are told that our society must be organized around the premise that we are all individual rational actors, seeking our self-interest on the free market; that this is how things get done. Let us consider instead an alternative and undeniable premise: that we are all the products of housework – not in a sentimental sense but in a material, embodied, economic sense. None of us exists outside of this labor. To begin envisioning and creating the foundations for another world, we don't have to go far. We can start where we are.

Acknowledgements

To Silvia Federici, Mariarosa Dalla Costa, Selma James, Margaret Prescod and Wilmette Brown, I express my deep, heartfelt gratitude. What they have taught me extends far beyond what I've had the space to write in these pages. I expect that not one among these five will agree with everything I've written here, and, in the end, this book can only convey my own perspective and interpretation. I also benefited from the generosity of many people connected to the Wages for Housework campaign, who took the time to speak with me, including Leopoldina Fortunati, Antonella Picchio, Lucia Basso, Mariarosa Cutrufelli, Jane Hirshmann, Beth Green (Ingber), Hedda Matza, Boo Watson, Cristel Amiss, Niki Adams, Sara Callaway, Anne Neale, Nina Lopez, Phoebe Jones, Tree Muldrow, Ida LeBlanc, Miriam Abrams, Kay Chapman, Judith Ramirez, Suzie Fleming (and Rachel-Mulford-Fleming), and everyone who welcomed me at the Crossroads Women's Centers in London and Philadelphia. My debt to these visionaries is too large to be repaid, but I hope I can begin to pay it forward.

Casiana Ionita knew this was a book before I did, and her vision, judgement and encouragement are more than I could ever hope for in an editor. She has made this a better book, and me a better writer. Thank you to her and to Emily Taber, and to everyone at Penguin Press UK and Seal Press for all their guidance and support.

I am so very grateful to Katrina Forrester, Giuliana Chamedes, and Simon Balto, who read the entire manuscript and provided feedback as well as camaraderie. My dear friend Pernille Ipsen, in addition to reading and commenting on part of the manuscript, has been my sounding board throughout this entire process. I think that I have discussed every aspect of this book with her on our long meandering walks around Madison. I cherish our friendship.

Ruth Wilson-Gilmore, Robin D. G. Kelley, Linda Gordon, Sarah Schulman, and April Haynes offered knowledge, advice and encouragement at critical moments along the way.

Many archivists generously offered their time and expertise. I am especially grateful to the staff at the Biblioteca Civica in Padua for accommodating me with access to the archives outside of regular business hours. Arlen Austin is a scholar-activist, creator of community, and, luckily for me, an incredible archivist. So much of the material about Wages for Housework and Lotta Femminista that I used in this book were available to me because of the work he has done collecting, archiving, and digitizing sources from the history of the Wages for Housework campaign. Mary Murphy at the Pembroke Feminist Theory Archives at Brown University welcomed me and facilitated my initial research while the Silvia Federici Papers were still in the process of being assembled and cataloged. I conducted research for this book before members of the London Campaign were finished depositing their materials in their official archive at Bishopsgate, and I am grateful to Selma James, Nina Lopez, Anne Neale and others who allowed me to sit and explore these materials at the Crossroads Women's Center.

I am grateful to the staff at archives that I was able to visit in person, including those at the Pembroke Feminist Theory Archives at Brown University; the Biblioteca Civica di Padova; the Bishopsgate Institute Special Collections and Archives; the Women's Library at the London School of Economics; the Feminist Archives South at the University of Bristol; and the Special Collections and Archives at Queens College, City University of New York. Because I researched and wrote so much of this book during the COVID-19 pandemic, when travel was impossible, I relied on the work of archivists who were willing to locate and scan materials for me. Thank you to staff at the Walter P. Reuther Research Library at Wayne State University; the Tamiment Library and Wagner Labor Archives at New York University; the Alma Jordan Library at the University of the West Indies, St. Augustine; the Lesbian Herstory Archives; the Schlesinger Library at the Radcliffe Institute; the

Briscoe Center for American History at the University of Texas; the San Francisco State University Special Collections and Archives; and the Bancroft Library at University of California, Berkeley. I also benefited immensely from the assistance of Julia Scheinbach, Jackie Coffey, Renee Cozier, and Collin Bernard, who found and scanned materials I was not able to access in person.

To write this book, I needed time and quiet space: scarce resources for a new parent, which is what I was throughout the duration of this project. I thank my friend Kathryn McGarr, who often let me use her empty house when I needed a spell of focus and solitude for writing. I wrote much of this book during multiple stays at the Holy Wisdom Monastery in Middleton, Wisconsin, and I finished this book during a residency at the UW Madison Institute for Research in the Humanities in the company of a wonderfully supportive community of scholars.

My deepest gratitude is for my family. Becoming a mother to Theo was the catalyst that led me to write this book. He and his brother Otis bring joy and curiosity to my life every single day. I can hardly believe how lucky I am to be their mother. Their father and my partner, Stephen, looks after our family with exquisite attention and care and love. While I was writing this book, he defended my time and supported me in body, mind and soul. He is the love of my life, and I could not have written this book without him.

While researching this book, I've spent a lot of time trying to understand the meaning and politics of housework. But it's when I see my mother, Debra Callaci, giving my children her energy, attention and love that I understand the generative, world-making power of this work, and understand myself to be part of a flow of generations. Her labor has made everything possible in my life. This book is for her.

Notes

Abbreviations

Archivio: Archivio di Lotta Femminista per il Salario al Lavoro Domestico, Donazione Mariarosa Dalla Costa, Biblioteca Civica, Padua

Glaberman Papers: Martin and Jesse Glaberman Papers, Walter P. Reuther Library, Wayne State University, Box 40, Folder 25

Campaign Archive: Wages for Housework Campaign Archive, Bishopsgate Institute, London

Introduction

1 Image by Nicole Cox, 1974, United States Library of Congress

2 Laura Briggs, *How All Politics Became Reproductive Politics* (University of California Press, 2017), 6–8

3 Andaiye, *The Point is to Change the World: Selected Writings of Andaiye* (Pluto Press, 2020), 129

4 Jill Tweedie, "Slave Wages," *Guardian*, May 3, 1975

5 Mariarosa Dalla Costa, "Women and the Subversion of the Community," in Mariarosa Dalla Costa and Selma James *The Power of Women and the Subversion of the Community* (Falling Wall Press, 1972), 49

6 Wilmette Brown, Time Off for Woman's Day, San Francisco, October 24. WINGS Archive and Audio Tape Collection, Briscoe Center for American History, University of Texas

7 Margaret Prescod, "Los Angeles Ripper, Women vs. Police Illegality and Racism," February 25, 1987, at Bristol InkWorks, UK, Bishopsgate Institute Archives and Special Collections, Papers of the English Collective of Prostitutes

1. Selma James

1 Selma James to Martin Glaberman, April 16, 1971, Glaberman Papers
2 *Women Talking*, 1970, dir. Midge Mackenzie
3 Selma James interviewed by Margaret Prescod, Sojourner Truth Radio with Margaret Prescod, April 24, 2012 <https://soundcloud.com/sojournertruthradio/april24_2012>
4 Becky Gardiner, "A Life in Writing: Selma James," *Guardian*, June 8, 2012
5 "Beyond Boundaries," interview with Selma James by Ron Augustin, *Monthly Review*, September 1, 2019
6 "'Sex, Race and Class' – Extended Interview with Selma James on Her Six Decades of Activism," Amy Goodman, *Democracy Now!*, April 18, 2012
7 James interviewed by Margaret Prescod, Sojourner Truth Radio with Margaret Prescod, April 24, 2012
8 Grace Lee Boggs, *Living for Change: An Autobiography* (University of Minnesota Press, 2016)
9 Selma James, interview Michelene Wandor, *Once a Feminist: Interviews with Michelene Wandor* (Virago Press, 1990), 188–9
10 Gardiner, "A Life in Writing: Selma James"
11 Selma James, February 22, 1951, Notes on Pearl S. Buck, Glaberman Papers
12 Selma James, "Report," 1954, Glaberman Papers
13 Selma James, "Miss Universe," *Correspondence*, 1954, reprinted in Selma James, *Sex, Race and Class: The Perspective of Winning* (PM Press, 2012)
14 James, "Report," 1954, Glaberman Papers
15 Boggs, *Living for Change*, 67
16 Selma James, "The Way I Work," *Big Issue North*, May 9, 2016
17 Selma James, "A Woman's Place," February 1953, Campaign Archive
18 James, "Report," 1954, Glaberman Papers
19 Ibid.
20 John L. Williams, *CLR James: A Life Beyond the Boundaries* (Constable, 2022), 239
21 "Beyond Boundaries," interview with Selma James
22 Ibid.
23 Williams, *CLR James*

24 Selma James to Freddy Paine, February 5, 1956, Frances D. and G. Lyman Paine Papers, Walter Reuther Library, Wayne State University

25 Transcript, CLR James Papers, University of the West Indies, Box 6, Folder 149

26 "Beyond Boundaries," interview with Selma James

27 James, interview in Wandor, *Once a Feminist*, 189

28 Williams, *CLR James*, 308–9

29 Benjamin W. Heineman Jr, *The Politics of the Powerless: A Study of the Campaign Against Racial Discrimination* (Institute of Race Relations, Oxford University Press, 1972), and Kennetta Hammond Perry, *London is the Place for Me: Black Britons, Citizenship, and the Politics of Race* (Oxford University Press, 2015)

30 Aldo Grandi, *La generazione degli anni perduti: Storie di Potere Operaio* (Einaudi, 2003), 269.

31 *Small Axe*, dir. Steve McQueen, BBC One, 2020

32 Selma James to Mariarosa Dalla Costa, November 11, 1971, Archivio

33 Selma James to C. L. R. James, July 1966, CLR James Papers

34 Selma James to Martin Glaberman, October 5, 1967, Glaberman Papers

35 Selma James to Mariarosa Dalla Costa, March 26, 1973, Archivio

36 James, interview in Wandor, *Once a Feminist*, 188–9

37 *People for Tomorrow, Our Time is Coming Now*, dir. Michael Rabiger, BBC, January 21, 1971

38 James, interview in Wandor, *Once a Feminist*, 193

39 Ibid., 194

40 *Shrew*, 3(8), September 1971

41 James, *Sex, Race and Class*

42 Transcript of Selma James speech in Milan, June 13, 1971, Archivio

2. Mariarosa Dalla Costa

1 Accounts of this appear in Grandi, *La generazione degli anni perduti*, 269, and James, *Sex, Race and Class*

2 "Ferruccio Gambino and Mariarosa Dalla Costa," audio recording, Archivio

3 *Essere donne*, dir. Cecilia Mangini, 1965

4 Maud Anne Bracke, *Women and the Reinvention of the Political: Feminism in Italy, 1968–1983* (Routledge, 2014)

5 "Biographical Note of Mariarosa Dalla Costa," Biblioteche Civiche Padova <https://www.bibliotechecivichepadova.it/sites/default/files/archivio/nota_biografica_mariarosa_dalla_costa_eng.pdf>

6 Angelo Ventura, *Padova* (Editori Laterza, 1989), 367–99

7 Robert Lumley, *States of Emergency: Cultures of Revolt in Italy from 1968 to 1978* (Verso, 1990); Steve Wright, *Storming Heaven: Class Composition and Struggle in Italian Autonomist Marxism* (Pluto Press, 2017)

8 Wright, *Storming Heaven*

9 Rachel Kushner, "Introduction," to Nanni Balestrini, *We Want Everything: A Novel* (Verso, 2022)

10 Mario Tronti, *Workers and Capital* (Verso, 2019) (originally *Operai e Capitale*, Einaudi, 1966)

11 *Porto Marghera: Gli ultimi fuochi*, dir. Manuela Pellarin, 2004; Wright, *Storming Heaven*

12 Draft and final version of the interview by Mariarosa Dalla Costa to *L'Espresso* for a report on '68, Archivio

13 Mariarosa Dalla Costa, "The Door to the Garden," in *Women and the Subversion of the Community: A Mariarosa Dalla Costa Reader* (PM Press, 2019), 230–31, 240

14 Ibid., 239

15 Ibid.

16 Interview by author with Leopoldina Fortunati, October 16, 2019, Padua

17 *Porto Marghera*, dir. Pellarin

18 Alisa Del Re, interview, July 26, 2000 <https://www.generation-online.org/t/alisadelre.htm>

19 Steve Wright, *The Weight of the Printed Word: Text, Context and Militancy in Operaismo* (Haymarket, 2022), 35

20 Stefania Sarsini in Aldo Grandi, *Insurrezione armata* (BUR Futuropassato, 2005), 290, quoted and translated in Wright, *The Weight of the Printed Word*, 35

21 Mariarosa Dalla Costa, "Women's Autonomy and Remuneration of Care Work in the New Emergencies of Eldercare," in *Women and the Subversion of the Community*, 161

22 Ibid., 162

23 Mariarosa Dalla Costa to C.L.R. James, December 29, 1970, Archivio

24 Selma James to Mariarosa Dalla Costa, Archivio

25 "Document 1," Movimento di Lotta Femminile di Padova, June 1971, Archivio

26 Mariarosa Dalla Costa, *Potere femminile e sovversione sociale* (Marsilio Editore, 1972)

27 Selma James to Mariarosa Dalla Costa, undated, Archivio

28 Mariarosa Dalla Costa, "Women and the Subversion of the Community," in *Women and the Subversion of the Community*, 48

29 Various letters, including Selma James to Antonella Picchio, October 24, 1973, Archivio

30 Mary Capps to Selma James and Mariarosa Dalla Costa, November 1971, Archivio

31 "Programmatic manifesto for struggle of housewives in the neighborhood," Lotta Femminile Padova, July 1971, Archivio

32 "Noi donne di Magistero," August 12, 1971, Archivio

33 "Donne del Quartiere," Lotta Femminile Padova, November 27, 1971, Archivio

34 "Questionnaire for women in neighborhood," Archivio

35 "Women, do you know how much work you do in a day?" flyer, Archivio

36 Interview with Mariarosa Dalla Costa, in Louise Toupin, *Wages for Housework: A History of an International Feminist Movement, 1972–77* (Pluto Press, 2018), 225

37 Dalla Costa, *Potere femminile e sovversione sociale*, 31

38 Ibid.

39 Ibid.

40 *L'Offensiva: Quaderni di Lotta Femminista*, 1, December 1972, Turin

41 Statement by Lotta Femminista Roma, July 7, 1972, Archivio

42 Serena Rossetti, "Femminismo/Se il Maschio: Picchia Con La Sinistra," *L'Espresso*, July 23, 1972

43 These letters to the editor are reprinted in *L'Offensiva*, 1, December 1972, Turin

44 Dalla Costa, "Women's Autonomy and Remuneration of Care Work"

3. Housework in Global London

1 Selma James to Martin Glaberman, April 16, 1971, Glaberman Papers

2 "The Miners Strike and Women's Liberation Movement," Women's Liberation Workshop, January 25, 1972, leaflet, Campaign Archive

3 Selma James, "Women Against the Industrial Relations Act, 1971," in James, *Sex, Race and Class*

4 Selma James, *Women, the Unions and Work, or What Is Not To Be Done*, Notting Hill Women's Liberation Group, April 8, 1972, Campaign Archive

5 Selma James to Mariarosa Dalla Costa, September 26, 1972; and Selma James to Suzie Fleming, undated, late summer 1972, Archivio

6 Suzie Fleming interviewed by Rachel Fleming-Mulford, August 30, 2019, Feminist Archive South, Bristol, UK

7 Selma James to Mariarosa Dalla Costa, September 26, 1972, Archivio

8 Selma James, "Introduction," in Dalla Costa and James, *The Power of Women and the Subversion of the Community*

9 Fleming interviewed by Rachel Fleming-Mulford

10 Selma James, "The Perspective of Winning," Detroit, 1973, in Selma James, *Sex, Race and Class*, 81

11 Ibid., 80

12 James, interview in Wandor, *Once a Feminist*, 197

13 Selma James, "Sex, Race and Working Class Power," *Race Today*, 6(1), 1974

14 Selma James, "The organizational perspective of wages for housework," Campaign Archive

15 Ibid.

16 Norma Steele, "We're in Britain for the Money," in Margaret Prescod-Roberts and Norma Steele, *Black Women: Bringing it All Back Home* (Falling Wall Press, 1980)

17 Speech by Norma Steele at the House of Commons, March 6, 1978, Stella Dadzie Collection, Black Cultural Archives

18 James, *Women, the Unions and Work*

19 Open letter from Power of Women Collective / Wages for Housework to the Claimants Unions, Feminist Archive Topic Box: Politics and Policy 27: Claimants' Unions, Feminist Archive South, Bristol

20 Monica Sjöö, interviewed by Viv Honeybourne, "Personal Histories of Second Wave Feminism," Feminist Archive South, Bristol

21 Suzie Fleming, *The Family Allowance Under Attack* (Falling Wall Press, 1973)

22 Selma James, "Family Allowance Campaign: Tactic and Strategy," July 9, 1973, Campaign Archive

23 Interview by author with Selma James, May 11, 2023, Zoom

24 Priscilla Allen, speech, March 30, 1974, Campaign Archive

25 "Statement of aims re: Women's Centre, 129 Drummond St," Campaign Archive

26 "After the news, work," Selma James interviewed by Nanette Rainone, broadcast November 28, 1974, WBAI <https://archive.org/details/pacifica_radio_archives-BC2072>

27 Zoë Fairbairns, review of "About Time," *Spare Rib*, 58, May 1977

28 Zoë Fairbairns, *Benefits* (Virago, 1979).

29 Amanda Sebestyen, "Rape Rally Wrangle," *Spare Rib* 62, September 1977

30 Dale Wakefield, interviewed by Viv Honeybourne, "Personal Histories of Second Wave Feminism," Feminist Archive South, Bristol

31 Lynne Segal, "Leftists of One Form or Another," Verso Blog, 14 November 2023 <https://www.versobooks.com/blogs/news/leftists-of-one-form-or-another>

32 Sheila Rowbotham, "The Carrot, the Stick, and the Movement," *Red Rag*, 2, 1972. See also Sheila Rowbotham, *Daring to Hope: My Life in the 1970s* (Verso, 2021)

33 Priscilla Allen, "Wages for Housework Collection Preface," *Women in Struggle*, 1, June 1973

34 "You Can't Make Ford Cars and Change Nappies at the Same Time," interview with Selma James, May 19, 1973, *Guerrilla*, 3(29), Toronto, Campaign Archive

35 "Wages for Housework and the Single Woman," *Women in Struggle*, 1, June 1973

36 "Why I Want Wages for Housework," *Women in Struggle,* 1, June 1973.

37 "Living Through the Crisis," in *All Work and No Pay: Women, Housework, and the Wages Due*, ed. Wendy Edmond and Suzie Fleming (The Power of Women Collective and Falling Wall Press, 1975), 37

38 "Interview with a Shoplifter," in *All Work and No Pay*, 56

39 Power of Women Collective, "Collectively Speaking," *Journal of the Power of Women Collective*, 1(1), March/April 1974

40 "Wages for Schoolwork," in *Power of Women*, 1 (2), 1973

41 James, "Sex, Race and Working Class Power"

42 Power of Women Collective, "The Home in the Hospital," in *All Work and No Pay*, 69

43 Ibid., 69, 73

44 Ibid., 85

45 "Rachel Smith's Speech at the House of Commons, 6 March 1978," Hall-Carpenter Archives, London School of Economics Library

46 "Resolution on Child Benefit," Dodie Seymour speech, March 13, 1980, Feminist Archive South, Bristol, DM2123/2/PP44 Politics/Policy 44: Wages for Housework Campaign

47 Ibid.

48 Joan Lesley White, "Nothing to Lose but My Children," transcript of speech, July 4, 1978, Hall-Carpenter Archives, London School of Economics Library

49 *All Work and No Pay*, dir. Michael Rabiger, BBC Open Door, 1976

50 Ibid.

4. Potere, Baci e Soldi!

1 "Manifestazione del Mestre, 8–10 March 1974," video, Archivio

2 Wright, *The Weight of the Printed Word*

3 "L'esperienza di Venezia," Archivio

4 Interview with Alisa Del Re, July 26, 2000, trans. Arianna Bove, in *Futuro anteriore. Dai "Quaderni rossi" ai movimenti globali: Ricchezze e limiti dell'operaismo italiano*, ed. Guido Borio, Francesea Pozzi, and Gigi Roggero (Rome: DeriveApprodi, 2002)

5 Mariarosa Dalla Costa, "Soldi Alle Donne! Salario per il Lavoro Domestico Come Leva di Potere," Archivio

6 Mariarosa Dalla Costa, "A General Strike," 1974 speech, in *All Work and No Pay*, 126

7   Leopoldina Fortunati, "Learning to Struggle: My Story Between Workerism and Feminism," *Viewpoint Magazine*, September 15, 2013

8   Interview by author with Leopoldina Fortunati

9   Mariarosa Dalla Costa to Susan Andres, 1976, Archivio

10 Silvia Federici to Mariarosa Dalla Costa, undated, Archivio

11 Interview by author with Leopoldina Fortunati

12 Mariarosa to Suzie Fleming and Selma James, 1975, month unclear, Mariarosa Dalla Costa to Susan Andres, 1976, Archivio

13 *Canti di Donne in Lotta: Il Canzoniere Femminista* (Dischi dello Zodiaco, 1975)

14 Miriam Abrams to Mariarosa Dalla Costa, December 1975; Mariarosa Dalla Costa to Susan Andres, 1976, Archivio

15 Renato Stroili Gurisatti, ed., *Solari: I Maestri del tempo* (Forum Edizioni, 2011)

16 Anna Gottardo, "Histoire d'une lutte de femmes en usine," *L'Italie au féminisme*, ed. Louise Vandelac (Éditions Tierce, 1978; "Documents of Le Donne della Solari," Archivio

17 "Tutto il nostro tempo di vita è sempre tempo di lavoro," *Le operaie della casa*, May 1975

18 "Documents of Le Donne della Solari," Archivio

19 "Tutto il nostro tempo di vita"

20 "Documents of Le Donne della Solari," Archivio

21 Ibid.

22 Serene Todesco, *Campo a due: Dialogo con Maria Rosa Cutrufelli* (Giulio Perrone, 2021)

23 Ibid.

24 Maria Rosa Cutrufelli, "Il Mondo visto da Gela" <http://www.universitadelledonne.it/cutrufelli72.htm>

25 Maria Rosa Cutrufelli, *Disoccupata con onore* (Mazzotta Editore, 1975)

26 Maria Rosa Cutrufelli, "Il Mondo visto da Gela"

27 *Adesso Basta! Bolletine Lotta Femminista Gelese*, vols 1 and 2, Archivio

28 "Esperienze dei gruppi femministi in Italia – Gela," *Sottosopra*, 1973; "Un'analisi della condizione della donna in Sicilia, a cura di Maria Rosa Cutrufelli con la collaborazione di Marilena Bongiovanni, Cettina Brigadeci, Paola Uscè e Maria Venuti Borruso," *Rendiconti*, 28, April 1975

29 Manuela Gandini, "Prefazione: Nel vortice degli anni Settanta!" in Milli Gandini and Mariuccia Secol, *La mamma è uscita: Una storia di arte e femminismo* (DeriveApprodi, 2021)

30 Jacopo Galimberti, *Images of Class: Operaismo, Autonomia and the Visual Arts (1962–1988)* (Verso, 2024)

31 Gandini and Secol, *La mamma è uscita*, 149

32 Mariuccia Secol, "Maria," *Le operaie della casa*, November 1975–February 1976

33 Mirella, "Isabella," *Le operaie della casa*, June/July 1976

34 Galimberti, *Images of Class*

35 Gruppo Immagine, "Vogliamo, Vo(g)liamo," Archivio

36 Caterina, Iaquinta "Domestic Anti-Trophies: Feminism in the Art of Clemen Parrocchetti," in *The Unexpected Subject: 1978 Art and Feminism in Italy* (Flash Art, 2019), 28–9.

37 *La Biennale di Venezia 1978: From Nature to Art, from Art to Nature* (Biennale Venezia, 1978)

5. Silvia Federici

1 Silvia Federici, "Wages Against Housework" (The Power of Women Collective and Falling Wall Press, 1975)

2 Ibid., 2

3 "Silvia Federici in Conversation," Brown University, Pembroke Library, November 22, 2019

4 Federici, "Wages Against Housework", 6

5 Silvia Federici, "Putting Feminism Back on Its Feet," in Federici, *Revolution at Point Zero: Housework, Reproduction, and Feminist Struggle* (PM Press, 2011)

6 Ibid.; Jordan Kisner, "The Lockdown Showed How the Economy Exploits Women. She Already Knew," *The New York Times Magazine*, February 17, 2021

7 "Silvia Federici in Conversation," 9

8 Interview with author, November 22, 2019

9 Ibid.

10 Federici, *Revolution at Point Zero*, 2

11 Interview with author, November 22, 2019

12 Ibid.

13 Ibid.

14 Ibid.

15 Giovanni Anceschi, "Introduction to Enzo Paci's Presentation at the 10th Triennial" (trans. John Cullars), *Design Issues*, 18(4) (Autumn 2002)

16 Michele Gulinucci, ed., "What Does It Matter Who Is Speaking? Dialogue with Luciano Anceschi [and Others]," in *Those Who Look from Afar Look Like Flies: An Anthology of Italian Poetry from Pasolini to the Present, Tome I: 1956–1975*, ed., Luigi Ballerini and Bepe Cavatorta (University of Toronto Press, 2017), 482–99

17 *Buffalo Town Crier*, February 18, 1969

18 Ruth Geller, *Seed of a Woman* (Imp Press, 1979), 225

19 Interview with author, November 22, 2019

20 Roberta Gold, *When Tenants Claimed the City* (University of Illinois Press, 2014), 193

21 "Women's Bail Fund," *Rat*, 17, Dec. 17–Jan. 6, 1970/1971); *Everywoman*, 32, May 1972; "Women's Bail Fund," flyers, Box 107, Tamiment Library and Robert F. Wagner Labor Archives, NYU Special Collections

22 Silvia Federici, "Notes on Lukács' Aesthetics," *Telos*, Spring 1972

23 Guido Baldi, "Theses on Mass Worker and Social Capital," *Radical America*, 6(3), 1972

24 Radicalesbians, "The Woman-Identified Woman," 1970; see <The Woman-Identified Woman / Women's Liberation Movement Print Culture / Duke Digital Repository>

25 Silvia Federici to Mariarosa Dalla Costa, 1972, Archivio

26 Silvia Federici to Mariarosa Dalla Costa, undated, Archivio

27 Mariarosa Dalla Costa to Silvia Federici, October 14, 1972, Archivio

28 Silvia Federici to Mariarosa Dalla Costa, undated, Archivio

29 Silvia Federici to Mariarosa Dalla Costa, undated; Mariarosa Dalla Costa to Silvia Federici, October 14, 1972, Archivio

6. The New York Committee

1 Silvia Federici to Mariarosa Dalla Costa, 1973, undated, Archivio

2 Various letters in Archivio

3 *Wages for Housework: The New York Committee 1972–1977: History, Theory and Documents*, ed. Silvia Federici and Arlen Austin (New York: Automedia, 2017), 19

4 Statement from Los Angeles Wages for Housework Committee, July 28, 1975, MRDC Archives, Faldone B, Cartella 2

5 Silvia Federici to Mariarosa Dalla Costa, May 20, 1975, Archivio

6 Silvia Federici, with Nicole Cox, "Counterplanning from the Kitchen," in Federici, *Revolution at Point Zero*

7 Federici, "Wages Against Housework"

8 Flyer, reproduced in, *Wages for Housework*, 46–7

9 Silvia Federici to Mariarosa Dalla Costa, undated, likely November 1974, Archivio

10 John Sibley, "'Storefront Psychiatry' Helps Brooklyn's Poor," *The New York Times*, April 21, 1970

11 Hedda Matza, phone interview, October 23, 2020

12 Jane Hirschmann, "Organizing on the Second Job," in *All Work and No Pay*, 111

13 Silvia Federici, "Notes on Organization," in *Wages for Housework*, 38

14 "The Right to Have Children," *Power of Women, Journal of the Wages for Housework Campaign*, 5

15 Silvia Federici, "Speech at the Brooklyn Storefront Opening (1975)," in *Wages for Housework*, 90

16 "Silvia Federici in Conversation," Brown University, Pembroke Library, Nov. 22, 2019

17 Federici, "Notes on Organization,"

18 Jane Hirschmann, interview with author, March 2020

19 Kim Phillips-Fein, *Fear City: New York's Fiscal Crisis and the Rise of Austerity Politics* (Metropolitan Books, 2017), 7

20 Mierle Laderman Ukeles, "Who Cares?", Discard Studies Conference, NYU, October 12, 2022

21 Phillips-Fein, *Fear City*

22 Jean Bergantini Grillo, "Wives Want Wages: or The Great Housework War," *Soho Weekly News*, January 15, 1976, reproduced in *Wages for Housework*, 175–7

23 Silvia Federici, "Women and Welfare (1975)," in *Wages for Housework*

24 Beth Green, interview with author, March 23, 2021

25 Walter Carlson, "Advertising: Window Dressing by Chase," *The New York Times*, July 6, 1965

26 Suzanne Kahn, *Divorce, American Style: Fighting for Women's Economic Citizenship in the Neoliberal Era* (University of Pennsylvania Press, 2021)

27 *Wages for Housework*

28 Kahn, *Divorce, American Style*

29 Silvia Federici, "On Rape Within Marriage (1976)," in *Wages for Housework*, 154

30 Pamphlet on forced sterilization, reproduced in *Wages for Housework*, 55–61

31 *Life Magazine*, April 1977

32 WFH / Barbara Silverman, undated film, Silvia Federici archives

7. Wilmette Brown

1 *Decade of Our Destiny – Women: A New Force for Change*, 1976; Motion Picture 220-IWY-1, Motion Pictures and Video Recordings Relating to International Women's Year, 1974–1977; Records of Temporary Committees, Commissions, and Boards, Record Group 220; National Archives at College Park, College Park, MD

2 "Housewives Choice," *The Voice Interview*, March 2, 1993, interview by Winsome Hines

3 Wilmette Brown, "Women, Poverty and Peace: Remembering Martin Luther King Jr.," *Sanity*, July 1985

4 Kevin Mumford, *Newark: A History of Race, Rights, and Riots in America* (NYU Press, 2008)

5 "Housewives Choice"

6 Ibid.

7 Minutes of the 1963 CORE National Convention, Dayton, OH, Library of Congress

8 Brown, "Women, Poverty and Peace"

9 Minutes of the 1963 CORE National Convention

10 Brown, "Women, Poverty and Peace"

11 Mumford, *Newark*

12 "Interview: Wilmette Brown, Building Power," by Sarah Schulman and Sophia Mirviss, *WomaNews*, November 1980

13 "PROC Elects Leaders," *Daily Californian*, March 14, 1964

14 "Peace Rights Organizing Committee," University of California, Berkeley Archives, Social Protest Collection, Carton 202, Folder 2017

15 "Wilmette Brown, Building Power"

16 Donna Jean Murch, *Living for the City: Migration, Education, and the Rise of the Black Panther Party in Oakland, California* (UNC Press, 2010), 75

17 Wilmette Brown, "Reviving the Movement: The Legacy of Malcolm X and Franz Fannon [*sic*]," Pacifica Radio Archives, recording of a speech, Broadcast on KFPK, 1991 <https://www.pacificaradioarchives.org/recording/kz1653>

18 Kitty Kelly Epstein and Bernard Stringer, *Changing Academia Forever: Black Student Leaders Analyze the Movement They Led* (Myers Education Press, 2020), 24

19 Martha Biondi, *The Black Revolution on Campus* (University of California Press, 2012)

20 "From Panthers to Parliament," *Gay News*, 1984

21 Wilmette Brown, "Oppose the Alton Bill," speech, Bristol Poly, July 27, 1988, Crossroads Women's Centre

22 "Wilmette Brown, Building Power"

23 "Black Studies Attacked," *Dock of the Bay*, Kathy Kettler, November 18, 1969

24 *San Francisco State College Bulletin*, 1969–1970, X(3), February 1969

25 Carol Long, "More Trouble at S.F. State," *Sun Reporter*, March 7, 1970

26 Brown, "Reviving the Movement"

27 "A Coalition of Liberation Movements," Wilmette Brown interviewed by Nuri Muhammed, April 12, 1991, KPFK <https://www.pacificaradioarchives.org/recording/kz1635>

28 "Housewives Choice"

29 Wilmette Brown, "Bushpaths," *Conditions*, 1(1), April 1977

30 Brown, "Women, Poverty and Peace"

31 Jamie Monson, *Africa's Freedom Railway* (Indiana University Press, 2009)

32 "U.S. Blacks Invited to Work in Zambia," *The New York Times*, August 2, 1970, 22

33 Hugh Macmillan, *The Lusaka Years: The ANC in Exile in Zambia, 1963–1994* (Jacana, 2013)

34 Wilmette Brown, "The Autonomy of Black Lesbian Women," transcript of speech, Toronto, July 24, 1976, Box 1, Wages for Housework Special Collections, Lesbian Herstory Archive, Brooklyn, New York

35 "Wilmette Brown, Building Power"

36 Brown, "Women, Poverty and Peace"

37 Brown, "Oppose the Alton Bill"

38 Tucker Pamella Farley, "Changing Signs," in *The Politics of Women's Studies: Testimony from Thirty Founding Mothers*, ed. Florence Howe (The Feminist Press, 2000)

39 CUNY Digital History Archive, transcript of interview with Tucker Pamella Farley, interviewed by Andrea Ades Vásquez and Yana Calou, May 15, 2016, New York; also: meeting minutes from Tucker Pamella Farley Papers, Sophia Smith Collection, Smith College

40 Farley, "Changing Signs"

41 *Queens College Bulletin*, 1976–77, Special Collections and Archives, Queens College Library

42 "Wilmette Brown, Building Power"

43 Ibid.

44 Brown, "Oppose the Alton Bill"

45 "Counting Women's Care Work: An Interview with Andaiye," interview by David Scott, *Small Axe*, 15, March 2004

46 "Napoli demonstration, May 1, 1976," video, Archivio

47 Photographs in Archivio

48 "Wilmette Brown," lecture on audiocassette, Archivio

49 Speech by "Mary Brant," conference of Women Prostitutes, Archivio

50 Brown, "The Autonomy of Black Lesbian Women"

51 Ibid.

52 Ibid.

53 Ibid.

8. *Margaret Prescod*

1 Diana Mara Henry Papers, Special Collections and University Archives, University of Massachusetts Amherst Libraries

2 *Safire*, 1(1), Fall 1977

3 Laura L. Lovett, "Johnnie Tillmon: Welfare as a Women's Issue," in *It's Our Movement Now: Black Women's Politics and the 1977 National Women's Conference*, ed. Laura L. Lovett et al. (University Press of Florida, 2022).

4 "Wages for Housework: 50 years of Campaigning," webinar, March 24, 2022 <https://globalwomenstrike.net/video-wages-for-housework-50-years-of-campaigning-selma-james-founder-of-the-wfh-campaign-in-conversation-with-margaret-prescod-co-founder-black-women-for-wages-for-housework/>

5 Margaret Prescod, in Selma James, ed., *Strangers & Sisters: Women, Race & Immigration* (Falling Wall Press, 1985), 83

6 Margaret Prescod-Roberts, "Bringing It All Back Home," in *Black Women*, 24

7 Margaret Prescod, in "Feminist Generations: A Conversation with Selma James, Margaret Prescod and Chanda Prescod-Weinstein," January 19, 2021, University of Toronto, transcript of Women and Gender Studies Institute Research Seminar, in partnership with Women in Dialogue Archives Speakers Bureau <https://wgsi.utoronto.ca/wp-content/uploads/2022/01/feminist-generations-closed-captions-converted.pdf>

8 Margaret Prescod, in "Radical Black Women Series Presents: Honoring the Radicalism of Margaret Prescod," May 10, 2022 <https://www.youtube.com/watch?v=QRNs5bJf6oQ>

9 Prescod-Roberts, "Bringing It All Back Home," 24

10 Frontispiece of *Black Women*

11 Prescod, in "Feminist Generations"

12 Matthew Parker, *The Sugar Barons: Family, Corruption, Empire, and War in the West Indies* (Walker, 2011); Jennifer. Morgan, *Laboring Women: Reproduction and Gender in New World Slavery* (University of Pennsylvania Press, 2004); Hilary McD. Beckles, *How Britain Underdeveloped the Caribbean* (University of the West Indies Press, 2021)

13 Prescod, in "Feminist Generations"

14 "Wages for Housework" webinar

15 Prescod, in James, ed., *Strangers & Sisters*, 81

16 Prescod, in "Radical Black Women Series Presents"

17 Margaret Prescod, in *Feminists: What Were They Thinking?*, dir. Johanna Demetrakas, 2018

18 *The Sun Rises in the East*, dir. Tayo Giwa, 2022

19 Jerald E. Podair, *The Strike that Changed New York: Blacks, Whites, and the Ocean Hill–Brownsville Crisis* (Yale University Press, 2004)

20 Margaret Prescod, "Introduction," Selma James, *Our Time is Now: Sex, Race, Class, and Caring For People and Planet* (PM Press, 2021)

21 Prescod, "Feminist Generations"

22 "Counting Women's Care Work: An Interview with Andaiye"

23 "Birth Announcement," 1976, in *Wages for Housework*, 116

24 Wilmette Brown, *Black Women and the Peace Movement* (Falling Wall Press, 1984)

25 Prescod, "Introduction," in James, *Our Time is Now*

26 Francie Wyland, "Wages for Housework a Lesbian Issue, Too," *Los Angeles Times*, July 3, 1977; Francie Wyland, *Motherhood, Lesbianism and Child Custody* (Wages Due Lesbians Toronto and Falling Wall Press, 1977)

27 Brown, "The Autonomy of Black Lesbian Women"

28 "Speakout," December 21, 1976, Papers of Margo St James, Schlesinger Library, Radcliffe Institute

29 Statement, "No Cuts, Just Bucks," Papers of Margo St James, Schlesinger Library, Radcliffe Institute

30 Queens College Action Group, "Women, Welfare and Unwaged Work," *Phoenix*, XVIII(13), November 30, 1976

31 Ibid.

32 Prescod-Roberts, "Bringing It All Back Home," 24

33 Spencer Chin, "SEEK speak-out at BHE draws 100 Students and Faculty," *Globe*, March 1, 1978

34 Press Release, Statement by Paula Henderson at the New York State Board of Education Expanded Education Opportunity Committee Public Hearing on Chancellor Kibbee's proposed draft of guidelines for the SEEK Program, February 23, 1978, Papers of Margo St James, Schlesinger Library, Radcliffe Institute

35 New York State legislative record and index, 1979 and 1980

36 Iris Cohen, "Women Lobby for SEEK," *Newsbeat*, October 10, 1978

37 Matthew Desmond, *Poverty, by America* (Crown, 2023)

38 Gail F. Baker, "Black Women Demand Wages for Housework," *Chicago Defender*, April 16, 1977

39 "An Attack on Prostitutes is an Attack on All Women," flyer, Papers of Margo St James, Schlesinger Library, Radcliffe Institute

40 "Money for Prostitutes is Money for Black Women," flyer, Papers of Margo St James, Schlesinger Library, Redaliffe Institute

41 Peter Gorner, "Prostitutes and Housewives Unite, Forming a Surprising Sisterhood," *Chicago Tribune*, April 18, 1977

42 Susie Linfield and Nina Brodsky, "Wages for Housework Stages Street Trial," *Sister Courage*, July 8, 1977

43 Script, Papers of Margo St James, Schlesinger Library, Radcliffe Institute

44 *Safire*, 1(1), Fall 1977

45 Prescod-Roberts, "Bringing it All Back Home"

46 Prescod, in James, ed., *Strangers & Sisters*, 37

47 "Plato Retreats, Pros Picket," *High Society Magazine*, October 1979

48 "P.O.N.Y. – Decriminalization of Prostitution," radio broadcast, WBAI, April 9, 1980 <https://archive.org/details/pacifica_radio_archives-IZ0440.01>

49 Kathleen Hendrix, "Passionate Pursuer's Crusade Against the South Side Slayer," *Los Angeles Times*, October 16, 1986

9. Reclaiming the Earth

1 Wilmette Brown, *Roots: Black Ghetto Ecology* (London: Housewives in Dialogue, 1986), first published in *Reclaim the Earth: Women Speak Out for Life on Earth*, ed. Léonie Caldecott and Stephanie Leland (The women's Press, 1983)

2 "Our Women's Centre Began as a Squat," short film, <http://crossroads women.net/our-story-our-film>

3 Ibid.

4 Prescod, in "Feminist Generations"

5 Workfare Protest, San Francisco City Hall, September 15, 1987, WINGS Archive, Briscoe Center for American History, University of Texas at Austin

6 Wilmette Brown, April 28. Time Off for Women's Day, San Francisco, October 24. WINGS Archive and Audio Tape Collection, Briscoe Center for American History, University of Texas at Austin

7 Clotil Walcott, *Fight Back, Says a Woman* (Institute of Social Studies, The Hague, 1980)

8 Wages for Housework Public Meeting, San Francisco, 1986 or 1987, WINGS Archive, Briscoe Center for American History, University of Texas at Austin

9 Clotil Walcott interviewed by Miss Rosalie Barclay, no date, University of the West Indies, St. Augustine, Department of Gender Affairs and Development

10 David Scott, "Counting Women's Work: An Interview with Andaiye," *Small Axe*, 15, March 2004, 196

11 Ibid.

12 Ibid., 207

13 Andaiye, *The Point is to Change the World*, 129

14 Elaine Sciolino, "Political Wars in the 'Peace Tent' in Kenya," *The New York Times*, July 13, 1985; Forum '85, UN World Conference on Women Opening Program, Swarthmore College Peace Collection Sound Recordings

15 Wages for Housework Public Meeting, San Francisco

16 "The Global Kitchen," Wages for Housework international campaign journal, special issue for End of First UN Decade for Women, summer 1985

17 *The Nairobi Forward-Looking Strategies for the Advancement of Women*, July 1985 paragraph 120

18 Fahnbulleh, *The UN Decade for Women: An Offer We Couldn't Refuse* (Crossroads Books, 1987)

19 Clotil Walcott to Prime Minister's Office, October 23, 1987, Campaign Archives

20 Andaiye, *The Point is to Change the World*

21 Brown, *Roots*

22 Thomas Belton, *Protecting New Jersey's Environment: From Cancer Alley to the New Garden State* (Rutgers University Press, 2010)

23 Audre Lorde, *The Cancer Journals* (Penguin, 2020)

24 Brown, *Roots*

25 Sasha Roseneil, *Common Women, Uncommon Practices: The Queer Feminisms of Greenham* (Cassell, 2000)

26 "A Black Voice in the Peace Movement," *Asian Times*, 202, January 1987

27 Virginia Woolf, *Three Guineas* (1938) (Mariner, 2006), 129

28 Ibid., 93

29 Mildred Calvert, quoted in Brown, *Black Women and the Peace Movement*, 32

30 Brown, *Black Women and the Peace Movement*, 32

31 Wilmette Brown, "Women, Poverty and Peace: Remembering Martin Luther King," *Sanity*, July 1985

32 Black Women for Wages for Housework Press Release, November 17, 1986, Campaign Archives

33 Refusing Nuclear Housework: Women's Case Against the Building of Hinkley "C" Nuclear Power Station, Summary of Proof of Evidence, December 18, 1988

34 Roseneil, *Common Women, Uncommon Practices*

35 Yasmin Alam, letter to the editor, *Time Out London*, 896, October 21–8, 1987

36 Interview with Sarah Hipperson, by Lyn E. Smith, Imperial War Museum, 2000 <https://www.iwm.org.uk/collections/item/object/80019678>

37 Brown, *Roots*, 14

38 Brown, "Reviving the Movement"

39 Olúfẹ́mi O. Táíwò, *Reconsidering Reparations* (Oxford university, Press, 2022)

40 Adom Getachew, *Worldmaking after Empire: The Rise and Fall of Self-Determination* (Princeton university, Press, 2019)

41 Brown, *Roots*, 14

10. Afterlives

1 Mariarosa Dalla Costa, "The Door to the Flower and Vegetable Garden," *Viewpoint Magazine*, June 20, 2017

2 Dalla Costa, "Women's Autonomy and Remuneration of Care Work," 165

3 Dalla Costa, "Women and the Subversion of the Community," in *Women and the Subversion of the Community*, 49

4 Mariarosa Dalla Costa to Selma James, March 4, 1973, Archivio

5 Mariarosa Dalla Costa to Selma James, July 27, 1978, Archivio

6 Letter, July 16, 1979, Silvia Federici Papers, Feminist Theory Archives, Pembroke Center, Brown University

7 Dalla Costa, "The Door to the Flower and Vegetable Garden"

8 Mariarosa Dalla Costa, "So That Fish May Flop in Vegetable Gardens: Biodiversity and Health in Movements for Peasant-Based Agriculture and Artisan Fishing" <https://thecommoner.org/wp-content/uploads/2020/06/so-that-fish-may-flop-in-vegetable-gardens.pdf>

9 Dalla Costa, "The Door to the Garden," 246

10 Ibid., 241

11 Mariarosa Dalla Costa, *Una Mattinata* (Bino Rebellato Editore, 1965)

12 Interview of Silvia Federici by Louise Toupin, January 31, 1996, Silvia Federici Papers, Brown University Library.

13 Letters on the motivations behind the internal break of the SLD/WFH committee in 1978, Archivio.

14 Dalla Costa, "Women and the Subversion of the Community," in *Women and the Subversion of the Community*, 47–9

15 Interview with author, November 22, 2019, Brown University

16 Federici, *Revolution at Point Zero*, 3

17 E. Alex Jung, "Wages for Facebook," *Dissent*, 2015

18 *Commoning with George Caffentzis and Silvia Federici*, ed. Camille Barbagallo, Nicholas Beuret, and David Harvie (Pluto Press, June, 2019)

19 Silvia Federici en la Villa 21–24 y Zavaleta, 2018 <https://www.youtube.com/watch?v=SLVOIM8niw4&t=8s>

20 "Caliban and the Witch Reading Group," Silvia Federici Papers, Brown University

21 Sarah Hipperson, *Greenham: Non-Violent Women-vs-Crown Prerogative* (Greenham Publications, 2005)

22 Margaret Prescod, San Francisco, 1987, WINGS Archive and Audio Tape Collection, Briscoe Center for American History, at Austin University of Texas

23 Margaret Prescod, "Los Angeles Ripper, Women vs. Police Illegality and Racism," February 25, 1987, at Bristol InkWorks, UK, Bishopsgate Institute Archives and Special Collections, Papers of the English Collective of Prostitutes

24 Scott Harris, "Coalition Joins Effort to End Killer's Reign," *Los Angeles Times*, July 16, 1986

25 Hendrix, "Passionate Pursuer's Crusade Against the South Side Slayer" *Los Angeles Times*

26 Ibid.

27 Anne Gray Fischer, *The Streets Belong to Us: Sex, Race and Police Power from Segregation to Gentrification* (University of North Carolina Press, 2022)

28 John Crust, "Gates Under Fire for Not Warning of Possible Serial Killer," *Los Angeles Herald Examiner*, February 22, 1989

29 Prescod, "Los Angeles Ripper, Women vs. Police Illegality and Racism"

30 <https://www.youtube.com/watch?v=MTDXCllSINU>

31 Suzie Fleming interviewed by Rachel Fleming-Mulford, August 30, 2019, Feminist Archive South, Bristol, UK

32 Madeleine Bunting, "Wages for Housework: Who is Telling the Truth?", *Guardian*, July 30, 1992

33 Margaret Prescod and Phoebe Jones, "Work Requirements for Child Tax Credits Are an Insult to Mothers," *Ms. Magazine*, April 13, 2022

Epilogue

1 Quoted in Mark Fisher, *Capitalist Realism: Is There No Alternative?* (Zero Books, 2009)

Index

Credit: Robert Streiffer

Emily Callaci is a professor of history at University of Wisconsin–Madison. She lives in Madison, Wisconsin.